"Walter Strickland's n   arched,
carefully organized,   ꜥortant
subject. The accompanying volume of well-chosen and well-introduced documents makes a valuable project even more useful. With its focus on Black Protestants, these books are landmarks for the exploration of the nation's past and its perennial struggles over race. Most of all they record a story that has been regularly neglected in accounts of American Christianity. It is the often unexpected, sometimes contentious, but enduring impact of the Christian gospel throughout African American history."

Mark Noll, author of *America's Book: The Rise and Decline of a Bible Civilization, 1794–1911,* and *C. S. Lewis in America*

"In *Swing Low*, Strickland takes readers on a profound journey by combining historical narrative (volume one) with primary resources (volume two) to illuminate the triumphs, struggles, and theological developments that have shaped and continue to shape Black Christianity's enduring legacy in the United States. Throughout the entirety of these volumes, readers are invited to deeply explore how the Black church in America continues to navigate the challenges and opportunities of our contemporary world. They are simultaneously encouraged to envision a future where the Black church remains a catalyst for holistic liberation and spiritual renewal and continues to be a voice for justice, reconciliation, and communal transformation. This book is essential reading for pastors, theologians, and all who seek to understand the unique and profound contributions of the Black church in America and to honor its enduring legacy, learn from its theological insights, and join in the ongoing pursuit of liberation, healing, and reconciliation in our communities and beyond."

Bryan Carter, pastor of Concord Church in Dallas, Texas

"In these complementary volumes, Walter R. Strickland II provides a detailed and profound rendering of the story of African American Christianity. The assembled documents, dating as far back as 1619 and as current as the present year, illustrate thought formed in response to various matters of concern. Among this wide range of ideas, Strickland brings to the fore the recurring, interrelated convictions about God, Jesus Christ, the Bible, conversion and sanctification, and freedom and liberation in each era."

Frederick L. Ware, professor of theology at Howard University School of Divinity

"Walter R. Strickland II has made an incredible contribution with both volumes of *Swing Low*, laying out a well-organized history of the African American Christian tradition, and supporting it with an expansive anthology of primary sources. His thorough work highlights people and movements that were instrumental in American religious history. It is a valuable resource for those studying the holistic story of the church in America."

J.D. Greear, pastor of The Summit Church in Raleigh-Durham, North Carolina

"There are many ways to tell a story; Walter Strickland tells the story of the Black church through a theological lens. These scholarly and accessible volumes tell the story of the Black church by introducing us to many faithful saints, some familiar but many less well-known. These lives show us how the Black church pursued and embodied a faith where beliefs matter as much as faithful and liberating practice. We encounter a holistic faith where we see many ways to walk faithfully in a world full of tremendous challenges. Strickland has given us a long-needed historical narrative and anthology."

Vincent Bacote, professor of theology and the director of the Center for Applied Christian Ethics at Wheaton College

VOLUME 1

SWING LOW

A HISTORY
of BLACK
CHRISTIANITY
in the
UNITED STATES

✝

WALTER R.
STRICKLAND II

ivp
Academic
An imprint of InterVarsity Press
Downers Grove, Illinois

InterVarsity Press
P.O. Box 1400 | Downers Grove, IL 60515-1426
ivpress.com | email@ivpress.com

©2024 by Walter Robert Strickland II

All rights reserved. No part of this book may be reproduced in any form without written permission from InterVarsity Press.

InterVarsity Press® is the publishing division of InterVarsity Christian Fellowship/USA®. For more information, visit intervarsity.org.

All Scripture quotations, unless otherwise indicated, are taken from The New King James Version®. Copyright © 1982 by Thomas Nelson, Inc. Used by permission. All rights reserved.

The publisher cannot verify the accuracy or functionality of website URLs used in this book beyond the date of publication.

Cover design: David Fassett
Interior design: Jeanna Wiggins
Images: Moment via Getty Images: © Tuomas A. Lehtinen, © Oxygen, © Witthaya Prasongsin, © Yifei Fang;
 © PixelCatchers / E+ via Getty Images, © Keith Lance / DigitalVision Vectors via Getty Images, © Glasshouse Images / The Image Bank

ISBN 978-1-5140-0936-9 (hardcover) | 978-1-5140-0420-3 (paperback) | ISBN 978-1-5140-0421-0 (digital)

Printed in the United States of America ∞

Library of Congress Cataloging-in-Publication Data
Names: Strickland, Walter R., II (Walter Robert), 1984- author.
Title: Swing low a history of Black Christianity in the United States / Walter R. Strickland II.
Description: Downers Grove, IL : IVP Academic, [2024] | Includes bibliographical references and index. | Contents: Transatlantic faith – Deliverance in the shadows – Faith reclaimed – The invisible institution becomes visible – "Alpha and omega of all things" – A new normal – budding theological movements – The road to the Civil Rights Movement : interlude : theologizing Black consciousness – Black evangelical identity – Black evangelical consciousness – Black evangelical diaspora – The arrival of Black liberation – Heirs of Black liberation – Into the twenty-first century.
Identifiers: LCCN 2024005764 (print) | LCCN 2024005765 (ebook) | ISBN 9781514004203 (print ; paperback ; volume 1) | ISBN 9781514009369 (print ; hardcover ; volume 1) | ISBN 9781514004227 (print ; paperback ; volume 2) | ISBN 9781514009000 (print ; hardcover ; volume 2) | ISBN 9781514004210 (digital ; volume 1) | ISBN 9781514004234 (digital ; volume 2)
Subjects: LCSH: African Americans–Religion–History. | Religion and culture–United States–History. | African Americans–Social life and customs–History. | African American churches–History. | BISAC: RELIGION / Christian Theology / History | RELIGION / Christian Church / History
Classification: LCC BR563.B53 S77 2024 (print) | LCC BR563.B53 (ebook) | DDC 277.30089/96073–dc23/eng/20240512
LC record available at https://lccn.loc.gov/2024005764
LC ebook record available at https://lccn.loc.gov/2024005765

To my grandmother

Belvia Jean Strickland

A quintessential daughter of the Black church

†

CONTENTS

Acknowledgments — ix

1 Introduction — 1
2 A Transatlantic Faith — 12
3 Deliverance in the Shadows — 28
4 Faith Reclaimed — 47
5 The Invisible Institution Becomes Visible — 64
6 "Alpha and Omega of All Things" — 84
7 A New Normal — 104
8 Budding Theological Movements — 120
9 The Road to the Civil Rights Movement — 134

INTERLUDE: Theologizing Black Consciousness — 153

10 Black Evangelical Identity — 161
11 Black Evangelical Consciousness — 175
12 Black Evangelical Diaspora — 189
13 The Arrival of Black Liberation — 206
14 Heirs of Black Liberation — 235
15 Into the Twenty-First Century — 249

General Index — 257
Scripture Index — 259

ACKNOWLEDGMENTS

This project is a labor of love that would have been impossible without a community who encouraged and assisted me along the way. I must begin by thanking my wife, Stephanie, for encouraging me through long hours of research and writing, and for your patience as I ruined countless dinners with family and friends discussing the gems I found in my study that day. I am also grateful for the motivation gained from my children, Kendra, Kaiya, and Walter III, so they would not have to search as widely to find a theological account of this wonderful tradition. I am also indebted to the cloud of witnesses in this book who modeled longsuffering as I wait to meet my oldest daughter, Hope, once again, in glory.

I am eternally indebted to the unyielding dedication of employee turned student and now friend Phabienne Anderson, who read every word of this book and whose enthusiasm for this project rivals my own. To Dr. Kelvin J. Washington, who is an incredible dialogue partner for all things theology, and in particular the details of twentieth-century African American Christianity. Likewise, the research of Trei Council was essential to the breadth of this project as he unearthed several figures featured in this narrative.

I am humbled to have colleagues, specifically Stephen B. Eccher, Matthew Mullins, Chip Hardy, Miguel Echevarría, Ross Inman, and Tracy McKenzie, who encouraged me as this project wore on. Among my colleagues, I cannot thank Keith Harper enough for a decade of sharpening my intellectual engagement with African American faith, and Chip McDaniel for teaching me how to write (beginning as an MDiv student). I would be remiss if I did not convey my gratitude to Jason Fowler for his formidable contribution to this project as he directs the Southeastern library.

This project has benefited from the generosity of Southeastern Baptist Theological Seminary for granting me a year-long sabbatical to make significant strides on this book. In addition, I'd also like to thank the anonymous donor who provided a summer book writing grant organized by Keith Whitfield that helped me acquire rare resources and facilitate interviews necessary to assure this project's depth and accuracy.

I would also like to think the leadership of California Baptist University, Missional Training Center (Pheonix), Grace College and Seminary, LeTourneau University, Southeastern Seminary, Second Presbyterian Church (Memphis), and First Baptist Church (Charleston) for giving me opportunities to hammer out some of the ideas contained in this book via lecture and asking thoughtful questions.

Finally, to my editor Jon Boyd who gently guided and encouraged me through this process; you are a blessing to me. To Rebecca Carhart for keeping this project on track, and to Allie Crumley, whose attention to detail produced a useful index.

It is with joy that I dedicate this book to my paternal grandmother, who inspires my faith with each passing year. Grandmommy, I hope this book makes you proud.

1

INTRODUCTION

It was April 24, 1823, and after months of braving the open sea, land was in sight. A passenger on the vessel, a woman with the complexion of cocoa, later recalled, "The sight chilled our very hearts. The ladies retired to the cabin and burst into tears; and some of the gentlemen turned pale: my own soul sickened within me, and every nerve trembled." She recollected thinking to herself during the voyage,

> I must look forward to that Sabbath which will never end—there to see, face to face, what we now see dimly through a glass; and to meet you, with my other friends, whom I have left behind. It is a source of consolation to me to be able to think that you, with many others in my native land, pray for me. Were it not for that, I should almost despair.

This is not a record of the dreaded Middle Passage but of missionary Betsey Stockton's transit from America's Eastern Seaboard to the Sandwich Islands (later named Hawaii). Stockton was born into slavery in 1798 and was soon without mother or father to look after her. She converted to Christianity in 1816 and was manumitted (freed) the following year. Stockton became a member at First Presbyterian Church in Princeton, and soon after she concluded that it was the sacred duty of every Christian "to offer themselves in humble obedience to God's call to carry out his plan of salvation through Jesus Christ for the world."[1]

Her conviction kindled a desire to depart for Africa as a missionary. Shortly thereafter, Stockton learned that Princeton Theological Seminary student Charles S. Stewart was planning to depart for the Sandwich Islands, and she joined her efforts with those of his family. Stockton was commissioned by the American Board of Commissioners for Foreign Missions and became the second single American woman sent overseas.

---

[1] Robert J. Stevens, *Profiles of African-American Missionaries* (Pasadena, CA: William Carey Library, 2012), 65.

While on the island, Stockton established a school for the Maka'ainana, the common people of Maui. After receiving some opposition from the local chiefs, in 1824 Stockton established a school and was its first teacher.[2] She taught algebra, English, Latin, and history. Her missionary strategy was upheld by the conviction that reading and writing were essential to ongoing discipleship. By 1826, the school Stockton founded had educated eight thousand Hawaiian students with the intention of imparting the gospel of Jesus Christ. In 1825, Stockton returned to Princeton due to the poor health of Stewart's wife, Harriet.

Like the tale of Betsey Stockton, the African American Christian story recounts a determined people driven by faith to pursue spiritual and social uplift for themselves and others to God's glory. The narrative contained in these pages tells the story of countless heroes and heroines of the faith who were often overlooked while they walked the earth, who have been forgotten in history, but whose names are written in the Lamb's book of life.

A STORY WITHIN A STORY

The Christian story is a global story composed of a "cloud of witnesses" (Hebrews 12:1) from "all nations, tribes, peoples, and tongues" (Revelation 7:9). Contributions from Black Catholics and other organized faiths notwithstanding, this volume is limited to professed Black Christians within Protestant denominations and communions in the United States, or missionaries who were sent from America to other nations. This volume's focus on African American Christianity means that the expansive witness of the broader African diasporic Christian community is not within the book's immediate scope despite their meaningful contributions to the faith. The tale of Black faith is interwoven into the tapestry of God's people but is often absent in the pages of church history. This Christian narrative steps into that void by featuring the stories of Hosea Easton, Zilpha Elaw, Elias Camp Morris, Harriett A. Cole Baker, Gardner C. Taylor, Mary McCleod Bethune, and others as they displayed how the gospel of Jesus Christ redeems sinners and restores them to walk faithfully within their cultural and historical context. This narrative highlights the beauty of the African American contribution to the universal Christian story, of which Jesus Christ is at the center.

THE THEOLOGICAL ANCHORS OF BLACK CHRISTIANITY

The story of Black Christianity in the United States has been told in a variety of ways. A common approach features denominational development. C. Eric Lincoln and

---

[2]Gregory Nobles, *The Education of Betsey Stockton: An Odyssey of Slavery and Freedom* (Chicago: University of Chicago Press, 2022), 115.

Introduction 3

Lawrence H. Mamiya's *The Black Church in the African American Experience* is a classic example of this method. Another approach focuses on African origins, and this is characterized by Albert J. Raboteau's *Slave Religion*. The most common method employed by trained theologians reflects the priorities of Black liberationists who evaluate African American Christianity with the rubric of radicalism.

Theologian James H. Cone argues that "the black church was born in protest" and that a radical posture is the hallmark that legitimizes a Black church.[3] Historian Gayraud S. Wilmore's 1973 publication of *Black Religion and Black Radicalism* cemented Cone's insistence on political protest as the means of belonging to the African American religious tradition.[4] This approach incorporates figures based on their opposition to slavery, resistance against Jim Crow segregation, and fight against social injustice, and often overlooks Conversion stories and the vibrant spiritual witness of Black Christianity.

The two-volume work *Swing Low* resists assessing the African American Christian tradition with a method that materialized in the middle of the twentieth century. Instead, this volume employs a theological criterion that emerged from the nascent days of African American faith. The rubric deployed in these volumes is defined as theological Anchors that conceptualize the doctrinal themes that emerge from within the story of Black Christianity in America. *Swing Low* volume 1 chronicles how the Anchors emerged and matured and developed in their sophistication and emphasis through history while maintaining independent viability until a calculated methodological shift led by Black liberation theologians.

By offering a historically detailed account with a keen eye toward its theological foundations, the Anchors maintain a familiar cord that traces its roots to the orthodox theological commitments of both African and non-African church fathers. While Black Christians did not set out to establish an organized doctrinal

---

[3] James H. Cone, *Black Theology and Black Power* (Maryknoll, NY: Orbis Books, 1997), 94.

[4] Cone and Wilmore's contemporaries also critiqued their historical approach. Chief among them was Cecil Cone, the brother of James Cone. Cecil Cone insisted that James Cone's deployment of Black power in his theological project bequeathed essential problems in his formulation. Cecil Cone writes, "Because [James] Cone used Black Power as the point of departure for this theological analysis of black religion, our argument is that he was unable to grasp its essence. He wrongly perceived black religion to be primarily political activity as found in Stokley Carmichael and Rap Brown. This led Cone to an affirmation of the pre–Civil War black religious traditions of Nat Turner, Denmark Vesey, and Gabriel Prosser, but to a rejection of the post-Civil War traditions as compensatory.... The confessional story of black people's relationship to the Almighty Sovereign God is replaced by the call to political activity." Cecil Wayne Cone, "The Identity Crisis in Black Theology: An Investigation of the Theological Interpretation of Black Religion in the Works of Joseph R. Washington, James Cone and J. Deotis Roberts" (PhD diss., Emery University, 1974), 63.

framework, these thought patterns consistently emerge from the literature. The following theological Anchors summarize the doctrinal commitments that African Americans have historically affirmed.

Anchor 1: Big God. A Big God is at the center of African American Christianity—the one who is "able to do exceedingly abundantly above all we ask or think" (Ephesians 3:20). The God who is able is affirmed without dispute throughout the tradition. In the Black community, African American theologians conclude that the ultimate question is not "Does God exist?" but rather "What is his character?"

During the Great Awakenings, Black converts received an overly spiritualized faith from evangelists. Despite accepting the Christian faith, they did not internalize all they received. African slaves contested a dualistic expression of God confined to the spiritual realm. From the beginning of the African American story, there was an expectation that divine interaction profoundly shaped every area of human existence—including the social, political, and economic spheres. Divine handiwork ascribed intrinsic value to God's creation and especially to his image bearers. Consequently, Black Christians were convinced that the oppression they endured and the counterfeit doctrine used to uphold Black inferiority were not beyond divine judgment.

God's sovereignty affirmed that neither slave masters nor bigots were ultimate—God is. The need for a Big God in the face of suffering did not expire at emancipation; it was necessary when Reconstruction unraveled, during Jim Crow segregation, and throughout decades of de facto racism and disenfranchisement. God's meticulous providence brought comfort to the faithful despite their circumstances because perfect love, grace, and mercy are essential to God's character. The tension created between life's barbarous circumstances and a sovereign God caused theodicy (that is, divine engagement with evil in the world) to emerge as a centerpiece of theological consideration. However, God's praiseworthy character deemed him worthy of confidence. God executes his divine will, which includes justice on earth as it is in heaven and hope in the life to come.

Anchor 2: Jesus. Christ is essential to the Christian faith, and his person and work are fundamental to the African American theological tradition. A driving motif of the incarnation is identification. For example, Jesus identified with God the Father, the Holy Spirit, and humanity at his baptism and once again with humankind during his wilderness temptations. For Black Christians, Jesus' identification with life's joys and sorrows forged meaningful solidarity with the marginalized.

Referring to the Savior as Jesus (his given name), rather than Christ (his office), emphasized Jesus' nearness to the plight of the least.

Jesus' kinship with those who are "despised and rejected" contradicts the social order's ongoing assault on their image-bearing capacity. Jesus' earthly life was a foretaste that casted seeds of love and justice that will fully bloom in his kingdom. While his life bespoke solidarity with the "least of these," this is only comforting because he is God. The God-man purchased redemption on Calvary's cross, and sinners who receive Jesus' death and resurrection for their sin are free from sin's deadly consequences.

African American Christians have long placed a strong emphasis on the blood of Jesus. "The blood," which is central in Black preaching and hymnody, testifies that the Savior is acquainted with grief, and his blood washes away their guilty stains. Blacks in the antebellum period were captivated by Christ's blood because unjust bloodshed by slaves draped over barrels, strapped to trees, and tied to fenceposts was a tragically common occurrence. But Jesus' redeeming blood, shed on the cross, granted hope in the pit of suffering, and his resurrection offered believers a foretaste of victory over sin and oppression that is theirs in Christ Jesus.

Anchor 3: Conversion and Walking in the Spirit. Conversion and Walking in the Spirit coalesce as an event and a process. Like two sides of the same coin, these distinct realities relate to each other. The Conversion (or salvation) event exchanges sin and condemnation for new life in Christ through his atoning death and resurrection. The moment of Conversion initiates the sanctification process, wherein believers are conformed to Christ's likeness by overcoming the power of sin in their lives by the Spirit's power. While the lion's share of the tradition affirms that sanctification is a lifelong process, those in the holiness tradition embrace Christian perfectionism, which affirms that believers are fully sanctified in a second blessing of the Spirit (distinct from salvation).

The concepts of sin, repentance, Conversion, and sanctification are prominent within African American Christianity because large numbers of Blacks converted to faith in Christ at revivals during the Great Awakenings. These themes were woven into the fabric of African American Christianity. From one generation to the next, these biblical concepts were passed down through discipleship because believers are prone to pass along notions that fanned their own belief into flame.

Walking in the Spirit is the means of demonstrating Christ's lordship in the believer's life. Sanctification encompasses pursuing personal piety expressed in the fruit of the Spirit (Galatians 5:22-23) and social awareness as described in Micah's summary of godly living (Micah 6:8). Spiritual warfare, in the form of racial terrorism, reinforces the need for God's Spirit in daily life. The need for a powerful spiritual experience marked Black church gatherings, which featured exuberant worship and dynamic preaching that made doctrine dance. Parishioners gathered with expectancy to encounter the Spirit to overcome the hurts of the past and prevail over the trials to come. The role of the Holy Spirit in the African American Christian tradition cannot be overestimated.

Anchor 4: The Good Book. The Bible is the Good Book. African Americans are a Bible-centric people with a healthy dependence on God's revealed Word. Despite high illiteracy rates, Bible knowledge increased dramatically as enslaved Blacks rehearsed biblical stories and sang spirituals in the fields and in their living quarters. Telling and retelling biblical accounts of Israel was far more than entertainment; it was an act of resistance. African Americans avoided making the Good Book an object of distanced analysis by thrusting themselves into the biblical narrative. Slaves identified with the Hebrew people and declared themselves participants in the biblical drama. Their identification with the story further cemented them within the people of God and reassured their inherent dignity.

During the antebellum period, few desires rivaled education within the Black community. Throughout Reconstruction, literacy skyrocketed as Blacks were educated. Reading was the primary goal of education, and in particular reading Scripture. The impact of the biblical narrative was amplified, especially among Black leaders, because pastors did not read theological treatises crafted by formally trained theologians; they mastered "telling the story." African Americans also desired to read Scripture to undo the exegetical abuses of slave owners who sought to justify Black subservience with the words of God.

African American Christians affirmed that Scripture was the sole divinely authored guide for salvation and godly living. The nineteenth century gave rise to debates about the sufficiency and inerrancy of Scripture that were primarily located in the ivory towers of theological academies to which Blacks had no access. Among African Americans, the most fundamental assertion concerning Scripture's nature has been regarding authority—does the Bible have the right to guide personal and public life? An affirmative answer has been virtually unquestioned because it is assumed that when the Bible speaks, God speaks. Among contemporary African American Christians, interpretative issues that question the Bible's authority are largely relegated to the academy, not the church. Rank-and-file Black Christians are a Bible-believing people.

Anchor 5: Deliverance. God is a liberator. This biblical theme directly applies the Christian faith to the African American experience. Sometimes also called freedom or liberation, Deliverance is established in significant biblical events that serve as an interpretative key for unlocking Scripture's message and discerning the unchanging character of God. Most prominently, the exodus reminded Israel of God's faithfulness and demonstrated that slavery was against his will and that divine power was available to deliver his people. Similarly, Jubilee was a celebration of canceling debts and freeing slaves that was intended to establish God's liberating character in the social consciousness of his people. These acts of Deliverance culminated in Christ's death and resurrection, which secured victory over every manifestation of sin for his people.

Liberation language describes a series of experiences in the Christian life. Three separate acts of Deliverance start with liberation from sin at Conversion and culminate with Deliverance in God's eschatological kingdom. Between the liberating acts of Conversion and glorification, sinfulness is palpable in the social, economic, and political realms of daily life. Consistent with his unchanging nature, God, by the power of Jesus' resurrection, is the deliverer from each of these dire circumstances.

Liberation's place in the biblical witness is nearly uncontested among African Americans, but the method employed to pursue liberation by God's people has been the locus of spirited discussion, especially since the civil rights movement. Wide-ranging proposals notwithstanding, two categories emerge in discussions of pursuing divine Deliverance. The first comprises those who insist that the gospel *is* liberation—with a nearly exclusive gaze toward political and social freedom. The second group constitutes those who hold that liberation is an imperative of the gospel and that the intensity of racial oppression warrants concerted attention to apply the balm of the gospel to this social wound. At its best, the tradition holds salvific, social, and eschatological liberation in tension and shrewdly applies this theme to the Black experience.

Inherent integration of the Anchors. African American theological reflection is a celebratory task. Passionate doctrinal expression is a means of extolling the God who can save his people from their sins and overcome life's trials. As the Anchors are assessed throughout the narrative, it is essential to note that thought, action, and worship are intrinsic to Christian faithfulness within historic Black faith. Theological reflection on the Anchors does not conclude with abstract concepts but with a living witness to biblical teaching. Said differently, for Blacks, Christianity is a practiced faith, so the Anchors have not achieved their purpose until they guide activity in both public and private life. In addition to serving as an instructional means of introducing the theological themes of African American Christianity, this story of Black faith incorporates a wide variety of self-confessed Christians, and these Anchors are a means of demonstrating whether their doctrinal commitments lie within or extend beyond the orthodox faith that African Americans have historically affirmed.

PERIODS AND CHAPTERS

Each chapter highlights significant ecclesiastical events and provides a nuanced historical context to trace the doctrinal Anchors of the African American Christian tradition. Following this introduction, chapter two documents manifestations of the Christian faith in Africa prior to the transatlantic slave trade, which refutes the fallacy that God used slavery to introduce Christianity to Africans. This chapter also recounts the circumstances of Africans arriving in the New World. Chapter three demonstrates how the Christian faith spread among Africans in America during the First and Second Great Awakenings. Chapter four explores how African Americans took the often-warped faith given to them by their masters, made it their own, and reclaimed it for freedom. This chapter is punctuated by exploring where Blacks worshiped and how faith energized the "invisible institution" and Black abolitionism.

Chapter five marks the beginning of a new era, initiated by the Emancipation Proclamation. Saying that the invisible institution became visible during this period is the best way to describe the establishment of Black churches and denominations, which became the central institution of the African American community.[5] Chapter six chronicles how the Black church remained the central organizational body in the Black community and provided services for Black people, including educational opportunities.

Chapter seven begins with the advent of Jim Crow segregation, which marked a new normal in America that was punctuated by the Great Migration. Chapter eight highlights two budding theological movements, namely, Black Pentecostalism and Black fundamentalism, that burst on to the scene amid the rapidly changing intellectual and ecclesiastical climate in America. Chapter nine accounts for the development of the intellectual foundations of the civil rights movement, along with the historical and theological foundations of its leaders and foot soldiers.

---

[5]George F. Bragg, *History of the Afro-American Group of the Episcopal Church*, Academic Affairs Library (Chapel Hill: University of North Carolina at Chapel Hill, 1922), 30-31.

Introduction

The book's interlude chronicles the advent of the Black consciousness movement. This movement was so profound in the African American community that it required a response from Black leaders in education, community development, and in the church. The response was so disparate among Black Christians that it results in a need to account for two distinct responses to Black consciousness. Whereas before the interlude, the story is told in chapters that advance chronologically, after the interlude, two stories will be told, one of Black evangelicalism and the other of Black liberationism, which are concurrent movements with overlapping chronologies.

Chapter ten documents the formation of the National Negro Evangelical Association along with its social, political, and theological priorities. Chapter eleven recounts a distinct shift in the association's ethos as it sought to bear witness to Christ amid a volatile cultural moment. Chapter twelve recounts the diasporic nature of Black evangelicals within historically Black denominations, evangelical institutions of higher education, and parachurch ministries.

Chapter thirteen accounts for the origin and early stages of Black liberation theology. In addition, this chapter highlights the contributions of select first-generation Black liberationists. Chapter fourteen accounts for second-generation Black liberationists and proposes a third generation. The final chapter offers a short account of developments in the twenty-first century that are not conclusive but worth noting because they will likely develop into a movement deserving attention as historical distance grants further clarity.

USING THESE VOLUMES

This volume is intended to be accessible enough to serve as a first-time foray into the African American Christian tradition, but it also provides an overarching narrative for those who are familiar with aspects of the tradition outside a consistent theological framework. With both readers in mind, here are some tips to help every reader get the most out of this book.

Two volumes working together. This book is part of a two-volume set. Each volume can be read independently, but their value is amplified when they are used together. Throughout both books, careful attention is given to tracing the development of the theological Anchors that emerge from the African American Christian tradition. The Anchors appear capitalized as proper nouns when they are assessed. The anthology, volume 2, highlights the theological Anchors as they appear throughout the primary sources. Another feature that integrates the volumes is the reference of over one hundred primary sources in volume 1 that are featured in volume 2. This allows readers to have a firsthand encounter with the literature that drives this theological narrative.

Representing Black dialects. To allow African American saints to speak for themselves, both volumes contain representations of Black dialects that remain as they were originally recorded. This authentically captures the strength, resilience, and beauty of African American faith in the words they were expressed in. This editorial decision insists that the strength of Christian faith is not awakened because of complex theological expressions. Faith's power emits from its object and living in faithful obedience to a praiseworthy God. In addition, the grammatical solecisms of Black dialects convey important regional and chronological details that would be otherwise lost.

Project scope. This volume's primary focus is African American Christianity. Exceptional African diasporic contributions to the faith are numerous but are only included in reference to Black Christianity in America. In this volume, it follows that the term *Black* is commonly a designation for African Americans. Further, the focus on Christian expressions of "God-talk" (i.e., theology) does not discount the impact of non-Christian religious expression in the Black community but is not featured in the narrative.

The purpose of a survey. Both volumes are surveys. Volume 1 provides a historical-theological narrative spanning several hundred years, and volume 2 offers a sampling of the literature produced by this theological tradition. As a result, neither volume is exhaustive, but they are the seedbed for more focused research and a foray into resources that are yet to receive the attention they deserve. After completing these volumes, I am dedicating my research and writing to this much-needed task of retrieval—and I encourage others to do the same.

Corresponding Chapters/Sections in Volumes 1 and 2

Volume 1 Chapter	Volume 2 Section
1	introduction
2, 3, 4	1
5, 6	2
7, 8, 9	3
10, 11, 12	4
13, 14	5
15	6

THE CONTINUED JOURNEY OF BETSEY STOCKTON

Upon returning to New England, Stockton was hired by the Committee for the Establishment of the Coloured Infant School in Philadelphia. The school was the first of its kind, and Stockton founded and served as the school's principal and as a teacher from 1828 to 1830. Soon after, she departed the United States as a missionary once again to establish a school in Grape Island, Canada, that instructed Native American children. Stockton's biographer notes, "Within two months, the fruits of Stockton's work were apparent—'She came for the purpose of setting up an Infant School, which has succeeded admirably'—and other teachers across the region built upon her success well into the 1830s."[6]

In September 1830, Harriet Stewart died, and Stockton cheerfully took over the care of her three children, who had previously become her family. In addition to her new maternal responsibilities, she established a school for Black children in Princeton, New Jersey, the only such school in Princeton at the time. In 1836, the African American members of First Presbyterian Church, where Stockton attended, were given permission to receive Communion at their own parish. She was one of the founding members of the church, the First Colored Presbyterian Church of Princeton, later named Witherspoon Street Church. Stockton transitioned to glory in 1865, and her services were held at Princeton University, where President John Maclean Jr. and theologian Charles Hodge presided.

African American Christianity is full of stories like Betsey's—tales of the faithful that will be forgotten if they are not told.

---

[6]Nobles, *Education of Betsey Stockton*, 147.

2

A TRANSATLANTIC FAITH

THE CONTEMPORARY TREND of disregarding Christian orthodoxy because it was used as a tool of Western hegemony and colonization is prevalent in America. The abuse of Christian doctrine to gain power is unfortunate and undeniable, but an honest look at the church's history demonstrates that "contending for the faith once for all delivered to the saints" (Jude 3), based on biblical authority, is an ancient African practice that predates colonization. The theological Anchors of Black faith have their roots in Africa and were transported to America and blossomed into a fully orbed Christian witness. In particular, the establishment of a Big God, Jesus, and the Good Book are prominent in Black transatlantic faith.

This brief sketch of African Christianity is not exhaustive but bears witness to precolonial African Christianity that was not established by coercion but as a free choice. These regional accounts of early African faith demonstrate that the African American Christian story begins in Acts 8 with the Ethiopian eunuch—not the transatlantic slave trade.[1] From the pages of the New Testament to the church fathers, African Christianity is an often-overlooked wellspring of the church's history. By the fifth century, four principal African civilizations were predominantly Christianized: North Africa, Egypt, Nubia, and Ethiopia. The Christian gospel spread throughout the continent from these early societies via trade routes where goods were exported, and religion was in tow.

> **In the New Testament, the term *Ethiopian* is commonly used to describe Black persons residing south of Egypt. Consequently, the biblical references to the queen of Sheba and the Ethiopian eunuch are not direct references to sub-Saharan nations.**

---

[1] This summary closely follows the work of Vince L. Bantu in *A Multitude of All Peoples: Engaging Ancient Christianity's Global Identity* (Downers Grove, IL: InterVarsity Press, 2020).

North Africa is a seedbed of Christian thought. Born in Carthage, Tertullian (b. 155/160, d. after 220) was one of Africa's most significant early church fathers. His theological treatises in Latin shaped the doctrinal vocabulary of the church around the world. Cyprian (200–258), a Carthaginian native, provided theological and ecclesiological leadership during a time of false teaching, schism, and persecution. His most profound treatise was *On the Unity of the Church*. Tertullian and Cyprian's influence in the church and beyond is difficult to overestimate.

However, the influence of Tertullian and Cyprian is eclipsed by that of Augustine (345–430), who is unquestionably the most influential Christian thinker outside Scripture. Augustine expounded a Big God for the universal church to anchor its hope. While his African roots are commonly neglected, he was born in the Numidian city of Thagaste (modern Souk Ahras, Algeria) and made references to himself as being African.[2] While he wrote his famous *Confessions* and *City of God* in Latin, Augustine continually identified with his people by speaking the common Nubian language.

In addition to theological formation, North Africa was the site of inspiring stories of faithfulness that spread throughout the region. Perpetua (182–203), a noblewoman from Carthage, was imprisoned for her faith and was later martyred. Her book, *The Passion of Saints Perpetua and Felicity*, is the first known Christian text composed by a woman, and as it spread throughout ancient North Africa, the gospel was broadcasted in its pages.

> **Anthony the Great** (251–356) was a famous Egyptian monk from Scetis who promoted asceticism, self-denial of all forms of sensual indulgence, as the model Christian lifestyle. Athanasius wrote his biography and promoted his ideas, and Anthony became a central figure in the Egyptian church.

While North Africa was a doctrinal fountainhead, Egypt and Alexandria were points of departure for the Christian faith onto the rest of the continent. Among Coptic (Egyptian) Christians, the long-held story remains that the apostle Mark introduced their region to the Christian faith. The apostle converted Egyptians, appointed natives as bishops, and continued with his missionary journeys. After the Council of Constantinople in 381, the Egyptian church fought to maintain orthodoxy, and Christianity became the dominant religion over against paganism.

---

[2]Bantu, *Multitude of All Peoples*, 114.

Benjamin of Alexandria (590–662) was an Alexandrian patriarch who fought for an indigenous African expression of the Trinity and combated Roman theological error.

> **The Council of Constantinople** in 381 was the second ecumenical church council. This assembly pronounced the trinitarian doctrine of equality of the Father, Son, and Holy Spirit.

After Egyptian missionaries shared the gospel with Nubians, the struggle to maintain an indigenous expression of the Trinity raged during the fifth century. Figures such as Julianus and Theodora resisted the spread of the trinitarian language from the ecumenical church councils in favor of an African expression of Christ's humanity and divinity. Theodora's help was essential. As the emperor's wife, she was able to stall an envoy of Chalcedonian bishops at the Egyptian boarder who were intent on carrying the Chalcedonian trinitarian formula into Nubia. Orthodox North African language for the divinity and humanity of Christ spread in Africa via Theodora's missionaries under Julianus's leadership.

> **Alexandrian trinitarianism** embraced the full humanity and divinity of Jesus but had difficulty with the language of two natures. Africans maintained that Jesus' humanity and divinity were migrated into one nature (*physis*) at the incarnation, in contrast with the "one person, two natures" affirmation of Chalcedon.

Ethiopia is one of the oldest world civilizations, and its influence is felt throughout sub-Saharan Africa. Ethiopia's dramatic precolonial story of Christian orthodoxy climaxed soon after Ethiopian King Ezana (303–350) was baptized, insisted on the construction of church buildings, and adopted Christianity as the national religion. The Roman emperor Constantinus (317–461), son of Constantine the Great, attempted to enforce heretical doctrine that made the Son inferior to the Father. Despite numerous acts of intimidation, King Ezana defended Christ's divinity while Rome was under heretical rule.

After King Ezana's reign, Christianity continued to spread through missionaries called the nine saints. These missionaries were especially active in northern Ethiopia, and they introduced monastic practices and built monasteries that are in existence today. The nine saints were highly effective and proclaimed Christ with contextualized language from Egypt and Syria.

After a millennium of the church maturing in Ethiopia, Emperor Zar'a Ya'qob (1399–1468) caused a reformation more than a century before Martin Luther sparked the European Reformation. During Ya'qob's reign (1434–1468), there was strife between sects that insisted on different days for observing the Sabbath. Ya'qob's marvelously written *Book of Light* brought peace between the factions by instructing them to observe the Sabbath on both days. The *Book of Light* also defines the doctrinal commitments of the Ethiopian nation; it states, "This Book of Light tells of the abolition of magic which was practiced in the land of Ethiopia, and it teaches the worship of God alone: without any mixing with [other] cults, astrology, or augury."[3]

Ya'qob gained significant political power and influence during his successful efforts to unify the Ethiopian church. This caused the Stefanites, a group of ascetic Ethiopians, to challenge the king's inflated authority in church matters and the elevation of any text in addition to Scripture. Ethiopian Christians identified the grievances that Martin Luther and other European Reformers lamented over one hundred years later. This story is virtually unknown but establishes the Good Book and its stories as central to African Christianity.

The story of the Christian faith in these regions demonstrates the free choice of Africans to follow Jesus before colonization. While this narrative does not negate the presence of African traditional religion and other faiths, it abolishes the notion that Christianity is strictly a White man's religion. The oral nature of African cultures precludes gathering modern demographic evidence for Christianity. Nevertheless, may this oral history maintain its truth value today as it did for Africans in the past.

During colonialization, European missionaries and explorers came to Africa proclaiming a mixed message of death and life to indigenous peoples. Their proclamation contained the life-giving message of Christ, but deadly manipulation tactics were added so Europeans could master fellow image bearers in God's name. The conscientious observer can untangle the web that colonists (and later slave owners) wove to dehumanize African people. This task is exactly what African Christians undertook in North America as they reclaimed the faith as the means of their deliverance.

BLACK CHRISTIANITY IN AMERICA

The relationship between Africans in America and the Christian faith changed dramatically during the pre-emancipation era. The story begins with Captain John

---

[3]Bantu, *Multitude of All Peoples*, 106.

Smith's 1619 description of a scene in Jamestown, Virginia. He recounts, "About the last of August came in a Dutch man of warre that sold us twenty Negars."[4] During the transatlantic slave trade, there was no data compiled on the percentage of captured Africans who were Christian, but it is evident that by emancipation (1865) Christianity was an unmistakable pillar in the Black community.

From Christopher Columbus's arrival in the "New World" in 1492 to the end of the slave trade in 1867, more than ten million Africans were transported to the Americas on approximately 27,000 expeditions (nearly 170 a year). More than half a million of those who endured the Middle Passage arrived in the American colonies (about 95 percent of the Africans transported across the Atlantic were sent to the tropical, sugar-growing regions of Brazil and the Caribbean).[5] In the later 1600s, the demand for slaves increased as colonial plantations grew larger, and the price of indentured servants from England and the Caribbean increased.

A SLAVE'S JOURNEY

Africans were captured on their native soil and taken to the Atlantic coast. They endured the dreaded Middle Passage—the transatlantic voyage from Africa to the Americas. Slaves suffered inhumane conditions on overcrowded and disease-ridden ships. The emotional, physical, and sexual abuse endured by captives resulted in mortality rates of 15 to 20 percent of the "cargo." Slaves disembarked, were sold on the auction block, and were taken to workplaces throughout colonial America.

The economic benefit of slavery was not enough to justify the troubled conscience of colonists. Consequently, slave owners created a mythos of the supremacy of Whites and the subhumanity of Blacks—the invention of race. Blackness and Whiteness are human fabrications produced by the process of racialization. Race is a socially constructed reality that attributes negative and/or positive meaning to biological traits and cultural manifestations that are used to categorize people. The concept of race (and the process of racialization) resulted in the ability to justify the mistreatment of Blacks. This dehumanization gave license to one group to assert dominance over another, and its vile repercussions echo throughout American history.

The distinction between slave masters and the enslaved was deeply religious. From the beginning of the American story, race and religion were intermingled

---

[4]John Smith, *The Generall History of Virginia, New-England, and the Sumer Isles* (London, 1624).
[5]Nell Irvin Painter, *Creating Black Americans: African-American History and Its Meanings, 1619 to the Present* (New York: Oxford University Press, 2006), 30.

because Christianity was a means of crystallizing notions of Whiteness and Blackness. Being Black was the equivalent to being a heathen (i.e., pagan) and signified diminished inherent worth, resulting in exploitation. Being European was equated with being Christian. This superior status was designated as being White. Despite the Christian faith being weaponized against Black people, Christianity was the means of Deliverance deployed by African Americans to begin dismantling the social implications of racialization.

> **DISTINGUISHING RACE, ETHNICITY, AND CULTURE**
>
> Race is an appalling social fabrication that weaponizes ethnic distinctions and cultural expression to categorize humanity. By contrast, the biblical word *ethnē* refers to God-given biological designations that distinguish people groups (Matthew 28:19; Revelation 5:9). In addition, the making of culture is a biblical undertaking given to humanity by God (Genesis 1:26-28).[a]
>
> [a] For more, see Walter R. Strickland II and Dayton Hartman, eds., *For God So Loved the World: A Blueprint for Kingdom Diversity* (Nashville: B&H Academic, 2020), xix-xxi.

SLAVE EVANGELIZATION

In the late 1600s, slaves converted to Christianity with increasing regularity, and colonists were forced to grapple with their English heritage, which insisted that Christians could not be slaves. During this time, large swaths of Christians insisted that the debate over slave evangelization was trivial because Blacks had no soul to proselytize. Missionary Morgan Godwyn (1640–1686) encountered this sentiment. While reporting his missionary efforts to slaves, a parishioner interrupted, saying, "You might well baptize puppies as Negros."[6]

As time passed, while some European colonists remained convinced that Blackness was irreconcilable with Christianity, the consensus affirmed that Blacks had souls. This conclusion forced colonists to wrestle with the question of whether baptism made slaves White—that is, free, intelligent, and fully human.[7] An affirmative answer threatened to undermine the social order because the British

---

[6] Morgan Godwyn, *The Negro's & Indian's Advocate: Sung for the Admission to the Church, or A persuasive to the instructing and baptizing of the Negro's and Indians in our plantations shewing that as the compliance therewith can prejudice no man's just interest, so the wilful neglecting and opposing of it, is no less than a manifest apostasy from the Christian faith: to which is added, a brief account of religion in Virginia* (London: Printed for the author by J.D., 1680), 38.

[7] Paul Harvey, *Through the Storm and Through the Night: A History of African American Christianity* (Plymouth, UK: Rowman & Littlefield, 2011), 19.

custom was that Christians are not fit for servitude, and thus slaves were freed upon baptism.

The intensity of the controversy escalated during the first half of the eighteenth century as Africans were imported to the colonies at a rate three times greater than that of the White population. By 1750, nearly 20 percent of the colonies' population was of African descent. The need to preserve the social hierarchy that necessitated White dominance and Black subservience was essential.

In 1701 the Society for the Propagation of the Gospel in Foreign Parts, an Anglican missions organization, was formed to share the gospel with Black and native people in the New World. Their missionaries insisted that their efforts would not threaten the social order by encouraging insurrection and rebellions. The society's pamphlets and publications declared that Scripture supported slavery, citing passages including Ephesians 6:1, "Slaves, obey your earthly masters" (NRSV).

Despite their assurances, acknowledging that Blacks had souls to evangelize threatened the social order. Proponents of slave evangelization appealed for the bishop of London to decree that baptism no longer granted slaves manumission—and the proposal passed. To further assuage the fear of slave masters, evangelists followed the lead of Francis Le Jau (1665–1717), who drafted a vow for slaves to sign before baptism. Le Jau's statement read, "You declare in the presence of God and before the congregation that you do not ask for the holy baptism out of any design to free yourself from the Duty and Obedience you owe your Master while you live, but merely for the good of Your soul and to partake of the Graces and Blessings promised to the Members of the Church of Jesus Christ."[8]

In time, the fear of slave evangelization and looming rebellion grew as the African population swelled—especially on large plantations and among churches with large Black populations. White concern for maintaining the social order was affirmed because slaves intuitively discerned the relationship between their faith and Deliverance. This was evident in 1723, when a group of Christian slaves sought legal action for their freedom. In a letter to an Anglican bishop, Edmund Gibson, Virginian slaves argued that their masters disallowed them from observing the Sabbath.

Two theological Anchors were manifest in this scene as these slaves deployed the Good Book and Deliverance, comparing their masters to the Egyptians who ruthlessly oppressed the Israelites in the book of Exodus, saying, "Our task mastrs

---

[8]Francis Le Jau, "Slave Conversion in the Frontier," in *African American Religious History: A Documentary Witness*, 2nd ed., ed. Milton C. Segnett (Durham, NC: Duke University Press, 2000), 27.

A Transatlantic Faith

are has hard with us as the Egypttions was with the Chilldann of Issrall." The slaves did not affix their names to the letter "for feare of our masters for if they knew that wee have Sent home to your honour wee Should goo neare to Swing upon the gassass [gallows] tree."

Despite the peaceful nature of this appeal, the debate raged as the fear of slave rebellion increased and opponents of slave evangelization claimed that Christianity made slaves headstrong because spiritual liberation insisted on bodily freedom. Still others argued that Christianizing slaves was appropriate because the faith served as in internal motivation to keep slaves docile and subservient. Amid the heated debate, one thing that both sides affirmed was the maintenance of the social hierarchy.

Slave masters and missionaries warped the Christian faith to serve their social agenda. Christian teaching was weaponized to uphold logic that disjointed the spiritual and physical existence that God declared very good (Genesis 1:31). This "plantation gospel" reduced the Christian faith to valuing the soul while disregarding the embodied state. Spiritual life was regarded over against physical well-being, which promoted a dualistic anthropology that maintained the status quo. Ironically, this theological deformity, formulated and employed to subjugate Black people, was internalized by its proponents.

For the first one hundred years of slavery, missionaries made limited progress evangelizing slaves, especially those who were brought to America by way of the Middle Passage. The language barrier and the cultural trappings of Anglo Christianity were off-putting to slaves. In addition, it was difficult for slaves to understand the redemptive value of a belief system used to justify their servitude.

PROSLAVERY CHRISTIANITY

Cotton Mather (1626–1710) and others formalized a version of the Christian faith in pamphlets and other writings that boasted a justification for the goodness of Black servitude. Consistent with his theological claims, Mather hosted a weekly gathering of the "Society of Negroes" in his home, intended to Christianize African attendees. Mather asserted that neither Scripture nor the Church of England's teaching insisted that Christianization was equated with freedom from servitude.

John Staffin made theological arguments that complemented Mather's slaveholding ideals. Staffin argued that Scripture decreed some men to be born slaves, and he authorized this claim by demonstrating that Abraham owned slaves.

Moreover, Staffin introduced a fallacy that is widely affirmed today, namely that slavery brought Africans out of a pagan land to a new world to be saved from divine judgment.

Proponents of proslavery Christianity eased the fears of Anglos who worried incessantly about insurrection by buttressing their theological convictions in the legal code. As slave codes were introduced, they supported the Christianization of Blacks while disallowing their freedom. Slave codes varied from one colony to the next, but they shared underlying similarities. The codes featured, first, exclusion from the legal process. This exclusion took various forms, including Blacks not having recourse to the court system, the allowance to testify in court against a White person, or the ability to vote.

The slave codes also regulated two fundamental social units central to God's design for society, namely, family and church. The codes denied slaves legal protections for marriage because "property" could not be party to a legally binding contract. Because slave unions were not recognized by states or commonwealths, slave masters split families to make a profit without legal interference, disregarding familial relationships. These dictates made slaves vulnerable to the physical, sexual, and emotional abuse that marked slave life.

The codes also ensured the perpetual state of oppression for those who had "one drop" of African blood in their heritage. One of the earliest legislative acts that ensured the domination of a pure White race was enacted in 1662. In December 1662 in Virginia, Act XII was enacted, concerning slave nativity:

> Whereas some doubts have arisen whether children got by any Englishman upon a Negro woman should be slave or free, be it therefore enacted and declared by this present Grand Assembly, that all children born in this country shall be held bond or free only according to the condition of the mother; and that if any Christian shall commit fornication with a Negro man or woman, he or she so offending shall pay double the fines imposed by the former act.

This code protected the dominance of Whites over Blacks, and mixed-race children (often conceived by a slave mother at the will of their slave master) were disenfranchised by ensuring that they were at the bottom of the social hierarchy.

Slave codes also regulated aspects of Black life that complicated Christian practice. The codes included prohibitions against slaves learning to read and criminalized teaching slaves to read. In the West, the ability to read the biblical text has been central to the Christian faith since the Protestant Reformation and is a foundational means of knowing God and his will. Black Christians were banned from reading Scripture firsthand by statutes, such as the South Carolina Act of 1740, which states,

> Whereas, the having of slaves taught to write, or suffering them to be employed in writing, may be attended with great inconveniences; Be it enacted, that all and every person and persons whatsoever, who shall hereafter teach or cause any slave or slaves to be taught to write, or shall use or employ any slave as a scribe, in any manner of writing whatsoever, hereafter taught to write, every such person or persons shall, for every such offense, forfeit the sum of one hundred pounds, current money.

Prohibitions against Blacks reading resulted in malicious biblical interpretations, used as a tool to manipulate slaves and maintain the social order.

The slave codes comprehensively imposed on the rights of slaves in order to shackle them to the status quo. The proliferation of the codes took place just before large numbers of slaves responded to the gospel message during the revivals that swept the colonies beginning in the early 1740s.

THE FIRST GREAT AWAKENING

The First Great Awakening swept through the British colonies during the mid- and late seventeenth century and sparked concern for the spiritual well-being and treatment of slaves. The revival reoriented Black religious life as slaves responded to the gospel's call at an unprecedented rate in the New World. The tent meetings that characterized the revival were marked by an unusual expression of racial unity and an insistence that the gospel was for all people. The sense was that the invitation to Christ was for everyone despite their station in life.

KEY FIGURES IN THE AWAKENING

In 1730, John Wesley traveled to Georgia as a Society for the Propagation of the Gospel in Foreign Parts missionary to Native Americans and African slaves. Wesley was followed by George Whitefield (1714–1770), who set off on his first preaching tour through the colonies (1739–1741), which arguably inaugurated the awakening. Jonathan Edwards (1703–1758) was a Congregationalist minister, evangelist, and theologian of the revival who gave direction to the emotionalism of the movement.

The theological tenets of the awakening were simple. The primary concern was establishing a personal relationship with God, initiated by repenting of sin. Revivalists traveled the colonies offering crowds the gift of unmerited favor (or grace) and new birth in Jesus Christ. Revivals were marked by celebration, including singing, dancing, and other highly emotional expressions giving gratitude to God for his salvific work. The personal faith promoted during the revival contrasted with the state church in England. Revivalists insisted that being a faithful churchgoer or a moral person did not earn salvation—justification came only through repentance and faith in Christ.

The emphasis on Conversion promoted the inclusion of Whites and Blacks in revival meetings. The personal nature of salvation devalued the place of social status, race, and wealth as prerequisites for participation. The atmosphere of the revivals was such a contrast to the times that it was common for the illiterate or enslaved to preach and pray at these public evangelistic events.

The success of the revivals provided a stark contrast with the initial evangelization efforts of Anglican missionaries, who focused on the slow process of memorization and catechesis. The emphasis on Conversion and being Spirit-filled took the focus away from wordy doctrinal statements that left slaves unmoved. The African American theological foundation was forged during the revivals, and deep commitments to Conversion and Walking in the Spirit remain prominent features in the African American theological tradition today.

The effectiveness of the Great Awakenings was also felt because practices in the revival had clear parallels to African religious rituals. The evangelistic emphasis on rebirth was reminiscent of rebirth rituals in African secret societies. Furthermore, baptism by immersion evoked the memory of African customs that featured being washed by submersion in water and emerging anew. These parallels do not necessarily imply syncretism but provided a sense of familiarity with African customs that were fulfilled by the Christian faith.

The Great Awakening was a countercultural movement. The methods of itinerant evangelists composed of clergy and laity challenged the clerical pecking order. The revivals also skirted the Church of England's oversight and ministered wherever evangelists deemed expedient. But despite the Awakening's countercultural disposition, it remained captive to the racial dynamics of the age—White dominance and Black subservience. One example is great preacher George Whitefield, who arrived in Charleston, South Carolina, as an avid opponent of slavery. Ironically, by the 1750s, Whitefield upended his biblical convictions and was happy to own slaves because it freed him for the work of evangelism. Whitefield adopted common Southern justifications including the fallacy that people were born into divinely intended social classes and must uphold God's intentions.

Whitefield's anemic gospel, which freed the soul while keeping the body enslaved, was unfortunately common during the First Great Awakening. Despite demonstrations of brotherhood and the affirmation that the gospel is for all—including Jew and Greek, slave and free, male and female (Galatians 3:28)—the revival's individualistic emphasis limited the faith's implications to spiritual realities. As a result, the gospel's restorative power was truncated, and the oppressive institution of slavery went unchallenged.

In light of the vast number of Blacks who converted during the First Great Awakening, there was already evidence of unique emphases within the faith that directly interfaced with the particulars of Black life. The early development of a Big God theology prioritized God's providence over all things, big and small. God's sovereignty insisted that nothing, even the sinful actions of people, was beyond his divine reach. Together, these divine characteristics insisted that God was "able to do exceedingly abundantly above all that we ask or think" (Ephesians 3:20).

Evidence of a Big God is apparent in the sermons and writings of Lemuel Haynes (1753–1833). Haynes was converted early in the First Great Awakening, and his theology was decidedly Calvinistic. As he was the first person of African descent ordained in America, his legacy as a pastor and theologian served to establish the category of a God who is able. Haynes expressed God's cosmic providence as Creator and sustainer in an 1805 sermon titled "Divine Decrees, an Encouragement to the Use of Means": "Not only events of great, but those of less magnitude, are ascribed to God; even the falling of a sparrow, or a hair on our head. It is difficult for us to distinguish between great and small events; there is not a superfluous link in the whole chain; they all depend on each other."[9] In the same sermon, Haynes connects God's sovereignty to human obedience and dependence:

> The humble Christian will feel his own weakness and insufficiency to do anything of himself and will see that all his sufficiency is of God, and his faith and hope will rest on His power and providence to do all—which will be a motive to diligence. This will be the foundation of his trust and will excite him to work out his salvation with fear and trembling, knowing that

---

[9]Lemuel Haynes, *Divine Decrees, an Encouragement to the Use of Means: A Sermon, Delivered at Grandville, N.Y., June 25th, 1805, AD Before the Evangelical Society, Instituted for the Purposes of Aiding Pious and Needy Young Men in Acquiring Education for the Work of the Gospel Ministry* (Herlad Office, 1805).

it is *God that worketh in him*, both to will and to do His good pleasure (Philippians 2:12-13).[10]

Despite the suffering in the foreground, the Big God that Haynes described was always working in the background.[11] In addition to Haynes's emphasis on the first person of the Godhead, the incarnation of Jesus loomed large in Black Christianity from the beginning. Jesus' humanity and sufferings forged a profound entry point into the faith amid the sorrows of life.[12]

Phillis Wheatley (1753–1784), the first published African American poet, captures Jesus' identification with the common struggle of losing a spouse while declaring the victory of the resurrection for God's children. In her 1773 poem "To a Clergyman on the Death of His Lady," the twenty-year-old Wheatley wonderfully embodies the way Black Christians brought Jesus into their struggles and claimed his victory as their own:

> There too may the dear pledges of our love
> Arrive, and taste with us the joys above;
> Attune the harp to more than mortal lays,
> And join with us the tribute of their praise
> To him, who dy'd stern justice to atone,
> And make eternal glory all our own.
> He in his death slew ours, and, as he rose,
> He crush'd the dire dominion of our foes;
> Vain were their hopes to put the God to flight,
> Chain us to hell, and bar the gates of light.[13]

In addition to the nearness of Jesus and resurrection power in the moment of trial, the Savior's blood is central in the salvific equation.[14]

In the faith of the Great Awakening, the crucified and risen Lord was central, but the emphasis among Black Christians intermingled with daily life in ways that were atypical compared to their fellow revivalists. The brutality of the African American experience necessitated an emphasis on the sufferings Christ endured

---

[10]Haynes, *Divine Decrees*.
[11]See vol. 2 for an excerpt from Lemuel Haynes's sermon on John 3:3.
[12]See vol. 2 for an excerpt from *Chavis's Letter upon the Doctrine of the Extent of the Atonement of Christ*.
[13]Phillis Wheatley, "To a Clergyman, on the Death of his Lady," in *Memoir and Poems of Phillis Wheatley, a Native African and a Slave. Dedicated to the Friends of the Africans* (Chapel Hill: University of North Carolina at Chapel Hill, 1834), 64-65.
[14]See vol. 2 for the text of Phillis Wheatley's "On Being Brought from Africa to America."

to achieve redemption. An untold multitude of Black Christians viewed their lives as the Friday of Passion Week looking ahead to the victory of Sunday. It follows that the 1823 sermon of Joseph Baysmore consistently echoed "the blood" amid the call to regeneration:

> This was God's scheme of redemption, that the blood of Christ should wash believers from the great sin of unbelief. And it is written: in that day there shall be a fountain opened to the house of David, and to the inhabitants of Jerusalem for sin and uncleanness, Hence:
>
> There is a fountain filled with blood,
> Drawn from Immanuel's veins:
> And sinners plunged beneath that flood,
> Lose all their guilty stains.
>
> And now the application of the blood, by faith, broke up the surface of sin and unbelief, and hence we are planted in the blood of Christ by our faith toward God, and we groweth in favor toward God, and we groweth in favor of God, by faith in the blood of Christ.[15]

Baysmore's progression from Jesus' blood, to redemption, followed by obedience strikes a note that continues to anchor Black conceptions of Jesus (Anchor 2) through history. Connecting these aspects requires faithful action to follow belief, which many Blacks lamented was missing in predominant American Christianity.[16]

FEATURES OF NASCENT BLACK CHRISTIANITY

After Blacks came to faith in large numbers during the revivals, unique emphases and trends marked Black faith in Christ. While harmonious with historic Christianity, distinctive actions highlighted loving God and neighbor within the antebellum context. These initial trends set trajectories for African American Christianity that are evident among Black Christians today. These theological Anchors of Black Christianity have explanatory power to demonstrate the faithfulness of Black Christians and the tensions antebellum saints faced during their time.

---

[15]Joseph Baymore, *A Historical Sketch of the First Colored Baptist Church Weldon, N. C., With the Life and Labor of Elder Joseph Baysmore, with Four Collected Sermons, First: The Harmony of the Law and Gospel. Second: Subject of the Pure in Heart. Third: How We Were Made Sinners and How We Were Redeemed from Sin and Made Heirs of God by His Love. Fourth: The Confirmation of Christian Faith* (Weldon, NC: Harrell's Printing House, 1887), 8-10.

[16]See vol. 2 for an excerpt from Joseph Baysmore's "Sermon Preached to the Convicts in the Penitentiary at Raleigh, N. C., Sept. 26, 1886."

The Great Awakenings changed the Christian landscape in the New World. Prior to the revivals, missionaries from the Society for the Propagation of the Gospel in Foreign Parts attempted to evangelize Blacks by requiring memorization and catechesis in English, but slaves were largely unfamiliar with the language. Africans did not associate rote memorization and repetition with religious practices. The passion and practices of the revivals were reminiscent of African religious practices, and Blacks came to Christ in droves. Historian Carter G. Woodson insists,

> While an Episcopal clergyman with his ritual and prayer book had difficulty in interesting the Negroes, they flocked in large numbers to the spontaneous exercises of the Methodists and Baptists, who, being decidedly evangelical in their preaching, had a sort of hypnotizing effect upon the Negroes, causing them to be seized with certain emotional jerks and outward expressions of an inward movement of the spirit which made them lose control of themselves.[17]

The parallels between African religion and Christianity extended beyond passionate worship and aspects of sacred practices. African traditional religion was ubiquitous in the ancestry of slaves and was not erased from memory during the Middle Passage. It was common for the message of Jesus to fulfill the religious longings wrought by African traditional religion while simultaneously disaffirming its non-Christian teachings. Despite the doctrinal incongruence between African traditional religion and Christianity, echoes of African religion shaped the thought patterns of African American Christianity from the revivals and are discernible today.

As non-Christian Africans were drawn to the faith, they found it not altogether unfamiliar. Conceptually, African traditional religion and Christianity both support the notion of a supreme being who is Creator and protector, which offered fertile religious soil to establish a Big God theology.[18] Also, both faiths affirm the existence of an afterlife. At times unhealthy syncretism occurred during evangelization and discipleship, but over time Christian doctrine was clarified, and many Black converts faithfully expressed Christian doctrine with appropriate echoes of their African heritage. The hallmarks of African religion pronounced

---

[17]Carter G. Woodson, *The History of the Negro Church* (Washington, DC: Associated Publishers, 1921), 143.
[18]The aspects of African traditional religion highlighted in this section follow the summary of John S. Mbiti in *Introduction to African Religion*, 2nd ed. (Halley Court, UK: Heinemann, 1991).

in African American Christianity are holistic spirituality, narrative orientation, and communal solidarity.

The notion of holistic spirituality is a striking commonality between Christianity and African traditional religion.[19] In both faiths, there is an absolute assumption that religion is all-encompassing and that there is no sector of life that God does not influence. As a result, faith profoundly shapes all areas of human existence, including social interaction, political involvement, and economic activities, a notion that gave rise to Deliverance becoming an anchor of Black faith. The holistic religious worldview of African traditional religion imparted a vital Christian principle into African peoples that emerged in African American Christianity. The assumption of holistic religious beliefs is one aspect that allowed Blacks to undercut the dualistic faith intentionally given to them to uphold the status quo of Black inferiority.

Second, Black Christianity took on a narrative (or oral) disposition shared with African traditional religion. Oral tradition was the primary method of chronicling religious truths and customs in African traditional religion and among illiterate Christians alike. Pre-emancipation education and legally mandated illiteracy reinforced the centrality of oratory in slave Christianity and inspired a natural disposition toward Old Testament narratives over against the propositional teachings of the apostle Paul.

Last, Black Christianity and African traditional religion share a sense of communal solidarity. In many cases, slaves had to imagine new ways to express communal solidarity because Black families and churches were held in little regard by their masters. The capture, transport, and sale of humans as chattel heightened the sense of communal responsibility. Despite laws that allowed for the destruction of the Black family, the spiritual family became a pillar in free Black and slave communities. The lingering emotional and psychological effects that slavery had on Black people have negative generational affects that still bear rotten fruit today, but the influence of the Christian faith has aided in preserving Black familial solidarity through generations. These aspects of African traditional religion tilled the religious curiosities of Africans that Christianity fulfilled in Africa and then again in the New World.

---

[19]Mbiti, introduction to *African Religion*.

3

DELIVERANCE IN THE SHADOWS

ACCOUNTS THAT INCLUDE BLACK CHRISTIANITY often feature what happened to African Americans rather than accounting for their spiritual agency. Retrieving scattered accounts of Black missionaries, evangelists, and ecclesial life accounts for not only a vibrant faith but a faith that emerges from doctrinal commitments that Anchored the tradition from the beginning. Missionary, evangelistic, and worship impulses testify to a faith that was forged under the weight of oppression and was often forced to thrive in the shadows.

AFRICAN AMERICAN MISSIONS

The Great Awakening catalyzed the missionary impulse among Black Christians. This movement demonstrates that from the beginning Black faith was both deeply pious and missiologically motivated, calling people to proclaim and live out the full scope of justice and righteousness. This missiological impulse was Anchored in a commitment to call others to Conversion and encourage them to Walk in the Spirit. While Black missionaries deployed to various locations, their African motherland maintained a special concern.

Missionary Nathaniel Paul (1793?–1839) captured the heart cry of numerous Blacks in America when he insisted that Africa's regeneration was dependent on biblical teaching and that African Americans had a special duty to participate in this effort. It is no exaggeration to insist that Christian missionaries began the pan-African movement. Augustus Washington (1820–1875) agreed by declaring that the uplift of Africa could occur only through evangelism. Native African Christians encouraged these missionary efforts because, with Rev. A. W. Hanson, they believed that the destiny of Africa was based on the Christian regeneration of the continent.[1]

---

[1] See vol. 2 for an excerpt from Nathaniel Paul's *An Address Delivered on the Celebration of the Abolition of Slavery in New York*.

Deliverance in the Shadows

The rich legacy of Black missionaries has been lost in the story of African American Christianity. Regrettably, the stories of these missionaries have been intentionally obscured among Anglo historians because they commonly sided with nationals as colonial powers stripped sub-Saharan Africa of its resources at the outset of the Industrial Revolution. Curiously, at times some of the problematic colonial impulses of Anglo mission agencies bled into Black missionary circles, yet those missionaries were still regularly neglected in official historical records. Decorated missionary Thomas Burch Freeman (1809–1890) is an example of a Black man whose service was expunged from the history of a missionary society because after years on the field Burch identified with the struggles of the nationals more than with the objectives of his sending agency.

> **The Industrial Revolution** began in the 1760s throughout Europe and the United States. During this transitional era, goods that were previously made by hand were mass-produced by machines. This evolution in manufacturing transformed demography as centers of production required manpower while producing a high volume of goods. Manufacturing was also exported to locations such as Africa that had unique natural resources.

Black missionary narratives were seldom recognized by the chroniclers of history because they employed unique missionary strategies. It was common for Blacks to deploy in large groups, including whole congregations embarking for distant lands. Paul Cuffe (1759–1817) and Samuel Mills (1783–1818) were Black ship owners who employed a mass-movement strategy and transported approximately sixteen thousand former slaves to Sierra Leone as missionaries between 1806 and 1816, including followers of John Marrant.

John Marrant (1755–1791) is an example of a Black missionary who converted during the Great Awakening and mobilized a large-group missionary movement. Marrant was born free in New York. Soon after his birth, his father died, and he relocated to the South with his mother. After living in Florida and Georgia, John and his mother settled in a free Black community in Charleston to find economic stability.

In Charleston, Marrant was educated and was a carpentry apprentice; he learned to play the French horn and violin. Marrant entertained English gentry at special events, and during this time, he explored drinking and various pleasures and became, as he recollected, "a slave to every vice situated to my nature and to my years."[2] As a teenager, Marrant heard that the renowned circuit-riding preacher George Whitefield was coming to town and decided to prank Whitefield by blowing his French horn in the middle of his sermon. Poised to disrupt the service, Marrant was struck to the ground with conviction and converted to Christianity.

Soon after, Marrant pioneered the earliest Black missionary efforts among Native Americans in the 1770s. He preached the gospel to Cherokee, Creek, Catawa, and Housaw Indians throughout his ministry. His efforts culminated with the African Methodist Episcopal Church's development of a missionary society among Native Americans. In his later years, he ministered to Blacks in Nova Scotia, Canada, and after his death nearly twelve hundred of his parishioners embarked for Africa. They settled in Sierra Leone and carried the Christian gospel to their kinsmen.

Among Baptists, Lott Carey (1780–1828) was the first recorded American missionary to West Africa. Carey was born a slave in Virginia and was raised by his grandmother, a devout Christian who regularly told stories of their family's heritage in Africa. After Carey's conversion in 1807, his unquenchable desire to read was directed toward Scripture. Over time, Carey was licensed as a Baptist minister by the First Baptist Church of Richmond. He later became the pastor of the African Baptist Church in Richmond, but despite his success in America, Carey never escaped his passion for Africa, which emerged from stories told to him during his childhood.

In 1819 Carey gained approval from the Baptist Board of Foreign Missions and the American Colonization Society to set up a mission in West Africa. In March 1821, Carey arrived in Freetown, Sierra Leone, with his wife, two children, and twenty-eight members of his church and their children. They began spreading the gospel and working for the common good of the natives. In 1828 Carey became the governor of Liberia, and he pastored Providence Baptist Church in Monrovia.

African American missions continue throughout the story of Black Christianity. However, these efforts were complicated by the yoke of racial injustice that placed legal limitations on Black communities and caused financial hardship. The more common American missions sending model, requiring individuals to access discretionary funds within their social network, was ineffective in underresourced communities. The mass-migration model was successful for Blacks because the community—the ecosystem of support—moved to a new land so those at home, living in the grip of racial oppression, did not carry the financial burden of supporting a missionary.

---

[2] John Marrant, *A Narrative of the Life of John Marrant, of New York, in North America: with an Account of the Conversion of the King of the Cherokees and His Daughter* (London: J. Gadsby and R. Groombridge, 1850), 6.

> **BLACK MISSIONS IN THE MODERN ERA**
>
> The seeming wane of the African American missionary impulse in the twentieth century came about because Blacks departed from the mass-migration model and mimicked the Anglo sending method, which highlighted the economic disparity between the communities. Methodological tensions aside, the missionary impulse remains alive within the structure of Black denominational life.

WOMEN EVANGELISTS

In addition to missionaries, the Great Awakening also mobilized Black women preachers. While male pastors affirmed their spiritual vitality and the effectiveness of their evangelistic proclamation, they rejected the idea of a woman being called to ministry. The distinction was that evangelists or exhorters could be nonordained itinerants who preached as the Holy Spirit led, but ministers were ordained men who had been formally vetted by an established church or denomination.

A centerpiece of this debate was Jarena Lee (1783–1855?), who was converted under the preaching of Richard Allen. In her 1849 autobiography, she recalls her dramatic Conversion after nearly attempting suicide:

> At this awful point, in my early history, the Spirit of God moved in power through my conscience, and told me I was a wretched sinner. On this account so great was the impression, and so strong were the feelings of guilt, that I promised in my heart that I would not tell another lie. But notwithstanding this promise my heart grew harder, after a while, yet the Spirit of the Lord never entirely forsook me, but continued mercifully striving with me, until his gracious power converted my soul.[3]

During this period, it was undisputed that upon Conversion believers were filled with the Holy Spirit and the process of Walking in the Spirit began immediately. Salvation accounts that feature an undeniable point of Conversion and Walking in the Spirit mark this era and established a tradition featuring powerful Conversion narratives.[4]

Lee was the first woman evangelist in the African Methodist Episcopal tradition and likely the first in America. Soon after her dramatic conversion, Lee was called

---

[3]Jarena Lee, *The Life and Religious Experience of Jarena Lee, a Coloured Lady, Giving Account of her Call to Preach the Gospel* (Philadelphia, 1849).
[4]See vol. 2 for an excerpt of *Religious Experience and Journal of Mrs. Jarena Lee, Giving an Account of Her Call to Preach the Gospel*.

to proclaim the gospel. Her ministry throughout the Northeast required her to travel by boat, carriage, and on foot despite ongoing bouts of debilitating sickness. Lee recalled that she traveled 2,325 miles with the help of a female companion. She addressed gatherings composed of both men and women, Black and White—which was unusual for that time, especially for a woman.

Another Black female evangelist, Zilpha Elaw (1790–1873), was born free in Pennsylvania into a pious Christian home. After her mother's death, when Zilpha was twelve, she lived with a Quaker family and began attending evangelistic Methodist gatherings. While attending Methodist camp meetings, she had a vision of Jesus drawing near to her, and at that point she was converted. Years later, after her husband's death, she received a call to proclaim the gospel. Elaw was convinced that her teaching was for men and women, despite her early affiliation with the Methodist church. Because the Methodists would not formally recognize her call to ministry with ordination, she did not formally affiliate with a denomination.

Her 1846 autobiography *Memoirs of the Life, Religious Experience, Ministerial Travels and Labours of Mrs. Zilpha Elaw, an American Female of Colour* recalled her itinerant ministry, which put her at risk of capture. After having great success in the United States, she departed to the United Kingdom for five years, where she preached over a thousand sermons before returning to America. Beyond her death at age eighty-three, nothing else is known about her life after the conclusion of her autobiography.[5]

Jarena Lee and Zilpha Elaw are two of the numerous women who powerfully proclaimed the gospel of Jesus Christ in this era. These early women evangelists set a precedent for women to boldly preach the gospel in the African American Christian tradition. The labors of these women of God set in motion a debate about women's role in the church, specifically in regard to ordination, that rages into the twenty-first century.

POSTREVIVAL CORPORATE WORSHIP

As large numbers of Blacks followed Christ during the revival, the challenge of ongoing corporate worship raised significant social issues. From the 1740s through the abolitionist movement, it was common for Blacks to worship corporately in three ways: (1) in independent Black churches, (2) in White churches, and (3) in the "invisible institution." Blacks may have participated in more than one form of

---

[5]See vol. 2 for an excerpt from Zilpha Elaw's *Memoirs of the Life, Religious Experience, Ministerial Travels and Labours of Mrs. Zilpha Elaw, an American Female of Colour.*

corporate worship, especially slaves who took part in the invisible institution in addition to other, more public forms of worship. However, by 1849 the Black church was so powerful in the community that popular Black intellectual and abolitionist Martin Delany wrote, "Among our people generally the church is the Alpha and Omega of all things."[6]

Independent Black churches. Independent Black churches served a variety of purposes in the community. Churches were a hub of spiritual fortification, political action, and community engagement. The independent Black church movement was encouraged by Baptists and Methodists, who licensed Blacks to preach beginning in the mid-1770s to shepherd their own people. The earliest Black pastors began reimagining the faith given to Blacks as a means of oppressing their social existence and repurposed it as a means of deliverance and freedom. Christian teachings and stories were taught and applied to the lives of slaves and free Blacks in a way that had not been done by White evangelists and missionaries. The explosion of Black Baptist and Methodist churches in the late eighteenth and nineteenth centuries shifted the American religious landscape as a whole.

> **EARLY INDEPENDENT BLACK CHURCHES**
>
> The first known independent Black congregation was recorded in 1758 on William Byrd's plantation near Mecklenburg, Virginia. Decades later, Black Baptists founded several other churches, including one on George Galphin's plantation in Silver Bluff, South Carolina, in 1773. Baptists also organized to establish congregations in Williamsburg and Petersburg, Virginia, in 1776.

In the South, independent Black churches were few before emancipation. These churches were crippled by restrictions driven by the fear of revolt. The most notable stipulation, beyond Black churches being assigned White ministers, was that services had to be supervised by Whites to minimize the threat of insurrection.

Silver Bluff, South Carolina, was an incubator for the Black Baptist church and missions. In 1773, slave George Liele (or Lisle, 1750–1820) converted to Christianity and was the first Black minister licensed to gospel ministry in the United States. Liele's master permitted him to establish a congregation on his plantation and later freed him to begin his preaching ministry. In 1778 Liele established the First African Baptist Church in Savannah, Georgia.

---

[6]*The North Star* (Rochester, NY), 1849.

Toward the conclusion of the Revolutionary War, Liele's former master died, and the master's children sought to reenslave him. To escape the threat of recapture, he and his family fled to Jamaica as indentured servants on a British ship. Seizing the opportunity to advance the gospel, Liele began a church in Kingston with four people. His ministry in Jamaica earned him the mantle of America's first international missionary. After the church's beginning in 1789, varying accounts record it having 350 to 500 members by 1791. Despite being imprisoned and forbidden by law to preach from 1805 to 1812, Liele continued proclaiming the gospel, and his efforts are said to have produced nearly eight thousand Christian converts in Jamaica.[7]

Liele is renowned not just for his ministry's numeric growth in Kingston; he also is known for his doctrinal fidelity, preserved in the form of a membership covenant that was recited monthly to theologically train members. Liele was also dedicated to multiplying disciples and churches. His advocacy for his sons in the ministry is evident in a 1791 missive to John Rippon in England, titled "Letters from Black Pioneers." The letter highlighted his expanding ministry in Jamaica but also drew attention to the work of Andrew Bryan, who led First African Baptist Church in Liele's absence to seven hundred members in 1800. The letter also included David George, Jeffy Gaulfing, and other Black ministers throughout North America.[8]

Independent Black churches were a welcome development, but the need for independent denominations was evident. Countless Black churches endured the sting of racism because independence often meant that Black churches remained within the same denomination while worshiping in ethnically homogeneous congregations. Ecclesiastical structures functioned as an ongoing means of control. Many of these churches were appointed White clergymen by their associational hierarchies, or, in rare cases, a Black minister was accompanied by a White overseer to mitigate the threat of revolt. When churches were led by Black pastors, they were commonly dismissed from denominational proceedings and forbidden to send delegates to annual meetings. In essence, these independent Black churches were anything but independent; they were disenfranchised denominationally, monitored incessantly, and harshly regulated to perpetuate the racialized status quo.

After the Revolutionary War, gradual ecclesiological emancipation took place in the North, and independent Black congregations increased in number because non-White clergy were permitted a primary shaping hand over church life.

---

[7]See vol. 2 for George Liele's *The Covenant of the Anabaptist Church*.
[8]See vol. 2 for Bryan and Liele's "An Account of several Baptist churches, Consisting chiefly of NEGRO SLAVES: particularly of one at Kingston, in JAMAICA; and another at Savannah in GEORGIA."

Deliverance in the Shadows

However, after persevering under structural oppression within White denominations, numerous independent Black churches followed the lead of Richard Allen (1760–1831) and Absalom Jones (1746–1818), whose leadership established the first Black denomination in America.[9]

In the North, where Allen and Jones were, to an extent the struggle over race was more embittered and complex than in the South because society fought to maintain Black subservience despite legal freedom. Blacks endured systemic marginalization in the church—such as segregated seating, which was referred to as "African Corner," "Nigger Pews," or, in the case of balcony seating, "Nigger Heaven"—and being forced to partake of a segregated Lord's Supper.

On a Sunday in 1787, church leaders at St. George's Methodist Episcopal Church in Philadelphia demanded that Allen and Jones move to a new segregated seating area during prayer. The men occupied their usual area, but renovations had changed the location of their segregated seating. After being confronted by a church leader, Black congregants refused to move until prayer was finished. Additional authorities confronted Allen and Jones, and they exited the service immediately. Allen had developed an extensive following among African American parishioners in the church by leading a 5 a.m. Sunday service for Blacks, and they followed the men out of St. George's sanctuary.

After their act of Deliverance, patterned after the exodus narrative—marked by a desire to worship God in freedom—parishioners began Bethel African Methodist Episcopal Church. Mother Bethel was part of the Methodist Church and was established as a congregation for Blacks to worship with dignity. These actions enraged the St. George's congregation, and for two decades they did all they could to gain control over Bethel's resources. Their actions failed, and Bethel's membership grew to approximately thirteen hundred by 1813.[10]

During the twenty-year struggle for independence, Bethel's leadership corresponded with Black Methodists across the Eastern Seaboard. A unique partnership developed with Methodists in Baltimore, where Daniel Coker (1780–1846), an escaped slave, served as a minister. Their partnership climaxed in 1816 with Black Methodists from various states incorporating themselves as the African Methodist Episcopal Church.

---

[9] See vol. 2 for an excerpt from Richard Allen's *The Life, Experience, and Gospel Labours of the Rt. Rev. Richard Allen.*
[10] Paul Harvey, *Through the Storm and Through the Night: A History of African American Christianity* (Plymouth, UK: Rowman & Littlefield, 2011), 38.

> **FIGHTING FOR FREEDOM WITH THE PEN**
>
> In 1810, Coker published *Dialogue between a Virginian and an African Minister*. This was a fictional conversation between a goodhearted yet misguided Virginia slaveholder who came to grips with the fallacies of his proslavery views through an African minister's biblically informed arguments.

Richard Allen was voted the African Methodist Episcopal Church's first bishop, which was an ideological statement for the young denomination. Coker represented an emerging movement that insisted that Blacks move back to Africa to flourish. On the other hand, Allen denounced colonization but also maintained that most African Americans claimed America as their home despite their troubled existence within its borders. After the establishment of the African Methodist Episcopal Church, Coker acted on his convictions and joined a pan-African movement. He served as a missionary in the motherland until he died in 1820.

Like Lott Carey, Daniel Coker worked with the American Colonization Society. Despite the society's motivation to colonize Africa, Black participants had their own mission of spreading the gospel in Africa using the society's resources. During Coker's long transatlantic journey to Sierra Leone, he founded the first African Methodist Episcopal Church that would be established in Africa. From 1833 to 1875, the Missionary Society of the Methodist Episcopal Church enlisted ninety-seven American-born missionaries to the Liberia Mission, and in the mid-1850s they stopped sending White missionaries due to Black missionary success in Africa.

In addition to the African Methodist Episcopal Church, other Methodists banded together in 1822 and formed the American Methodist Episcopal Zion Church in New York City, electing James Varick as its first bishop. These new denominations embodied the purity of Methodist virtue that welcomed a continuously dehumanized people as God's children. They simultaneously affirmed their African roots while asserting themselves in the struggle for Black equality.

Among Baptists, departure from White churches was easier than for the Methodists, but establishing a national convention was a challenge. In 1845, independent Black Baptist churches ballooned by nearly 150,000 members when Baptists split over slavery. The Baptist conviction of local church autonomy had advantages and disadvantages because it gave every church, regardless of age or size, the ability to assert its will in any matter as a requirement for partnership.

Churches managed to gather into regional conventions and local associations dating back to 1834, but a national convention did not exist until the merger of three bodies in 1895 to form the National Baptist Convention, U.S.A. These independent societies shared a concern for missions both at home and abroad. They included the National Baptist Education Convention, the Baptist Foreign Mission Convention of the United States of America, and the American National Baptist Convention. This new denomination represented the largest and most powerful African American family of churches to date, and the anticipation of its impact on Black education, social change, and cultural formation was unprecedented.

Blacks in White churches. Blacks continued to have limited opportunities to worship freely. During the pre-emancipation era, White churches were a mixture of life and death for Blacks. On the one hand, the church provided a venue for Blacks to hear about spiritual regeneration. On the other hand, church practices and structures regularly dehumanized Blacks in corporate worship. The pressure to divorce spiritual freedom from physical liberation was pervasive and caused Black Christians to wed them with increased enthusiasm. These oppressive forces bolstered the theological theme of Deliverance within Black Christianity.

Despite the explosive growth of independent Black congregations, most Blacks had little access to them—and this was especially true for slaves. If slaves attended regular services, most masters insisted that they receive spiritual guidance from White churches or attend services held on plantations. This arrangement was driven by the fear of religiously motivated slave revolts, which intensified after Nat Turner's rebellion in 1831. Throughout the antebellum South, it was common for slaves, seated in back pews or galleries, to outnumber White church members on any given Sunday.

In addition to peddling misshapen theology to Blacks and insisting on segregated seating, Black subservience was reinforced by abhorrent practices throughout church life. Preaching is the most visible element of weekly church gatherings. Congregants regularly gathered around the pulpit to hear a word from the Lord, but theological manipulation characterized these moments as church leaders proclaimed a gospel of Black subordination. Preachers warped Scripture and the pulpit itself to insist that submission to slave masters and the social order was tantamount to obeying God.

Ministers inserted meaning into Scripture that was alien to the biblical witness. Biblical narratives were misinterpreted. For example, Israel's unrest in the wilderness was projected onto escaped slaves and insisted to mean that they would desire to return to captivity, just like Israel. A former slave recalled a similarly manipulative worship gathering led by their master. He recounted his master's words:

You slaves will go to heaven if you are good, but don't ever think that you will be close to your mistress and master. No! No! There will be a wall between you; but there will be holes in it that will permit you to look out and see your mistress when she passes by. If you want to sit behind this wall, you must do the language of the text "Obey your masters."[11]

Similarly, a former slave reported his disgust with a White preacher's summary of the Christian faith, saying: "The preacher came and . . . he'd just say, 'Serve your masters. Don't steal your master's turkey. Don't steal your master's chickens. Don't steal your master's hawgs. Don't steal your master's meat. Do whatsomever your master tell you to do.'"[12]

Another example of manipulative biblical teaching is the curse of Ham, based on Genesis 9:18-27. Proponents of slavery taught that Genesis 9 had two primary implications. First, Genesis 9:25 demonstrated that God, not humanity, had inaugurated the institution of human bondage. Second, Noah's curse singled out Blacks for perpetual service to the White race. In addition, a "plain reading" of the text also promoted the New Testament's affirmation of slavery. The book of Philemon was the primary source used to support this claim and was referred to as "the Pauline mandate" for slavery. Ministers also cited Jesus as a proponent of slavery because of his silence on the issue despite its prevalence during his lifetime. This argument from silence was rationalized by insisting that Jesus was the fulfillment of the law of Moses, which does not renounce slavery. They insisted that since neither the law of Moses nor Jesus condemned slavery, it must not be contrary to the will of God.

> **BIBLICAL VERSUS CHATTEL SLAVERY**
>
> The use of biblical slavery to justify American chattel slavery was a manipulation of Scripture. Biblical slavery was a means of one party paying off a debt to another. This arrangement resembles a contemporary job or credit lending. Chattel slavery, however, was predicated on one person owning another.

Overall, the preaching ministries of many White pulpiteers were a source of conflicting messages for Black Christians. The pulpit was further compromised

---

[11] Albert J. Raboteau, *Slave Religion: The Invisible Institution in the Antebellum South*, updated ed. (New York: Oxford University Press, 2004), 213.

[12] Albert J. Raboteau, *Canaan Land: A Religious History of African Americans* (New York: Oxford University Press, 2001), 43.

because churches read the slave codes from this sacred space. The exploitation of the pulpit led to the supposition that Scripture and the codes maintained the same divine authority. This practice leveraged counterfeit authority to the oppressive social order the codes promoted. Beyond the pulpit, Black subordination was asserted through the sacraments.

Blacks were forced to take the Lord's Supper separate from White members. This demonstration of White supremacy undercut a significant function of an ordinance intended to display the unity of God's people depicted in Christ's broken body and shed blood. Likewise, catechesis was a weapon of theological manipulation. As the basic curriculum for child and adult converts, catechesis exerted incredible influence on a disciple's conception of the faith. William Caper's catechism, approved by the Methodist General Conference, is an example of curriculum used to instill Black inferiority. Despite the institutional racism embedded in White churches, the spirit of freedom was not trampled out of Black Christians. Although slaves were captive, their minds were not enslaved, and they reimagined the oppressive dogma of Caper's catechism into a liberating faith manifested in the "invisible institution."

The invisible institution. The phrase "invisible institution" refers to the religious life of slaves that was hidden from their masters. This holy phenomenon existed alongside White-led churches, and slaves often attended both. This experience is largely undocumented due to its intentionally secretive nature, but its existence is undeniable based on numerous slave testimonies. These secret meetings, often held in slave quarters with an overturned pot to absorb the sounds of worship, forged a Christian tradition that responded to the concerns and the plight of slave existence. The invisible institution was a sign of spiritual vibrancy among Black Christians and resistance against White supremacy in White churches.

"Hush Harbor" is a play on the phrase "brush arbors" and is another phrase to describe meetings of the invisible institution in the corners of a plantation. Brush arbors were secret places in the woods where a canopy was made with tree branches to minimize the sounds of worship.

A Reverend Green recounted how slaves gathered in secrecy to worship:

At night, especially in the summertime, after everybody had eaten supper, it was a common thing for us to sit outside. The old folks would get together and talk until bedtime. Sometimes somebody would start humming an old hymn, and then the next-door neighbor would pick it up. In this way it would finally get around to every house, and then the music started. Soon everybody would be gathered together, and such singing! It wouldn't be long before some of the slaves got happy and started to shouting.[13]

These worship services were akin to a typical church service; they often included preaching and singing songs that addressed the depths of the Black experience. However, the elements of worship were reminiscent of traditional African worship patterns that spontaneously fused enthusiastic singing, intentional spiritual warfare, and dancing. These gatherings were cloaked with secrecy via symbolism and messages indiscernible to Whites. In this context, Negro spirituals developed along with the beginnings of the Black preaching tradition, whose spontaneous rhythmic and tonal quality persists today.[14]

Slave preachers upheld the Good Book by masterfully retelling the biblical narratives learned from their masters to address the slave condition. In the face of legally enforced illiteracy, Blacks passed along the faith orally, which was customary in Africa. Clara Young, a former slave, testified about the power of the slave preacher, saying: "De preacher I liked de best was named Mathew Ewing. He was a comely nigger, Black as night, and he sure could read out of his hand. He never learned no real readin' and writin' but he sure knewed his Bible and would hold his hand out and make like he was readin' and preadh de purtiest preaching' you ever heard."[15] Slave preachers masterfully encouraged their hearers while simultaneously developing a code of indirect references to fool any Whites who might be listening.

These secret gatherings also featured singing that Anchored Black Christians in the doctrines of the faith. This hymnody, called spirituals (sometimes called Negro spirituals), is the most iconic development of pre-emancipation Black faith. The spirituals engaged the deepest longings in the slave's soul. "He's Jus' de Same Today," "Joshua Fit de Battle of Jericho," and "Ride on Moses" feature the Deliverance of a biblical character (or people) from suffering. Each of these songs insists that the God who delivered people in the past can rescue them in the present. Another prominent theme of the spirituals is divine fatherhood. The personhood derived from being part of God's family is evident in "Sometimes I Feel Like a Motherless

---

[13]Clifton H. Johnson, *God Struck Me Dead: Religious Conversion Experiences and Autobiographies of Ex-Slaves* (Philadelphia: Pilgrim, 1969), 87-88.

[14]See vol. 2 for the lyrics to "Roll, Jordan, Roll."

[15]Fisk University Social Science Institute, *Unwritten History of Slavery: Autobiographical Accounts of Negro Ex-slaves* (NCR Microcard Editions, 1968), 46.

Child," "O Glory, Glory, Hallelujah," and "Get Onboard Little Children," which countered the dehumanizing reality of slavery.[16]

Frederick Douglass recounted the role of the Negro spirituals among slaves, recalling: "They told a tale of woe which was then altogether beyond my feeble comprehension; they were tones loud, long, and deep; they breathed the prayer and complaint of souls boiling over with the bitterest anguish. Every tone was a testimony against slavery, and a prayer to God for deliverance from chains."[17]

The nature of Deliverance in the spirituals can be interpreted in two distinct ways. On the one hand, spirituals are about the slave's lived experience and have primarily social implications. In this sense, spirituals reflected on slave life and resisted dehumanizing treatment from slave traders, auctioneers, and slave masters, and energized Black social consciousness to stand against oppression's reign in society. On the other hand, the spirituals contain spiritual fortification and otherworldly implications that upheld slaves amid hardship. However, these two meanings of the spirituals are not mutually exclusive.[18]

It is overly simplistic to insist on a single reading of the spirituals. The two coincide as the social reading opposed immediate threats to Black well-being, and the otherworldly reading encouraged the Black soul with the promise of Christ himself in the "sweet by and by." The merits of both understandings are undeniably beneficial and together foster the prophetic and priestly scope of African American Christianity. Booker T. Washington states,

> Most of the verses of the plantation songs had some reference to freedom. True, they had sung those same verses before, but [slaves] had been careful to explain that the "freedom" in these songs referred to the next world, and had no connection with the life in this world. Now they gradually threw off the mask; and were not afraid to let it be known that "freedom" in their songs meant freedom of the body in this world.[19]

Spirituals communicated on more than one plane of meaning. This was essential for slaves because the ambiguous nature of spirituals allowed the hymns to contain coded messages discernible to slaves that were undetected by their masters. The

---

[16]See vol. 2 for the lyrics to "Sometimes I Feel Like a Motherless Child."
[17]Frederick Douglass, "Narrative of the Life of Frederick Douglass," in *The Oxford Frederick Douglass Reader*, ed. William L. Andrews (New York: Oxford University Press, 1996), 38.
[18]See vol. 2 for the lyrics to "Didn't My Lord Deliver Daniel."
[19]Booker T. Washington, "Up From Slavery: An Autobiography," in *The Booker T. Washington Reader* (Radford, VA: Wilder, 2008), 16.

spirituals are marked with memorable lyrics that retell stories from the Good Book, insist on Black image bearing, and feature the Deliverance of God's people.[20]

> **RING SHOUT**
> As slaves sang, they drove the words into their souls by engaging their whole bodies with handclapping and foot-stomping as they danced in a circle called a "ring shout."

During these worship gatherings, freed slave Peter Randolph testified, "The slave forgets all his sufferings, except to remind others of the trials during the past week, exclaiming: 'Thank God, I shall not live here always!' Then they pass from one to another, shaking hands, and they sing a parting hymn of praise."[21] The invisible institution served multiple purposes, including as an emotional safe haven that encouraged slaves to pursue faithfulness to God. In sum, the invisible institution was a covert religious movement where slaves worshiped God as respected persons and applied the Christian faith to daily life. Despite its secret meetings, the invisible institution's impact is undeniable as it emboldened slaves to pursue their freedom and psychologically withstand the abuses of servitude with spiritual resources.

Pre-emancipation Blacks were a Bible-centered people despite it being illegal for Blacks to read for much of the period. Their dependence on Scripture did not begin with written words but rather oral accounts of God's mighty hand in the Bible. As educational opportunities expanded for Blacks, literacy was an urgent matter for the purpose of going beyond oral summaries of Scripture to reading and interpreting the Good Book itself.

Jupiter Hammon (1711–1806?) captured the urgency of literacy and its strategic purpose in his 1787 speech, "An Address to the Negroes in the State of New York":

> Those of you who can read I must beg you to read the Bible, and whenever you can get time, study the Bible, and if you can get no other time, spare some of your time from sleep, and learn what the mind and will of God is. But what shall I say to them who cannot read . . . get those who can read to learn you, but remember, that what you learn for, is to read the Bible. . . . Reading other books would do you no good. But the Bible is the word of God,

---

[20]See vol. 2 for the lyrics to "Steal Away to Jesus."
[21]Peter Randolph, *Sketches of Slave Life Or, Illustrations of the "Peculiar Institution"* (Boston, 1855), 30-31.

and tells you what you must do to please God; it tells you how you may escape misery, and be happy for ever. . . . The Bible is a revelation of the mind and will of God to men.[22]

Hammon's appeal is characteristic of pre-emancipation Blacks who passed down stories from the Good Book in both oral and written form, but the impact of both mediums is the same: the unmistakable centrality of Scripture among Black Christians.

Against all odds, a unique theological voice developed among Black Christians prior to emancipation. Despite being the recipients of manipulative interpretative practices, Blacks developed a theological framework that accorded with Scripture yet differed from that of their masters. During this period, much of the tradition was oral, but it was preserved in spirituals, sermons, oratory, and poetry. Despite adversity, the foundation for these theological Anchors was laid by a people existing in chains and under a cloud of oppression.

THE REVOLUTIONARY ERA AND THE SECOND GREAT AWAKENING

The revolutionary period raised the logical contradiction of slavery in the British colonies. The call for revolution was based on the natural rights of colonists to freedom. Slaves identified the truth value of this logic and its inconsistent application to their lives. The claim to freedom from British oppression was no different from a slave's claim to freedom in America. When called on to give a speech celebrating American independence in 1852, Frederick Douglass raised this grievous paradox:

> Fellow-citizens, pardon me, allow me to ask, why am I called upon to speak here to-day? What have I, or those I represent, to do with your national independence? Are the great principles of political freedom and of natural justice, embodied in that Declaration of Independence, extended to us? and am I, therefore, called upon to bring our humble offering to the national altar, and to confess the benefits and express devout gratitude for the blessings resulting from your independence to us? Would to God, both for your sakes and ours, that an affirmative answer could be truthfully returned to these questions! . . . But such is not the state of the case. I say it with a sad

---

[22]Jupiter Hammon, *An address to the negroes in the state of New-York* (New York: Samuel Wood, no. 362 Pearl-street, 1806), www.loc.gov/item/24015736/.

sense of the disparity between us. I am not included within the pale of glorious anniversary! Your high independence only reveals the immeasurable distance between us. The blessings in which you, this day, rejoice, are not enjoyed in common. The rich inheritance of justice, liberty, prosperity and independence, bequeathed by your fathers, is shared by you, not by me. The sunlight that brought light and healing to you, has brought stripes and death to me. This Fourth July is yours, not mine. You may rejoice, I must mourn. To drag a man in fetters into the grand illuminated temple of liberty, and call upon him to join you in joyous anthems, were inhuman mockery and sacrilegious irony. Do you mean, citizens, to mock me, by asking me to speak to-day?[23]

The revolutionary period, coupled with the revivals, raised a growing number of questions about the legitimacy of the slave system in the last quarter of the eighteenth century. This confluence of questions led to the gradual abolition of slavery in the North, but in the South, where most slaves were held, slavery remained an accepted practice.

The final decade of the eighteenth century marked the arrival of the Second Great Awakening. In contrast to the First Great Awakening, which remained largely in the North and along the Eastern Seaboard, the second revival expanded farther south and west. Revivalism burst on the scene with the Cane Ridge revival in Kentucky.

> **The Cane Ridge revival** began in August 1801 and was arguably the largest camp meeting of the Second Great Awakening. The beginning of this camp meeting marked the arrival of the revival to the frontier, drawing some twenty-five thousand participants.

The camp meeting at Cane Ridge sparked an increasing number of slave converts in the frontier. The enthusiastic worship, dramatic preaching, and emotional atmosphere were welcomed by Blacks to counterbalance the overwhelming sorrow that characterized the slave experience. Much like the camp meetings in the First Great Awakening, the dancing, weeping, shouting, and fainting appealed to slaves because it was reminiscent of religious gatherings in their African motherland.

---

[23]Frederick Douglass, *Oration Delivered in Corinthian Hall, Rochester* (Rochester, NY: Lee, Mann, American Publishing, 1852), 16. See vol. 2 for an extended excerpt of Frederick Douglass's "What to the Slave Is the Fourth of July?"

In the wake of the Second Great Awakening, the revivalist emphasis on Conversion and Walking in the Spirit are evident in Maria Stewart's farewell address to her friends in Boston. Steward declared,

> I found that sin still lurked within; it was hard for me to renounce all for Christ, when I saw my earthly prospects blasted. O, how bitter was that cup. Yet I drank it to it very dregs. It was hard for me to say, thy will be done; yet I was made to bend and kiss the rod. I was at last made willing to be any thing or nothing, for my Redeemer's sake. Like many, I was anxious to remain in the world in one hand, and religion in to other. "Ye cannot serve God and mammon," sounded in my ear, and with giant strength, I cut off my right hand, as it were, and plucked out my right eye, and cast them from me, thinking it better to enter life halt and maimed, rather than having to hands or eyes to be cast into hell.[24]

Stewart's words illustrate the gravity of sin in the lives of converts and the serious means she took to annul its power in her life. The Spirit's work in believers was underscored by the necessity for supernatural strength and endurance via Walking in the Spirit to exist under the yoke of racial tyranny.

The explosive growth of Christianity among Blacks and Whites alike during the awakening is attributed to unique factors that catalyzed the gospel's expansion.[25] The first factor was the widespread conversion of the planter class coupled with the proliferation of proslavery Christianity. The plantation's patriarchal authority structure was said to be divinely instituted, and planters were lord over their wives, children, and slaves. It was widely affirmed that the planter patriarch was a Christian steward who was tasked with introducing slaves to a proslavery version of Christ. By the 1830s, this divinely appointed family hierarchy—with God at the top, White men as God's human representative, and slaves on the bottom—was a nearly uncontested way of life for White Southern evangelicals. The mentality of the paterfamilias, the male head of the household with supposed divinely commissioned authority, projected discernible patterns into America's racialized society through time.

The second factor was that Blacks and Whites benefited from Methodist and Baptist circuit-riding preachers, who evangelized the interior of the country as

---

[24]Maria Stewart, *Mrs. Stewart's Farewell Address to Her Friends in the City of Boston*, in *Productions of Mrs. Maria W. Stewart, presented to the First African Baptist Church and Society of the City of Boston* (Boston: Friends of Freedom and Virtue, 1835).

[25]The catalysts for gospel expansion closely follow developments in Harvey's *Through the Storm*.

people moved from the Eastern Seaboard to Mississippi, Alabama, Tennessee, and Kentucky. In particular, Blacks benefited from Baptist governance, which emphasized local church autonomy, allowing a group of Christians to establish a church and call a minister without denominational oversight. The freedom to forswear White ministerial norms, which included formal education that Blacks had not been allowed to participate in, caused Baptist churches to proliferate among African Americans.

The awakening offered the possibility of a new racial dynamic among Christians. During revival meetings, Blacks and Whites worshiped together and called each other brother and sister as they wept aloud and cried out to God in repentance. But much like the First Great Awakening, there were only subtle changes to the social order that oppressed Blacks and bound them as slaves. Moreover, the seminaries, colleges, and mission boards the awakening produced internalized the social hierarchy and perpetuated it in their ministries.

Pre-emancipation Black Christians casted all their cares on the Lord and looked to the resources of the faith to engage social problems. This holistic faith sought to conform souls, churches, and society to God's will. White Christians also integrated their faith into social life, but that integration was made to justify slavery—not resist it. Because Anglo-American Christianity came of age with a lesser need to critique the social order, there was no internal motivation to scrutinize society with the faith. As a result, White Christians casted social concerns onto other institutions, such as the government, that more consistently had their best interests in mind. This allowed Anglo Christians to dichotomize their faith, striving to keep it "pure" by looking to it to do what no other entity could do, namely, save souls. Consequently, social sin was declared a secular concern.

The result of these historical developments produced two distinct trajectories during America's infancy. One path boasted a pure gospel that was undefiled by the cares of the world, and another insisted that the rule of Christ encompassed all of creation and there was no segment of the world that should not be subject to God's will. The former resulted in a faith that sparked the Great Awakenings but left the institution of slavery untouched despite being countercultural in other ways. The latter is the trajectory that produced individuals who were simultaneously spiritual leaders and social reformers. Such leaders were present among abolitionists, during Reconstruction, and in the civil rights movement.

4

FAITH RECLAIMED

DESPITE THE SHOW OF BROTHERHOOD at camp meetings that characterized the Great Awakenings, the relationship between slaves and masters hardened. This became an increasing concern for Whites as industrial advances, including the cotton gin, required a much larger slave population to realize their production potential. These new Black-to-White ratios caused Whites to feel more vulnerable to slave revolt, so many underscored the slave-master distinction to maintain the social order with the development of new laws, shifts in educational practices, and denominational positions on slavery. This pressure accentuated the Deliverance imperative of Black faith, which manifested in Black abolitionism and an increased number of attempted and actualized slave insurrections. This included, most notably, those orchestrated by Denmark Vesey (1767–1822) and Nat Turner (1800–1831).

> **CHANGING BLACK-TO-WHITE POPULATION RATIOS**
> The cotton gin increased cotton production from 720,000 bales in 1830 to 2,850,000 bales in 1850. During the Second Great Awakening, these developments caused the slave population to swell from approximately seven hundred thousand in the 1790s to nearly 3.2 million in 1850.[a]
>
> [a] Jeremy N. Smith, "Making Cotton King," *World Trade* 22, no. 7 (July 2009): 82.

SLAVE CODES AND BLACK EDUCATION

In the South, ministers grew accustomed to presiding over gatherings where Whites were severely outnumbered. These disproportionate numbers also influenced local church congregations. In 1846, a church in Georgetown, South Carolina, claimed 33 White members and 798 Black attenders. In the same year, a church in Mississippi counted 62 White members and 380 Black attendees.[1]

---

[1] E. Franklin Frazier, *The Negro Church in America* (New York: Schocken, 1974), 24.

The master class and ministers grew in their agreement concerning the need to discourage independent Black religious expression because it threatened the increasingly fragile order of society. With the heightened threat of slave revolt, it was vitally important to ensure that the Christian faith was an apt tool to make slaves docile. In addition to forcing an overly spiritualized faith on slaves to keep them submissive, increased legal measures were taken, and shifts in slave education were made to keep Blacks in bondage.

The result of the population shift was a need to muzzle the liberative impact of the Christian faith in Black life. This resulted in intentional efforts to stifle the Anchors of African American Christianity, which consisted of disjointing the restorative message of Jesus that Black Christians insist had both spiritual (Anchor 3) and social (Anchor 5) implications. Initial measures to disconnect Blacks from the narrative of Deliverance included slave codes to silence the witness of the Good Book.

The slave codes became more comprehensive and put Blacks in a legal straitjacket, and punishments intensified to increasingly dehumanize Black offenders. The slave codes also heavily regulated religious meetings for Blacks and often barred Black-led convenings. These regulations were intended to preclude worship gatherings and educational efforts. One example is Georgia Statute Law Section II, number 17, from 1848:

> Punishment for preaching or exhorting without license. Any free person of color offending against this provision, to be liable on conviction, for the first offence, to imprisonment at the discretion of the court, and to a penalty not exceeding five hundred dollars, to be levied on the property of the person of color; if this is insufficient, he shall be sentenced to be whipped and imprisoned at the discretion of the court: Provided, such imprisonment shall not exceed six months, and no whipping shall exceed thirty-nine lashes.

The slave codes enabled slave masters to impose unregulated retribution as they worked to keep an orderly plantation and maintain social supremacy. While there was a spectrum of masters, and some were considered kindly by their subjects, this testimony was the exception. Punishments ranged from a specific number of stripes "well laid on" to being burned at the stake. Other instances of legalized brutality include whippings with the additional dehumanizing step of rubbing red pepper into lacerated flesh. If a slave did not respond favorably to discipline, some masters cut off an ear or plucked out eyes as a demonstration of domination and control to onlooking slaves.

In addition to intensified slave codes to ease the power of Black faith, the philosophy of educating slaves also shifted to accommodate the ongoing need to obscure the Deliverance motif Anchored in African American Christianity. Revolts led by literate Black men swayed public opinion to conclude that educated Blacks were no longer fit for slavery. White Southerners determined that the best way to keep a slave in bondage was with the shackles of ignorance. Likewise, Northern Whites feared being overrun by runaway slaves. Consequently, Black education was not a means of genuine education but a means of control.

Despite the controversy, some well-meaning Southern clergy continued to educate Blacks, but the influence of the anti-education movement altered the teaching offered to Blacks nonetheless. Initially, the primary goal of those who taught Blacks was literacy, so pupils could flourish in the book-oriented Christian faith. During the Second Great Awakening, educators sought to strike a balance between instructing Blacks in the Christian faith and appeasing a society that was increasingly suspicious of their work. In doing so, many educators made a subtle yet significant transition from *education* to *instruction*. The shift away from education that encouraged literacy morphed into to instructing "biblical principles" saturated with the instructor's interpretative biases. As a result, Blacks were distanced from interpreting Scripture for themselves and were left to internalize the prejudiced reading of their teachers.

At best, Whites who championed Black education disseminated content that upheld the status quo. Their biblical teaching did not answer to the needs of Blacks, especially their struggle with racial oppression and systemic injustice. At worst, the curriculum used Scripture to guilt slaves into docility. The instruction that Blacks received during Sunday (Sabbath) schools and night schools highlighted the ideological disconnect between the faith of slaves and that of masters. Unfortunately, the best education that Blacks could hope for was an awakening of the capacity to mimic the mental and moral habits of their White instructors, which freed the soul and kept the body bound. In sum, education imposed the religious ideas and practices of White dominance on Blacks cloaked in Christian pietism.

The mounting racial tension during the Second Great Awakening was not relegated to the legality of Black educational philosophy. The same period featured both Methodists and Baptists reversing their antislavery positions and allowing legal authorities to dictate their evangelistic efforts among Blacks. During a time that produced glimmers of Black and White brotherhood, White Christians increasingly emulated the social norms of White superiority and Black subordination.

METHODISTS AND BAPTISTS ABANDON ABOLITIONISM

At the conclusion of the Great Awakenings, Methodists and Baptists boasted the highest saturation of Black congregants, resulting from their shared abolitionist heritage, which dated back to the 1780s. Regretfully, by 1820 both denominations renounced their explicit opposition to racism and slavery.

Methodist founder John Wesley began a discipleship movement with an overtly antislavery conviction that crystallized when the Methodist Episcopal Church was established in 1784. At the inaugural gathering, delegates felt duty bound (except in the Virginia commonwealth) to expel members of Methodist societies for owning slaves. Following Methodism's courageous formation, a slow erosion of the antislavery conviction ensued.

The shift away from their founding position began with a motion at the 1812 General Conference to "inquire into the nature and moral tendency of slavery." The motion was tabled. In 1816 a committee was appointed to examine the inquiry, and their conclusion was that "No slaveholder shall be eligible to any official station in our Church hereafter where the laws of the state in which he lives will admit of emancipation and permit the liberated slave to enjoy freedom." This affirmation reduced church governance to following popular secular opinion and stripped the church of its prophetic voice. After four years of continued vacillation on its antislavery stance, the General Conference was advised to protest the antislavery political party, and in doing so they established a new position on slavery that was unrecognizable to their inaugural conference in 1784.

Much like the Methodists, Baptists displayed a steady trend away from fighting slavery. Following the First Great Awakening, Baptists were overwhelmingly against human chattel. In 1785 the Virginia Baptist General Committee, home to twenty thousand of the nation's sixty-five thousand Baptists, made a decisive declaration that slavery was "contrary to the Word of God." Soon after the Virginia statement, the Carolinas and Georgia affirmed a declaration of their own that endorsed gradual emancipation. In 1790 the antislavery momentum began unraveling when the Virginia General Committee adopted a resolution on gradual emancipation that did not gain approval by all its local associations. This marked the beginning of proslavery ripples throughout Baptist life.

In the wake of the failed resolution, from 1790 to 1805 associations began splitting throughout the South over slavery, and the tide was forever changed for Baptists on the issue. Affirmation of the inverted Baptist stance toward slavery crystallized in the aftermath of Denmark Vesey's failed slave revolt in 1822. During

Vesey's trial, the denomination's stance on slavery was clear when he was accused of being bereft of the gospel's influence because he did not submit to his "divinely appointed serfdom." In 1845, Baptists in the South broke away from Northern Baptists to further codify their proslavery position.

BLACK ABOLITIONISM

Despite the broader American church's vacillation on slavery, Black Christians were Anchored by a faith that insisted on Deliverance. Abolitionism was a pillar of Black Christianity's public witness in the antebellum period. Black churches in the North were the backbone of the antislavery movement and upheld the position that many White Methodists and Baptists abandoned. This movement was an organized effort to end American chattel slavery and emerged from the revivalism of the Great Awakenings, which stressed the sinfulness of slavery and the logic of natural rights that energized the Revolutionary War effort.[2]

Black abolitionists paralleled and at times joined the efforts of White abolitionists despite abolitionism's slow start among White Christians in the 1820s. These gradualists believed the primary role of the church was evangelism and discipleship and that changing individuals caused social problems to dissolve. However, in the 1830s White abolitionism was renewed by a passion for a nation that was ruthlessly consistent with its Christian ethic. It demanded immediate, uncompensated emancipation and regarded slave masters as woman whippers, child stealers, and thieves.

Abolitionism grew increasingly among Black churches in American political life between 1830 and the conclusion of the Civil War. For Northern Blacks, the antislavery movement was deeply personal because some were former slaves, they often still had family members in bondage, and the presence of fugitive slaves was a continual reminder of the plight of their kinsmen in the South. Of their motivations to pursue slavery's abolition (re: Deliverance), the Good Book was at the forefront. The biblical theme of liberation was dear to an oppressed people. More importantly, God himself as the liberator was inseparable from the African American Christian story. God's deliverance is most evident in the exodus narrative. A slave named Polly described the meaning to her mistress, saying: "We poor creatures have need to believe in God, for if God Almighty will not be good to us some day; why were we born? When I heard of his delivering his people from

---

[2]See vol. 2 for an excerpt from Hosea Easton's *An Address: Delivered Before the Coloured Population, of Providence, Rhode Island on Thanksgiving Day, Nov. 27, 1828.*

bondage I know that it means the poor African." Albert J. Raboteau, who quotes this account, goes on to say, "The story of Exodus contradicted the claim made by defenders of slavery that God intended Africans to be slaves. On the contrary, Exodus proved that slavery was against God's will and that slavery would end someday."[3] With Polly, the tradition testifies that Deliverance is rooted in the character of God, and the same God who intervened for Israel could act on behalf of enslaved Blacks.

Bishop Richard Allen also affirmed a belief in God that emphasized God's ability to deliver his people. Belief in God's liberative action drove him to warn slaveholders that they were toying with divine judgment. Allen thrust slaveholders into the biblical narrative as the character of Pharoah, who endured divine wrath: "When you are pleaded with, do not you reply as Pharoah did, 'Wherefore do ye Moses and Aaron let the people from their work, behold the people of the land now are many, and you make them rest from their burthens.' We wish you to consider, that God himself was the first pleader of the cause of slaves."[4]

In an 1808 New Year's sermon, Absalom Jones encouraged Blacks that God the liberator heard their cries. Drawing on Exodus 3:7-8, Jones assured his listeners that God saw their suffering and had not forgotten them:

> They were not forgotten by the God of their fathers, and the Father of the human race. Though, for wise reasons, he delayed to appear in their behalf for several hundred years; yet he was not indifferent to their sufferings. Our text tells us, that he saw their affliction, and heard their cry: his eye and his ear were constantly open to their complaint: every tear they shed was preserved, and every groan they uttered was recorded, in order to satisfy, at a future day, against the authors of their oppressions.[5]

The biblical theme of divine Deliverance offered temporal hope to Christians that the God of their salvation and their future had not forgotten about them in their present sufferings. Overwhelmingly, in the pre-emancipation era Black Christians

---

[3] See Albert J. Raboteau, *African-American Religion* (New York: Oxford University Press, 1999), 49.
[4] Richard Allen, *The Life, Experience, and Gospel Labours of the Rt. Rev. Richard Allen. To Which is Annexed the Rise and Progress of the African Methodist Episcopal Church in the United States of America. Containing a Narrative of the Yellow Fever in the Year of Our Lord 1793: With an Address to the People of Colour in the United States* (Philadelphia: Martin & Boden, 1833), 46.
[5] Absalom Jones, "A Thanksgiving Sermon, Preached January 1, 1808, in St. Thomas's or the African Episcopal, Church, Philadelphia. On Account of The Abolition of the African Slave Trade, on That Day, By the Congress of the United States," in *Preaching with Sacred Fire: An Anthology of African American Sermons, 1750 to the Present* (New York: Norton, 2010), 70.

employed a non-Western interpretative practice common in oral cultures that places the "reader" in the context of the biblical story. Their identification with biblical characters—especially the Hebrew people in the Old Testament—established their place within God's people.

A hermeneutic of participation. Entering a story necessitates action. The goal of participatory interpretation is not a contemporary reenactment of biblical stories exactly how they appear in Scripture. Rather, it is to identify circumstances in the text and in the lives of its interpreters that parallel Scripture, and then to apply the dictates of God from the text to the lives of the readers. This interpretative approach offers explanatory power for the actions of Black Christians in this era. Gabriel Prosser, whose story is told below, participated in the life of Samson at the level of even small details, including not cutting his hair, as well as in his larger exploits of doing battle with an opposing people. Similarly, deploying the exodus interpretative paradigm, Denmark Vesey participated in the story of Israel as he applied God's command to himself and so engaged in holy war against the master class.

This hermeneutical tradition insists that the acquisition of biblical knowledge necessitates action. The inseparability of thought and action (or theology and ethics) is a staple in the Black Christian tradition. This feature of Black biblical interpretation allowed African American Christian thought to in large part escape the Western impulse to generate knowledge (or theories) detached from life implications (or practice). This interpretative dynamic has some explanatory power for the consistent cadence of biblically based social and political activism that emerged from the Black church through the years.

The Committee of Vigilance organized to protect fugitive slaves on their way to freedom in New York City because it was a common refuge for runaways. The committee held its first official meeting November 30, 1835, led by journalist David Ruggles and ministers Henry Highland Garnet, Theodore Wright, and Christopher Rush.

Because of their commitment to the doctrinal Anchors of African American faith, it follows that some of the most prominent Black antislavery advocates were pastors who organized local demonstrations and antislavery societies, including the Committee of Vigilance in New York. In 1830, the American Society for Free Persons of Color met at historic Bethel Church in Philadelphia to deliberate ways to end slavery. This group, predominantly composed of ministers, purposed to "improve conditions for Black people in the United States and established a settlement in Canada for those driven from their homes by anti-Black laws."[6] Black ministers boldly taught that slavery was irreconcilable with Christianity and that the God of Deliverance could act, as he did against Egypt, on behalf of the enslaved. Ministers acted not only in public; many sheltered runaway slaves in their churches, such as Richard Allen and his wife, Sarah, who sheltered fugitive slaves in their home along the Underground Railroad.

> The **Underground Railroad** was a covert network of people and safehouses that sheltered fugitive slaves and helped them escape to freedom in the Northern states and Canada.

The Underground Railroad was perhaps the most iconic abolitionist development that was never seen. Legend has it that some thirty thousand people escaped slavery through a network of well-hidden safe houses where escaped slaves found shelter, food, and guidance along their dangerous journey to freedom. While Black churches and African American citizens provided the most dependable safehouses, it was truly a multicultural undertaking. The display of slave autonomy, despite its potentially deadly consequences, challenges the common yet foolish notion that Blacks were happy as slaves. The railroad, and its secrecy, was increasingly important as legislation such as the Fugitive Slave Act of 1850 restricted the freedoms of Blacks in the North.

The story of the Underground Railroad is powerfully illustrated in the life of Harriet Tubman (1821–1913). Tubman escaped from slavery from Maryland's Eastern Shore in 1849 and made nineteen trips back into the slaveholding South. She led close to three hundred slaves into freedom following the North Star. As one of the most successful conductors on the railroad, she earned the nickname "Moses" because of her widely known devotion to Scripture and her ongoing commitment to lead her people out of bondage.

Voices of abolition. Another pillar of the abolitionist movement was Sojourner Truth (1797–1883), who aptly embodied the faith-driven abolitionist movement. Born as Isabella Baumfree, Truth is renowned for her famous quote, "Ar'n't I a woman," asserted in her efforts to free slaves and humanize Black women. In her

---

[6] Albert J. Raboteau, *Canaan Land: A Religious History of African Americans* (New York: Oxford University Press, 1999), 31.

Faith Reclaimed

autobiography, she documents her calling from God to fight for freedom. After announcing her departure to join the ranks of the abolitionist, Isabella was asked, "What are you going east for?" Her answer was, "The Spirit calls me there, and I must go." At this point she declared her name to be Sojourner because her renewed purpose was to carry the message of God's truth that delivers the captives.[7]

Truth's abolitionist efforts were driven by a robust theological vision that reclaimed the oppressive faith bequeathed to Blacks by Whites. During her journey east, she arrived in the vicinity of Hartford, Connecticut, where she encountered an outpost of Blacks who emphasized "second advent doctrines"—as many Whites hoped for all Black Christians. Their teachings expressed hope in God to alleviate racial oppression and slavery upon his second coming. To judge their beliefs fairly, Truth participated in their religious exercises that in her perspective appeared escapist in nature. These doctrines seemed to be a means of suppressing the surrounding racial terror. Truth's overarching concern was that this teaching would relieve these people from being agitated to action.

After gaining favorable standing in the camp, Truth climbed a stump and chastised the people for their otherworldly emphasis, captured in their seemingly passive activity of "watching and praying"; she announced,

> "You seem to be expecting to go to some parlor away up somewhere, and when the wicked have been burnt, you are coming back to walk in triumph over their ashes—this is to be your New Jerusalem! Now I can't see anything so very nice in that, coming back to such a muss as that will be, a world covered with the ashes of the wicked! Besides, if the Lord comes and burns—as you say he will—I am not going away; I am going to stay here and stand the fire, like Shadrach, Meshach, and Abednego! And Jesus will walk with me through the fire, and keep me from harm. Nothing belonging to God can burn, any more than God himself; such shall have no need to go away to escape the fire! No, I shall remain. Do you tell me that God's children can't stand fire?" And her manner and tone spoke louder than words, saying, "It is absurd to think so!"[8]

Truth proclaimed that God's people were to aid in the purification process, and he would protect them as they participated in the divine plan to bring about his kingdom—marked by Deliverance—on earth.

---

[7]See vol. 2 for an excerpt from Sojourner Truth's autobiography, *Narrative of Sojourner Truth*.
[8]Sojourner Truth, *Narrative of Sojourner Truth, a Northern Slave, Emancipated from Bodily Servitude by the State of New York, in 1828* (Boston, 1850), 111-12.

> In 1831, **William Lloyd Garrison** established the Boston-based periodical *The Liberator*, which evolved into the legendary American Anti-Slavery Society. The society employed several gifted orators, including Frederick Douglass, Maria Stewart, Theodore D. Weld, Lucy Stone, and other nonviolent abolitionists.

Renowned abolitionist Frederick Douglass (1818–1895) was also motivated to action by his Christian faith. He was Anchored in the African American Christian tradition, but his faith is often lost by secular historians because of his social and political successes. Douglass testified to his faith in Jesus after mounting a vicious critique of Christianity as it was used against Black people. He stated,

> What I have said respecting and against religion, I mean strictly to apply to the *slaveholding religion* of this land, and with no possible reference to Christianity proper; for, between the Christianity of this land, and the Christianity of Christ, I recognize the widest possible difference—so wide, that to receive the one as good, pure, and holy, is of necessity to reject the other as bad, corrupt, and wicked. To be the friend of the one, is of necessity to be the enemy of the other. I love the pure, peaceable, and impartial Christianity of Christ: I therefore hate the corrupt, slaveholding, women-whipping, cradle-plundering, partial and hypocritical Christianity of this land.[9]

Douglass's nuanced analysis of the faith represents scores of Blacks who were able to parse out the bitter roots of religious abuse from the biblical faith that empowered daily life.

Douglass's careful theological integration is evident throughout his corpus, but especially in his most widely known address—the previously mentioned Independence Day address subsequently titled "What to the Slave Is the Fourth of July?" He argued against Black exclusion from American independence by arguing that Blacks are made in God's image. He demonstrated the injustice in the legal process in its inconsistent treatment of African Americans by arguing that Blacks, unlike animals, are assumed to be moral agents because they are held accountable by the rule of law. Douglass also equated Black and White humanity by insisting that Blacks were required to undertake work that demanded equal cognition to that of

---

[9]Frederick Douglass, "Narrative of the Life of Frederick Douglass," in *The Oxford Frederick Douglass Reader*, ed. William L. Andrews (New York: Oxford University Press, 1996), 93. See vol. 2 for a larger excerpt from the appendix to Frederick Douglass's autobiography.

their White counterparts. Douglass concluded that Blacks were human and therefore were also made in God's image.[10]

Despite motivation from a shared faith, Black Christian abolitionists did not always agree on the most effective methods. Douglass mobilized Black entrepreneurs such as James Forten, Robert Purvis, and Harriet Jacobs to devote their time and resources to catalyze the efforts of the American Anti-Slavery Society. Douglass also utilized coalitions with influential White leaders that employed political persuasion tactics and nonviolent protest.

By contrast, Methodist David Walker's (1796–1830) interpretation of Scripture required radical social action against the institution of slavery. The implications of his Christian faith were explained most clearly in his 1829 *Appeal to the Coloured Citizens of the World*, which featured violent and revolutionary language. Walker's audience was free Blacks in the North and slaves in the South, but he was aware that the *Appeal* would garner White attention as well. Walker called for slaves to revolt against their masters. He argued, "They want us for their slaves, and think nothing of murdering us.... Therefore, if there is an *attempt* made by us, kill or be killed.... And believe this, that it is no more harm for you to kill a man who is trying to kill you, than it is for you to take a drink of water when thirsty."[11]

Many well-known abolitionists renounced Walker's approach as impractical and deemed its ethics questionable. The *Appeal* coupled with Nat Turner's famous revolt a year after its publication resulted in additional legislation that further oppressed slaves and free Blacks alike. Similarly, militant abolitionist Henry Highland Garnet (1815–1882) called for all slaves to rebel because God's law was better obeyed in freedom. Garnet's aggressive pursuit of Black deliverance fueled an 1843 speech titled "An Address to the Slaves of the United States," which called slaves to rebel. He argued,

> In every man's mind the good seeds of liberty are planted, and he who brings his fellow down so low, as to make him contented with a condition of slavery, commits the highest crime against God and man. [God] requires you to love him supremely, and your neighbor as yourself—to keep the Sabbath day holy—to search the Scriptures—and bring up your children with respect for

---

[10]See vol. 2 for an excerpt from Frederick Douglass's speech "What to the Slave Is the Fourth of July?"
[11]David Walker, *Walker's Appeal, in Four Articles; Together with a Preamble, to the Coloured Citizens of the World, but in Particular, and Very Expressly, to Those of the United States of America, Written in Boston, State of Massachusetts, September 28, 1829* (Boston: David Walker, 1830), 29-30.

his laws, and to worship no other God but him. But slavery sets all these at nought, and hurls defiance in the face of Jehovah. The forlorn condition in which you are placed, does not destroy your moral obligation to God. . . . Let your motto be resistance! resistance! RESISTANCE![12]

Garnet's address called for ultimate allegiance to Christ rather than the institution of slavery, which hindered faithfulness to God's law. After Garnet's address, seventy delegates held a lengthy and emotional debate on whether to endorse or reject his ideas, but the vote to accept the resolution was defeated, with Frederick Douglass as one of its chief detractors.

Most Christian leaders decried Garnet's call for violence, but it is evident that Douglass and Garnet's leadership established two distinct trajectories of Black activism that are discernible most poignantly in the civil rights struggle in the twentieth century. Douglass's legacy is apparent in the work of Martin Luther King Jr. and later J. Deotis Roberts. By contrast, Garnet's "by any means necessary" mantra was utilized most notably by Malcolm X and Huey Newton of the Black Panthers.

THE INSURRECTION MOVEMENT

Faith-driven resistance was not limited to Garnet. As many Whites anticipated, the Christian faith motivated insurrections because slaves were emboldened to pursue their divinely intended freedom. While the faith drove some to revolt, radicalism was not the sole criterion to discern whether a slave was Christian. An untold number of Christian slaves leveraged the faith to resist mental and emotional captivity amid slavery. One example is Leonard Black.

In an autobiographical account, titled *The Life and Suffering of Leonard Black*, the author painstakingly details his inhumane treatment as a slave. Yet, in a passage describing the dispersal of his family to plantations around the region, he does not discount the sovereign hand of God at work, inspired by Habakkuk 3:17-19:

> As near as I can remember, my mother and sister were sold and taken to New Orleans, leaving four brothers and myself behind. We were all placed out (or sold to other plantations as property). At six years of age I was placed with a Mr. Bradford, separated from my father, mother and family. But the eye of God was upon me, and blessed me.[13]

---

[12]Henry Highland Garnet, "An Address to the Slaves of the United States," 1843.
[13]Leonard Black, *The Life and Sufferings of Leonard Black, a Fugitive from Slavery: Written by Himself* (New Bedford, MA: Benjamin Lindsey, 1847), 6. See vol. 2 for a longer excerpt.

The meticulous providence of God, the Creator, worked in the background despite the sinful deeds of humanity. For Leonard Black and other African American Christians, God was ultimate, not the racists who oppressed them. Trust in God's sovereign hand over all things was a profound form of resistance and answer for evil. However, Black's form of resistance was not the sole means of responding to Black servitude.

The looming threat of individual and mass revolts deeply troubled the master class. Despite their efforts to veil insurrection attempts to avoid copycat revolts, uprisings continued because the motivation for freedom was not the precedent set by other revolutionaries but the internal resolve imparted by Scripture. Exploring Christianity's role in slave insurrections is not a sweeping affirmation of murderous revolts. Rather, it is an effort to understand the faith's role in insurrections. The accounts of Gabriel Prosser, Denmark Vesey, and Nat Turner demonstrate how the Good Book motivated their attempts toward freedom.

Gabriel Prosser (1775–1800) was born a slave on a tobacco plantation in Henrico County, Virginia. Standing at six feet two inches tall, Gabriel was known for his physical stature, great intellect, and skill as a blacksmith, but most exceptionally his courage. Blessed with the gift of literacy, Prosser was a dedicated student of Scripture, and his interpretation of the book of Judges incited a plan for a slave revolt in 1800.

Prosser patterned his life after his favorite Bible character, Samson, and practiced aspects of the Nazirite vow, including not cutting his hair (Judges 16:17). Like Samson, he sincerely believed that God chose him during his childhood to deliver his people from bondage. His vision of deliverance culminated in the desire to establish a Black "kingdom" in Virginia that would be populated by runaway slaves. The kingdom would be established by a rebellion that included seizing arms from the arsenal in Richmond, killing Whites who resisted their efforts, and plundering the state treasury.

Inspired by the Samson narrative, Prosser inspired others to join his cause by motivating recruits with the Israelite judge's story. The highest estimates boast that nearly fifty thousand Blacks (slave and free) rallied to participate in his revolt. The city reported that one thousand people congregated at the designated rendezvous point, and Prosser estimates that ten thousand men were in remote locations ready to do battle. Despite meticulous planning, the plot was foiled by a storm that sent resisters into confusion the night of the rebellion. Due to the religious undercurrent of the revolt, some would-be insurrectionists interpreted the storm as God's disapproval of the rebellion. Although the people scattered, the revolutionary spirit of the participants did not dissipate. Twenty-two years later, another large-scale insurrection was motivated, at least in part, by the Christian faith.

Denmark Vesey (1767–1822) was likely born in St. Thomas, Danish West Indies. In 1781 he was sold to the captain of a slave ship, and after two years Vesey settled with his owner in Charleston, South Carolina. In 1800 Denmark purchased his freedom for six hundred dollars and established a business as an independent carpenter. Despite being a free man, Vesey remained dissatisfied with the inferior status of Blacks in society, and he vowed to himself to relieve the oppressed condition of Blacks in Charleston.

While establishing his business, Vesey was active in the Second Presbyterian Church. Between 1816 and 1818 he helped establish an independent African Methodist Episcopal Church that would later be called Mother Emanuel (the same church that arrested national attention in 2015 when terrorist Dylann Roof murdered nine congregants during a Bible study). As the first independent Black congregation south of Baltimore, Mother Emanuel was established as a beacon of hope in the South.

As a committed "class leader," Vesey regularly taught the Bible, and in each meeting the exodus narrative was read and parishioners were taught how God rescued his people from bondage in Egypt. Vesey's biblical exploration emboldened him to wage war against slavery and racial oppression. Inspired by depictions of the day of judgment in Zechariah 14 and how "Joshua Fit the Battle of Jericho" (Joshua 6), Vesey organized an uprising of Blacks in the Charleston region.[14]

Vesey rallied followers by capturing them with a biblical vision that situated the Black experience in Israel's conquest of the Canaanite land. He compared the children of Israel having crossed the Jordan with Blacks having crossed the Atlantic; he insisted that both peoples stood on the precipice of a new land with a rich and powerful enemy thwarting their inhabitance of a new territory. In the same way that war was divinely declared against the Canaanites, Vesey was convinced that God affirmed a war against slavery and racial oppression in America.

As plans for the revolt solidified, George Wilson, a fellow Mother Emanuel class leader and house servant, was convinced that the revolt did not uphold the biblical admonition to love one's neighbor. On June 14, 1822, the eve of the revolt, Wilson informed his master of the plot, and a large-scale military presence was marshaled to forestall the insurrection. In the wake of the foiled conspiracy, nearly 130 Blacks

---

[14]"Joshua Fit the Battle of Jericho" is the title of a Negro spiritual.

were arrested; 67 were convicted of inciting an insurrection (of whom 35 were hanged—including Vesey), and 32 were exiled, and the original meeting place of Mother Emanuel church was burned down.

Last, Nathaniel "Nat" Turner (1800–1831) is often reduced to an unsophisticated rebel against the slave system because he organized the most famous slave revolt in US history. In August 1831, Turner led a multiday slave uprising in Southampton, Virginia, that arrested the attention of the nation. Undercutting the false assertion that Blacks were content in their servitude, Turner led his murderous band of followers on a bloody march to Jerusalem, Virginia, that left sixty White people dead. Turner and his followers intended to commandeer weapons from the county armory, but they were stalled by three thousand men composed of state militia and local residents. Turner's followers were either captured or killed during the insurrection. Although Turner himself evaded arrest for six days, he was captured, tried, and hanged.[15]

While he is often assumed to be a rebel without a cause, in reality, Turner's actions were in his view a response to Scripture's call to "Seek first the kingdom of God and His righteousness, and all these things shall be added unto you" (Matthew 6:33). As a child, Turner was allowed to read and explore religion, and his faith became the driving force of his life. Biblical revelation, coupled with miraculous signs and divine voices, convinced Turner that he was called by God to deliver fellow slaves from their captivity.

After arriving in Southampton County, Virginia, Turner was known by neighboring slaves as a passionate preacher and was eventually nicknamed "the Prophet." Following Turner's revolt and arrest, he was interviewed by Thomas Ruffin, a court-appointed lawyer, which resulted in a published account of his story. Nat Turner's *Confessions* includes a childhood account of elders agreeing that he would be a prophet. As an adult, he described the Holy Spirit giving him "knowledge of the elements" that kindled his prophetic leadership. *The Confessions* depict him both as an avid student of Scripture who pursued obedience and as a mystic who was submissive to what he concluded was his divine calling.

These accounts of a people restless in their servitude depict those who were motivated by the Good Book to pursue Deliverance. The faith drove most enslaved believers to have secret worship gatherings, some to escape, and others to violently revolt.[16]

---

[15] Patrick H. Breen, *The Land Shall Be Deluged in Blood: A New History of the Nat Turner Revolt* (New York: Oxford University Press, 2015), 57-72.
[16] See vol. 2 for an excerpt from Nat Turner's *The Confessions of Nat Turner*.

THE DAWN OF BLACK FREEDOM

Over time, abolitionists converted goodwilled Northerners and further aggravated slaveholding Southerners. The tension between the North and South caused Confederate states to secede from the Union in 1860. The South's action sparked the Civil War, beginning in 1861, and the slow death of slavery continued at the cost of American lives on battlefields. Amid the war, President Abraham Lincoln issued the Emancipation Proclamation in 1863, and the war ended with Confederate surrender and Congress passing the Thirteenth Amendment, which abolished slavery except for convicted criminals.

In an 1862 address commemorating the emancipation of slaves in Washington, DC, Daniel Alexander Payne (1811–1893) welcomed former slaves to freedom and a way of living that honored God their deliverer:

> Enter the great family of Holy Freedom; not to lounge in sinful indolence, not to degrade yourselves by vice, nor to corrupt society by licentiousness, neither to offend the laws by crime, but to the enjoyment of a well regulated liberty, the offspring of generous laws; of law as just as generous, as righteous as just—a liberty to be perpetuated by equitable law, and sanctioned by the divine; for law is never equitable, righteous, just, until it harmonizes with the will of Him, who is "King of kings, and Lord of lords," and who commanded Israel to have but one law for the home-born and the stranger. We repeat ourselves, welcome then ye ransomed ones; welcome not to indolence, to vice, licentiousness, and crime, but to a well-regulated liberty, sanctioned by the Divine, maintained by the Human law.[17]

In the pre-emancipation era, Black Christianity developed from an unmeasured phenomenon to being the soul of a people at emancipation. During this period, Black Christians endured the Middle Passage, the auction block, chattel slavery, and for some, freedom. In every station of life, from legal disenfranchisement to sexual abuse, the oppressive social fabric developed the context in which Black Christianity matured and simultaneously was challenged. The Christian faith was a significant motivator for Black spiritual and social engagement. For those who remained in servitude and those who escaped, as well as those who lived free and those who emigrated elsewhere, the Christian faith was integral in every station in life.

---

[17] See vol. 2 for an extended excerpt from Alexander Payne's *Welcome to the Ransomed, or Duties of the Coloured Inhabitants of the District of Columbia.*

At the end of this period, Black Christians had limited ability to marshal a social or political response to racism. Pre-emancipation faith constituted a spiritual force that upheld Black believers through unimaginable suffering. By the end of the era, the Christian faith strengthened individual believers, but the fight for liberation rarely took institutional form. After the Emancipation Proclamation, the struggle for Black equality took on institutional form and Black political agency. A new era of freedom had dawned.

5

THE INVISIBLE INSTITUTION BECOMES VISIBLE

CHANGES IN THE LEGAL CODE allowed for the development of new institutions that provided Blacks an environment to explore the Christian faith and integrate its truths into their daily lives. During Reconstruction, the institutional Black church emerged as the cornerstone of the African American community. At the dawn of the twentieth century, prominent Black intellectual W. E. B. DuBois asserted, "The Negro Church of to-day is the social centre of Negro life in the United States, and the most characteristic expression of African character."[1]

> **Reconstruction** marked when the South began rebuilding after the Civil War. This process differed in each state but spanned from 1865 to 1877. Reconstruction was followed by what is colloquially called "deconstruction," which featured the undoing of legal protections for Black citizens granted soon after emancipation.

Within these institutions, the fundamental driver of doctrinal change was the ability to express a commitment to the Good Book through literacy and spreading an interpretation of Scripture that bolstered each Anchor of Black Christianity. Increasingly, the deepened theological expression of the Reconstruction era matured into the harmonizing tones of a trained ministerial note and the faithful note of the layperson.[2]

The period began with the hope of freedom for Blacks but ended with a noose of oppression around their necks. At the conclusion of the Civil War, Blacks were awarded legal freedom, but the stronghold of racism remained. The postwar social and political landscape offered new opportunities yet posed new challenges for Blacks as citizens and church people. The church and schoolhouses were the first

---
[1] W. E. B. DuBois, *The Souls of Black Folk* (repr., New York: Barnes and Noble Classics, 2005), 137.
[2] See vol. 2 for an excerpt from John Jamison Moore's sermon "The Unpardonable Sin."

environments where Blacks could convene under their own leadership and work together at the nexus of faith and politics. These ecclesiastical and educational developments among Blacks became the bulwark for spiritual vitality and the fight against racial injustice throughout the period.

THE LEGAL CONTEXT OF RECONSTRUCTION

The Reconstruction amendments of the United States Constitution upheld the social and political imperatives of emancipation. Ratified between 1865 and 1870, this series of reforms began with the Thirteenth Amendment, which ended slavery except for convicted criminals. The Fourteenth Amendment granted citizenship to all persons born in the United States, including slaves, and the Fifteenth Amendment afforded Black men the right to vote.

The legal context of this period can be characterized as the skirmish between the laws of the land and the will of the majority. At the beginning of Reconstruction, the laws of the land empowered Blacks to be full participants in society. Despite the new legislation, throughout the North and South many Whites lamented the newfound legal status of Blacks. This tension undergirded a social dynamic that granted Blacks freedom without the daily liberties enjoyed by other Americans.

After emancipation, jubilation among freed slaves was crushed by the realization of their dire economic straits. Countless Blacks were in the impossible position of having no land and no farming equipment in an agrarian society. These dynamics resulted in the economic fate of newly freed Blacks resting on their former masters, and sharecropping became a regular part of Black life. Sharecropping was an agreement wherein Black tenant farmers used farmland in return for a share of the money that the crops produced. There were no legal protections to ensure that tenant farmers were not overcharged or to keep landowners from changing their profit share after an agreement was established. This oppressive system often left sharecroppers in insurmountable debt with little hope of economic recovery. Indebtedness was later criminalized to provide another means of ensuring cheap labor in the South via the convict leasing system.

> **The convict leasing system** was a government-based program that leased prisoners to private companies or individuals. The individuals or companies used convicts as laborers in fields, on railroads, and in mines but were required to house, clothe, and feed them. This arrangement allowed the government to make money on convicts and for plantation owners to recoup cheap labor lost at emancipation.

Labor conditions for postemancipation convicts were arguably worse than slavery. Prior to emancipation, slave masters were motivated to "care" for their slaves—to some degree—because they were an investment. By contrast, the leasing system was based on renting a designated number of laborers for a specific amount of time. Consequently, managers could work their convicts to death and have them replaced, without penalty, per the terms of the lease agreement.

> **Convict death rates** fluctuated year to year, but it was common for more than 10 percent of leased convicts to be worked to death. In 1881, 14 percent of convicts died when leased, and nearly 10 percent died in Arkansas between 1885 and 1887. Worse still, in Mississippi the death rate was 16 percent in 1887.[a]
>
> [a]Matthew J. Mancini, *One Dies, Get Another: Convict Leasing in the American South, 1866–1928* (Columbia: University of South Carolina Press), 67; see also David M. Oshinsky, *Worse than Slavery: Parchman Farm and the Ordeal of Jim Crow Justice* (New York: Free Press Paperbacks, 1997).

To bolster the number of convicts for the leasing system, laws were fabricated that criminalized the actions of poor Blacks. A new battery of laws transformed relatively minor crimes into offenses punishable by state imprisonment. For example, the Mississippi pig law specified that theft of any cattle, pigs, or property over ten dollars in value led to a sentence of up to five years. Such crimes were common because Blacks resorted to stealing to feed their families when landowners paid less than contracted wages. Other laws manufactured to bolster convict numbers included vagrancy laws that criminalized being in a public place without actively working. There was also debt peonage or debt slavery, which was imprisonment to decrease debt. These efforts made the prison population swell by 50 percent between 1876 and 1882.[3]

In addition to convict leasing, the Reconstruction amendments were immediately challenged by Black codes. Black codes were akin to pre-emancipation slave codes and restricted freedom for Blacks in Southern states. This regimen of laws restricting African American freedom resulted in Blacks working for low wages and incurring significant debt. The challenge of Black codes catalyzed newly enfranchised Blacks—and their White allies—to elect African Americans to state legislatures throughout the South and to the United States Congress. By 1870,

---

[3a]Matthew J. Mancini, *One Dies, Get Another: Convict Leasing in the American South, 1866–1928* (Columbia: University of South Carolina Press), 120.

African Americans comprised a voting majority in four former Confederate states—Mississippi, South Carolina, Louisiana, and Florida. Newly enfranchised African Americans helped elect 16 Blacks to serve in Congress, 120 Blacks in state legislatures out West, and over 600 in state legislatures in the South during Reconstruction, many of whom were ordained ministers.

NEW CHURCHES AND DENOMINATIONS

During the Reconstruction era, the invisible institution became visible.[4] Social freedoms gave rise to ecclesiastical liberation as Blacks exited White churches en masse. Citing Matthew 25:25, longtime African Methodist Episcopal minister and scholar Benjamin Tucker Tanner (1835–1923) justified the pursuit of ecclesiastical liberation by drawing a parallel between African Americans who remained in White-led churches and the biblical story of the unacceptable steward who buried his God-given gifts (Matthew 25:14-30; Luke 19:11-27). Turner insisted,

> If we are not to think, for what purpose were reasoning faculties bestowed? if not to talk, why were our tongues created? If there be a fitness of things in creation; "considered they in their sober reflection," and the intellect was given to one class, with which it was to think and reason, and the tongue for utterance, and the muscular strength for every sphere of action, surely for the same high purposes were they conferred on all. But if it be true, that our White brethren must do all the thinking and controlling, all the preaching with the multiplied ministrations of the Gospel, then indeed is there an unfathomable mystery in the fact that we are made like them, with mind and voice and strength—we whose normal condition, they teach, is *only to work*.[5]

Because exercising divinely bestowed gifts was a matter of Christian obedience, Tanner cited the biblical example of Lot and Abram, as well as Paul and Barnabas, as those who parted ways in ministry to serve as God intended. He also cited a contemporary instance of parting ways in Richard Allen and Daniel Coker and insisted that Blacks follow their liberating example:

> When it becomes clearly impossible for peoples to worship together to mutual edification, they commit not that heinous offence by separating, and forming anew such organizations as best redounds to the glory of God; if so,

---

[4]George F. Bragg, *History of the Afro-American Group of the Episcopal Church* (Baltimore: Church Advocate, 1922), 30-31.
[5]Benjamin Tucker Tanner, *An Apology for African Methodism* (Baltimore: S. N., 1867), 17.

then indeed would Abram, by separating from Lot, and Paul from Barnabas, become the princes of the schismatics. Richard Allen, Daniel Coker and others, unable to endure the mad prejudices of their White brethren, which pulled them off their knees, drove them from the body of the church, thrust them into galleries, resolved to leave them in peace, and worship under such circumstances as would be to edification, and not condemnation—as would dignify and not debase. Allen was no advocate of Church divisions; he had read with trembling, the thundering imprecations against all who dare to rend the visible body of the Saviour (1 Corinthians 1:12).[6]

This ecclesiastical liberation underscores the theological Anchor of Deliverance that characterized African American Christianity as Blacks sought to worship God without racially motivated hinderances.[7]

Despite the emergence of Black churches and independent Black denominations, there was an insistence on the brotherhood of all humanity based on theological grounds. The Anchor of Conversion remained a vitally important doctrine during Reconstruction, resulting in an emphasis on the ethnic universality of the gospel offer. This theme was evident in the ministry of Elias Camp Morris (1855–1915), the first president and a longtime leader of the National Baptist Convention. Morris stressed the important and countercultural link between his convictions about the offer of salvation made to all people—despite ethnicity or culture—and the brotherhood that supersedes social norms.[8]

In a sermon from Genesis 45:4, titled "The Brotherhood of Man," Morris asserted that essential to biblical anthropology was a familial connection that transcended race and united the people of God. Morris argued, "'Christ Jesus came into the world to save sinners,' not White sinners, nor Black sinners, nor red sinners, but sinners." He went on to explicitly state, "Christ is not the Saviour of any particular race or class, but 'whosoever may will take the water of life freely.'"[9] The implication was that, through salvation in Christ, the family of God was composed of all ethnicities.

Morris lamented that the Christian doctrine of brotherhood was often overrun by social norms awash with racism, saying, "Sad to say, many church members have

---

[6]Tanner, *Apology for African Methodism*, 18.
[7]See vol. 2 for an excerpt from Benjamin Tucker Tanner's *Theological Lectures*.
[8]See vol. 2 for an excerpt from Elias Camp Morris's presidential correspondence.
[9]Elias Camp Morris, *Sermons, Addresses and Reminiscences and Important Correspondence, With a Picture Gallery of Eminent Ministers and Scholars* (Nashville: National Baptist Publishing Board, 1901), 38.

too often sided with the world, and especially so when this doctrine of the fatherhood of God and the brotherhood of man is presented." He argued, "Class and race antipathy has been carried so far in this great Christian country of ours, that it has almost destroyed the feeling of that common brotherhood, which should permeate the soul of every Christian believer." Morris was convinced that the church's complicity in racial division "silences one of the most effective weapons of the Christian religion," namely, the strength of a collective witness and the efficacy of united service to Christ and his mission.[10] Despite his doctrinal convictions, Morris concluded that pursuing dignity in worship was necessary for Black Christians to flourish in their faith considering the oppression endured in White churches. In short, the Anchor of Deliverance and the fruit of a liberated Black Christian witness was more valuable than a veneer of brotherhood undergirded by oppression.[11]

The liberative and reconciling action necessitated by Morris's convictions was unreciprocated by White Christians, so Northern Black denominations became national, and new denominations emerged. African American church membership swelled from 2.6 million in 1880 to 3.6 million in 1906.[12] In addition to numerous small denominationally unaffiliated congregations, by the end of the period two prominent denominations began, namely, the African Methodist Episcopal Church and the National Baptist Convention U.S.A. By 1906, African Methodist Episcopal and National Baptist Convention churches accounted for 74.4 percent of Black church membership in the United States.[13]

The expansion of Black Methodists. Postemancipation church growth is better appreciated in contrast with the growth of the African Methodist Episcopal Church's first two years in existence (1816–1818). The denomination claimed approximately 7,000 congregants in twenty-four months. While impressive, the denomination's antebellum growth pales in comparison to its postemancipation expansion, when it increased from 20,000 people at the onset of the Civil War to nearly 400,000 by 1884, and to 450,000 by 1896.[14] Growth among other Methodist denominations is also noteworthy, as the African Methodist Episcopal Zion

---

[10] Morris, *Sermons, Addresses and Reminiscences*, 37-39.
[11] See vol. 2 for an excerpt from Nannie Helen Burroughs's "How the Sisters Are Hindered from Helping."
[12] Paul Harvey, *Through the Storm and Through the Night: A History of African American Christianity* (Lanham, MD: Rowman & Littlefield, 2011), 72.
[13] William E. Montgomery, *Under Their Own Vine and Fig Tree: The African-American Church in the South, 1865–1900* (Baton Rouge: Louisiana State University Press, 1993), 343.
[14] C. Eric Lincoln and Lawrence H. Mamiya, *The Black Church and the African American Experience* (Durham, NC: Duke University Press, 1990), 54.

Church increased in membership from 20,000 in 1860 to 200,000 in 1870.[15] The Colored Methodist Episcopal Church also expanded and claimed membership exceeding 103,000 by 1890.[16]

Rapid Methodist growth did not occur without dedicated ministers who established new churches throughout the South. The story of minister James Lynch (1839–1872) illustrates the strategic work done by Methodist ministers to establish churches in the South so Blacks could worship with dignity. Less than two days after General William Sherman had taken Savannah, Georgia, Lynch convinced Blacks affiliated with Southern Methodists to join the African Methodist Episcopal Church. Of formerly enslaved Georgian Blacks, Lynch said, "Ignorant as they may be, on account of long years of oppression, they exhibit a desire to hear and learn that I never imagined. Every word you say while preaching, they drink down and respond to, with an earnestness that sets your heart all on fire, and you feel that it is indeed God's work to minister to them."[17]

Lynch led a parade of other Methodist ministers including his teacher, Bishop Daniel Alexander Payne (1811–1893). Bishop Payne was a native of Charleston, South Carolina, where he established a school for Black children. The school blossomed from three students from its establishment in 1829 to sixty in 1835. The school was forced to close unexpectedly when the South Carolina General Assembly passed Act 2639, An Act to Amend the Law Relating to Slaves and Free Persons of Color.

> **Act 2639** was part of an ongoing national response to the Nat Turner rebellion that forbade teaching Blacks to read or write. Disobeying the act resulted in a monetary fine and prison time for Whites. Blacks were punished with a monetary fine and fifty lashes.

Two years after the school closed, Payne was called to ministry. He was licensed by the Lutheran Church in June 1837 and ordained in New York two years later. Throughout his career, Payne transformed the education process for African Methodist Episcopal ministers. He was essential in establishing Wilberforce University in 1963, which was the first institution of higher education owned and operated by African Americans. In 1891 the Wilberforce University Board of Trustees approved

---

[15] Albert J. Raboteau, *Canaan Land: A Religious History of African Americans* (New York: Oxford University Press, 1999), 68.

[16] Lincoln and Mamiya, *Black Church*, 63.

[17] Quoted in Leon F. Litwack, *Been in the Storm So Long: The Aftermath of Slavery* (New York: Vintage Books, 1979), 455.

the theology department's wish to separate and establish the nation's first freestanding African American–led seminary. The seminary was named in Payne's honor.

Throughout Payne's career, he continually focused Methodists on the task of ministerial training and missions rooted in the study of a Big God. In an 1874 General Conference presentation, Payne insisted,

> Now each local church is nothing more and nothing less than a Chamber of this Spiritual Temple, and the Divine Master is equally interested in its purity, perfection, and beauty. But to do this the Workman should study the character of his Master as well as the work that is to be done. And This leads us to the first thing in the text that is to be expounded—the question, what is to be studied? First, he must study God in order that he may learn the character of the Master's will. Now God has manifested and is manifesting Himself in three different ways. The Workman, therefore, will do well to study these manifestations of the Deity.[18]

His thoroughly theological orientation marked his life and ministry and drove him back to his native Charleston after emancipation to expand the reach of the African Methodist Episcopal Church.

Payne arrived in Charleston in 1865 to organize a South Carolina Conference for the denomination. That same year, the structure of Emanuel African Methodist Episcopal Church was rebuilt after having been burned down when one of its members, Denmark Vesey, plotted a revolt in 1822 (see chap. 4). A year after Payne's arrival, there were five Methodist churches in Charleston, but by 1878 the African Methodist Episcopal Church grew so quickly that it forged a second conference in South Carolina. Baptists also shared the success of Methodists throughout the South.[19]

The expansion of Black Baptists. As the Baptist church expanded, the autonomous nature of Baptist ecclesiology made its growth difficult to track until the development of the National Baptist Convention in 1895. Before the denomination was established, there were various attempts to unite Baptists beyond regional associations. The first attempt was the Consolidated American Baptist Missionary Convention in 1866. This convention comprised the American Baptist Missionary Convention, which included the famed Abyssinian Baptist Church in New York City, and was the first Black postemancipation convention. The Consolidated

---
[18]Daniel Alexander Payne, "The Divinely Approved Workman: Semi-centennial Sermon (1874)," in *Proceedings of the Semi-centenary Celebration of the African Methodist Episcopal Church of Cincinnati, Held in Allen Temple, February 8th, 9th, and 10th, 1874*, ed. Rev. B. W. Arnett (Cincinnati: H. Watkin, 1874), 72-80.
[19]See vol. 2 for an excerpt from Daniel Alexander Payne's "The Quadrennial Sermon."

Convention had its first meeting in 1867 in Nashville and by 1876 reported a constituency of one hundred thousand members and two hundred ministers.

Despite its numerical growth, the Consolidated Convention met its demise by 1879. In addition to the trial of financial viability, tensions included internal conflict between educated and cultured Blacks in contrast to the emotive worship and political activism of former slaves in the South. The convention's collapse gave rise to three new organizations: (1) the Baptist Foreign Mission Convention of the United States, founded in 1880; (2) the American National Baptist Convention, organized in 1886; and 3) the National Baptist Educational Convention of the U.S.A., established in 1893.

At the 1894 annual meeting of these bodies, a motion was made proposing their merger into a single convention; the proposal was ratified on September 28, 1895. The organization established with the merger was the National Baptist Convention, with subsidiaries of Foreign Mission, Home Mission, and Education boards. By 1906, National Baptists claimed 61 percent of Black churchgoers.

In addition to Abyssinian Baptist Church in the North, Richmond's historical First African Baptist Church was a pillar in the South. The church began in an old building that White Baptists donated to the slave members of their fellowship in 1841 with a White minister, Robert Ryland (1805–1899). In 1867, Ryland resigned so the church could have Black leadership. His pastoral apprentice, former slave James Henry Holmes (1826–1900), was appointed to lead the church. Holmes, who was awarded an honorary Doctor of Divinity from Shaw University, led the church until his death at the turn of the twentieth century, and the church grew to a membership of several thousand under his leadership.

An enduring hallmark of Reconstruction was the formation of racialized church membership, which extends into the present. By 1875, the rise of Black denominations nearly depleted White congregations of Black members. Black membership among White South Carolinian Methodist churches is representative of this exodus, as it fell from 42,469 in 1860 to 653 in 1873. Among Baptists, the staggering rate at which Blacks withdrew from White churches was also exemplified in South Carolina, as the state convention counted 29,211 Black members in 1858, a number that dwindled to 1,614 by 1874.[20] Despite the justifiable departure of Blacks from White churches and denominations, the burden of explaining the proliferation of racialized congregations in America remains a wound in the Christian conscience

---

[20]Raboteau, *Canaan Land*, 68-69.

that is yet to be healed. As the most powerful organization in the African American community, the church frequently deployed its resources in the political realm to combat the oppression that typified the Black experience.

The church's priestly and prophetic mission. Just as important as denominational growth was the mission of the Black church. The mission can be summarized as two necessary sides of the same coin—priestly and prophetic. The priestly elements of church life foster spiritual maturation and are easily explained by "Love the Lord your God with all of your heart, with all of your soul, and with all of your mind" (Matthew 22:37). This command necessitates ministries of biblical proclamation, Scripture memorization, prayer, fasting, and fostering other spiritual disciplines. The prophetic witness is God's people, corporate and individually, bearing testimony to the healing power of the liberating gospel wherever the ravages of sin are manifest. This fruit of the Christian life is commanded when Jesus called his people to "Love your neighbor as yourself" (Matthew 22:39). The priestly and prophetic mission of the church is rooted in the longstanding doctrinal Anchors of Conversion and Deliverance.[21]

The Black church is not monolithic, and each church manifests its priestly and prophetic missions uniquely. Some fellowships emphasize the pietistic implications of the priestly call, while others focus more heavily on the prophetic. Division emerges when a single pole of the binary is made into the full scope of the church's mission. The danger of oversimplifying the Black church's mission to its priestly call is to forfeit the church's public witness. On the other hand, defining Christian faithfulness as an activity, rather than faith in Christ, is to offer those resisting social sin a false foundation for salvation. Furthermore, neglecting spiritual fortification while engaging the stench of death in American racism disallows the ability to persist in the face of demonic resistance. Without minimizing the spectrum between the extremes of being exclusively either priestly or prophetic, God's people boasted a host of Black Reconstruction Christians who pursued both. This two-pronged approach was led by the most visible figure in the Black community during Reconstruction, the Black minister.

THE BLACK MINISTER

The Black pastor was both spiritual leader and social advocate, and embodied the priestly and prophetic scope of the church's mission. Priestly refrains from Black

---

[21] See vol. 2 for an excerpt from John Jasper's sermon "The Sun Do Move!"

pulpits included the theological claims that Anchor the African American Christian tradition, including the need for repentance, righteous living, and love for others.

> Throughout the African American tradition **the prophetic task** is not *foretelling* the secret things of God but *forthtelling*, which most commonly refers to proclaiming the revealed truths of God in specific social and political circumstances.

Walking in the Spirit persisted as a hallmark of Black faith during Reconstruction. African Methodist Episcopal Zion Church minister James Walker Hood (1831–1918) sermonically illustrated the demonstrative action of walking with Jesus, saying:

> Finally, we must make a public entrance upon the divine service. We must get up boldly and leave the Devils camp, renounce our allegiance to him and publicly declare ourselves the servants of the Lord. Why not? We have served the devil publicly, why not forsake his service openly? Otherwise, Satan may charge us with sneaking away from him. He may claim our service on the ground that we have not given him proper notice that we have quit him. All work for God must be done in his vineyard.[22]

Hood's bold declaration of walking accordingly in Christ's vineyard is a crystallization of Walking in the Spirit made possible by Conversion. Hood's message was illuminated by Charles Octavius Boothe's charge for disciples of Christ. A minister and scholar, Boothe, whose story is told further in chapter six, insisted that "disciples of Christ should clearly understand that every sin, in thought, in Word, in action, dims their light, and unfits them for the blessed work to which their Lord calls them."[23]

Boothe explored radical Christian faithfulness by expounding on the Great Commandments—love of God and love of neighbor—during a time when Whites treated Blacks as less than human. He stated, "This subject of love to God, of love to his people, and of love that goes out as did the love of Christ toward all men, even toward enemies." After drawing on passages from Paul, Peter, and John, Boothe formulated two distinct Christian characteristics: "First, that love to God and love to our neighbors should be cultivated by the believer in Christ with the deepest earnestness. 'God is love.' . . . Second, we learn from these passages that increase in the love for God and in the love for our neighbor must go on together."[24]

---

[22]James W. Hood, *The Negro in the Christian Pulpit* (Raleigh, SC: Edwards, Broughton, 1884), 27.
[23]Charles Octavius Boothe, *Plain Theology for Plain People* (Philadelphia: American Baptist Publication Society, 1890), 86. See vol. 2 for an excerpt from this work.
[24]Boothe, *Plain Theology for Plain People*, 92, 95.

During this period, it was common for Boothe and other Reconstruction-era Blacks to cite love for others as the litmus test for genuine faith. This assertion does not discount an articulation of "Jesus is Lord," but that cannot be the proof of salvation alone because the demons and the Adversary possess that information (Mark 1:24; James 2:19). The test of genuine faith is love because it is the fruit of a converted life. The priestly duties of preaching, pastoral counseling, and admonishment were the midwife of these Christian doctrines during Reconstruction.[25]

The twin responsibilities of Black ministers consisted of the priestly and the prophetic burden—proclaiming "Thus saith the Lord" beyond the church's walls. The enduring insistence on these ministerial expectations was hermeneutically motivated and intensified due to the racism of the day. The Deliverance motif in Exodus marked pre-emancipation Black interpretation and is apparent also in Solomon Buckaloo's February 1892 sermon:

> We is de Lord's chillen of Israel of de nineteenth century; dere ain't no doubt at all about dat. . . . If we go to Liberia any oder way, de Lord he'll just open up a parf through the 'Lantic ocean jes' as he did for dem oder chillen through the Red Sea. The 'Lantic ocean is a might big pond, they tells me, and Liberia it lies a heap ob a way oft, but de Lord's equal to the occasion, brudders; don't you go and be forgettin' dat.[26]

While the anchor of divine Deliverance in the exodus remained during Reconstruction, Jubilee was also a welcomed expression of liberation during this period. Reconstruction featured a previously enslaved people who were liberated in an agrarian society without the requisite land and resources to sustain a family. The hope of Jubilee, with its focus on land and property rights after enslavement, leaped off the pages of Scripture and into the hopes of Blacks in America.

Charles H. Pearce (1817–1887), an African Methodist Episcopal cleric and public office–holding minister from Florida, said that it was impossible for Black ministers to separate religion from politics because the two coincided when advocating for the well-being of the Black community.[27] As a result, after emancipation, social and political advocacy for their parishioners' holistic being was a vital part of a Black clergyman's ministry assignment.

---

[25] See vol. 2 for an excerpt from Harriett A. Cole Baker's "Behold the Man."
[26] Cited in John Coffey, *Exodus and Liberation: Deliverance Politics from John Calvin to Martin Luther King Jr.* (New York: Oxford University Press, 2014), 187–88.
[27] L. H. Whelchel Jr., *The History and Heritage of African-American Churches: A Way Out of No Way* (St. Paul, MN: Paragon House, 2011), 138.

Pastors were ideal candidates for the prophetic task because they often embodied the convictions of the Black community, were generally the most educated, and possessed the rhetorical ability to advocate with clarity and persuasion. Ministers employed full time in large congregations were especially situated to advocate for the Black community because their financial security was shielded by the adverse effects of appeasing a White employer with their social activity. During Reconstruction, more than 230 Black clergymen held state or national office, and the 1868 Constitutional Convention of Mississippi included sixteen Black representatives, six of whom were clergymen.

Jesse Freeman Boulden (1820–1899) began the proliferation of Black clerical leadership in Mississippi. Boulden first ministered at Zion Baptist Church in Chicago, where he founded a missionary society to establish churches in the South after the Civil War. At the conclusion of the war, he moved to Mississippi and was a spokesman for Black suffrage. After being appointed to the state legislature in Mississippi, he was essential in the election of the first African American, African Methodist Episcopal cleric Hiram Revels (1827–1901), to the US Senate in 1870.

Like Mississippi, Georgia's Constitutional Convention included nine African American ministers, one of whom was Henry McNeal Turner (1834–1915). Turner was convinced that church organization, civil rights, and racial uplift were complementary aspects of the Black minister's task.[28] This conviction is evidenced by his assignments as the twelfth African Methodist Episcopal bishop, a local church pastor, and a public servant. When Turner served the Georgia Constitutional Convention, Black representatives significantly contributed to a new state constitution that was affirmed by 80 percent of Black voters but rejected by 82 percent of Whites. Turner was also elected to the Georgia House of Representatives, where he introduced a bill that popularized the eight-hour workday, legislatively prohibited segregated seating on public transportation, and supported universal public education.[29]

After Black legislators led multiple victories, White lawmakers expelled Blacks from the Georgia House of Representatives. This was a crossroads for Turner, and his political methods to advance Black causes gave way to more radical approaches. As the editor of *Voices of Missions* from 1892 until his death in 1915, Turner used his platform to decry race-based segregation and disenfranchisement laws that engulfed the South in the 1890s. In addition, he was also a public proponent of

---

[28]Harvey, *Through the Storm*, 80.
[29]Whelchel, *History and Heritage*, 140-41. See vol. 2 for an excerpt from Henry McNeal Turner's *Civil Rights. The Outrage of the Supreme Court of the United States upon the Black Man.*

emigration to Africa. Turner himself relocated to Africa, spending significant time in South Africa, Sierra Leone, and Liberia to better promote opportunities for African Americans in their motherland.

Minister Richard Harvey Cain (1825–1887) was an African Methodist Episcopal cleric and congressman known to make powerful theological arguments at Congressional gatherings rooted in a Big God of Deliverance. While ministering at Emanuel African Methodist Episcopal Church in Charleston, he shepherded the church to a membership of four thousand people and engaged their social needs as a member of the Reconstruction Constitutional Convention. He was elected to Congress in 1879 and did not leave his theological moorings when he left the church house. When advocating for a civil rights bill on the floor of Congress, Cain said, "We simply come and plead conscientiously before God that these are our rights, and we want them. We plead conscientiously before God, believing that these are our rights by inheritance, and by the inexorable decree of Almighty God."[30]

As representatives of the Black community on social issues, ministers were often highly revered, and churchgoers insisted they be well adorned with fine cars, clothes, and homes to legitimize their standing among leaders from other—especially White—communities. This included the use of formal titles including "Reverend" or "Doctor" to distinguish leaders as worthy of respect. Formal designations such as "Deacon" or "Mother" were also important to laypeople because they granted self-worth in the face of being verbally berated outside the church. The formality of Black church culture was and remains an assertion of Black dignity by image bearers continually treated as commodities.

> **"First lady"** is the title given to Black pastor's wives. This title developed as an allusion to the first lady of the United States, whose husband is the appointed voice of a nation. Likewise, the first lady in the Black church is the wife of the Black community's chosen representative.

The tradition of intermingling politics and theological themes is common in the African American Christian tradition and is alive and well in the twenty-first century. To capture the religious imagination of Black voters, presidential candidate Barack Obama employed biblical imagery in his campaign speeches in 2008. At a speech in Selma, Obama was aware of the deeply religious roots of political

---

[30]Cited by Benjamin E. Mays in *The Negro's God: As Reflected in His Literature* (repr., Eugene, OR: Wipf & Stock, 2010), 63 (originally published in 1938).

progress for African Americans.[31] He affirmed their religiously informed political imaginations, saying:

> But the Lord said to him, every place that the sole of your foot will tread upon, I have given you. Be strong and have courage, for I am with you wherever you go. . . . Be strong and have courage. It's a prayer for a journey. . . . Be strong and have courage, brothers and sisters . . . in the face of a mighty river. . . . Be strong and have courage and let us cross over [to] the Promised Land together.[32]

While not every Black minister ran for public office, on the whole it is evident that African American ministers were cognizant of their parishioners' social concerns and deemed engaging those needs to varying degrees to be part of their ministerial responsibility. Despite the ongoing attention given to the prophetic activity of postemancipation Black clergy, it was always coupled with their priestly responsibilities, as highlighted throughout this chapter. The importance of church leadership notwithstanding, ordained ministers were not the sum of the church; the laity in the pews were essential contributors to the church's work and mission.

BLACK CHURCH FOLK

During Reconstruction, the theology of trained ministers grew in complexity, but lay-level Christianity resembled the faith of pre-emancipation saints that sustained Blacks through dehumanizing strife and abuse. While simplistic, the depth of faith and trust in God among common Black believers was deepened by trials and buttressed by biblical narratives and scriptural passages often committed to memory. These barely literate saints—many of whom were born in slavery—were capable of plumbing magnificent biblical truths with ease. Doctrine summed up in the oral tradition contained cosmic truths that rolled off the tongues of Black Christians and Anchored the souls of Black folks for generations.

> **Oral tradition** was a mode of instruction composed of storytelling, poetry, music, and compact theological truths rehearsed in public venues—often in a call-and-response format—and in the recesses of the soul. It provided strength amid hardship.

---

[31]See Coffey, *Exodus and Liberation*, 1-2.
[32]Coffey, *Exodus and Liberation*.

The Invisible Institution Becomes Visible

Intimate and immediate contact with the divine was an essential notion of postbellum Black Christianity.[33] Close proximity to the Big God "who brought them a mighty long way" sustained Blacks during the trials of Reconstruction and deconstruction. Black Christians were convinced that the "God who is able" had not left them to endure trials on their own. This truth was often expressed in the oral tradition through the hymn lyrics, "Jesus is a rock in a weary land and a shelter in a time of the storm" (from the hymn "Jesus Is a Rock in a Weary Land").

A strongly emotive religious experience was also characteristic of African American faith during Reconstruction and its aftermath. The failure of Reconstruction marshaled significant external (social, political, and economic) pressure on Black people. In response, the average Black Christian had few powerful allies to expunge these daily hardships. As a result, faith was the primary recourse to stand amid the storm. Exuberant worship was a means of proactive resistance against the racial cruelty that characterized the period. Demonstrative church experiences provided an equally powerful experience to combat the emotional toll of racial oppression and sustained Blacks amid political powerlessness. Black worship served as a bridge between the theological Anchors of Black faith and daily life.

Among laypeople, the theological discourse is largely undocumented but is well accounted for in the oral tradition.[34] Among nonclerical Blacks, the Anchors of the African American theological tradition are unmistakable. During the preemancipation era, there was a commitment to the biblical narrative and the stories that comprised it, but legally mandated illiteracy disallowed widespread Bible reading among Blacks. During Reconstruction, attention radically shifted toward the biblical text, which was available to a growing number of people who were previously illiterate.

The shift toward a written text did not nullify the legacy of orality in biblical interpretation. Emphasis on biblical narratives remained central to Black faith. The continuity of the overarching narrative and its micronarratives is evident in "A Prayer for the Mourner's Bench," written by "an anonymous 'colored' woman":

> O father almighty, oh sweet Jesus, most glorified King, will you be so pleased to come dis way input you I on dese poor mourners? O Sweet Jesus, ain't you the Daniel God? Didn't you deliber de tree [three] chillum from the fiery

---

[33] For more on this and the following characteristic see Mark A. Noll, *God and Race in American Politics: A Short History* (Princeton, NJ: Princeton University Press, 2008), 55-56.
[34] Noll, *God and Race*, 51-52.

furnis? Didn't you heah [hear] Jonah cry in de belly ub de whale? O, if dere be one seekin' mourner here dis afternoon, if dere be one sinkin' Peter, if dere be one weepin' Mary, if dere be one doubtin' Thomas, won't you be pleased to sin no moah? . . . Won't you be so pleased to shake dese here souls over hell, an' not let 'em fall in![35]

This prayer is the outworking of a thoroughly biblical faith Anchored in the narrative of the Good Book and insists that Christians participate in that story in the present. The prayer emerged from a Deliverance hermeneutic rooted in the exodus during the pre-emancipation era, which gave rise to faith that was enacted in the church in the Reconstruction period.

THE WITNESS OF BLACK WOMEN

Men occupied most pulpits and assumed a lion's share of power within the Black church throughout this era. Despite these dynamics, resourceful and talented Black women found ways to utilize their God-given gifts on behalf of their communities and in the church. The Women's Convention, an auxiliary to the National Baptist Convention, actively pursued the spiritual well-being of parishioners and joined men by insisting on voting rights, equitable treatment by the justice system, unbiased school funding strategies, equal treatment on public transportation, and a moratorium on lynching. Fanny Jackson Coppin and Kate Drumgoold are two of the many Black women who asserted their intelligence, ingenuity, and determination to further the work of education and missions during Reconstruction and its aftermath.

After being born a slave in Washington, DC, Fanny Jackson Coppin (1837–1913) had her freedom purchased by her aunt. As a young woman, she enrolled at Oberlin College, the first American college to accept Black and female students. Against all odds, and with scholarship assistance from Daniel Alexander Payne, Jackson graduated with a bachelor's degree in 1865 (only three years after the first African American woman to achieve the honor).[36] Immediately following her graduation, she relocated to Philadelphia to serve as an instructor of Greek, Latin, and mathematics at the Institute for Colored Youth, the first public coeducational historically Black college, where she later served as the first Black female principal in the country.

---

[35] James Melvin Washington, ed., *Conversations with God: Two Centuries of Prayers by African Americans* (New York: HarperCollins, 1994), 51.

[36] Mary Jane Patterson was the first African American woman to graduate with a bachelor's degree, also from Oberlin College.

Jackson and the communities she served reaped great benefit from her education, so she committed her life to education advocacy for women and poor Blacks to have first-rate scholastic opportunities. In 1881, Jackson married African Methodist Episcopal minister Levi Jenkins Coppin, who had an abiding affection for South Africa. After Fanny served almost four decades at the Institute for Colored Youth, the Coppins relocated to South Africa to serve as missionaries. Amid their efforts in Africa, they founded a theological training and self-help school called the Bethel Institute.

The driving force behind Fanny Coppin's educational model was a robust sapiential (i.e., wisdom) theology Anchored in Jesus. She was convinced that the goal of education was embodied wisdom, which began with a Big God and emanates from the Good Book. She writes, "Whatever we do, the first thing is to have the child know about his Heavenly Father." Knowledge of God and Scripture offered learners a point of departure and granted teachers a basis for instruction. Coppin writes, "We must know that we can depend on his word. Obedience, truthfulness, love of right, and sincerity, must be instilled and inculcated by precept and by example, but always in kindness." Her instructional methodology assumes that a teacher expresses a Christlike witness in both word and deed, because the instructor's testimony has transformative power over children as they learn. Coppin encouraged teachers and parents, "Love wins when everything else will fail. You say that your child resists all your efforts to break him of his bad habits and make him become good. Have you tried kindness? Have you tried love?"[37] This moral foundation for learning is the cornerstone of Coppin's educational legacy.

Kate Drumgoold (1858/59–?) personifies the determination and boldness exhibited by an untold number of Black men and women during Reconstruction. Much of what is known about Kate is found in her unfinished autobiography, titled *A Slave Girl's Story: Being an Autobiography of Kate Drumgoold*. This incomplete memoir and her unknown birth and death dates are a parable of her life and many like her during this period who sacrificed deeply in the shadows without an agenda of self-promotion. Consistent with many of her peers, it is evident that Drumgoold was pleased not to reap the return of her investment but to pay it forward to the next generation.

Drumgoold was one of eighteen children and was born in "Old Virginia, in or near the valley, the other side of Petersburg."[38] Kate's family was disbanded because

---

[37]Fanny Jackson-Coppin, *REMINISCENCES of School Life, and Hints on Teaching* (Philadelphia: A. M. E. Book Concern, 1913), 58.
[38]Kate Drumgoold, *A Slave Girl's Story: Being an Autobiography of Kate Drumgoold* (Brooklyn, 1898), 4.

of her master's disregard for Black family ties. Her mother was sold so that her owner could pay a "poor White man" to fight in the Civil War in his place. At the conclusion of the war, Kate was overjoyed at being reunited with her mother, but when she returned, her mother found her husband remarried, her daughters separated, and her only son missing after having fought for the Confederacy. Kate, her mother, and a few reunited siblings moved north, where she spent the majority of her life in Brooklyn, New York, and Washington, DC.

A year after the war concluded, Kate recalled, "I followed my Lord and Master in the Jordan . . . , and those sweet moments have never left me once." She recounted:

> I told my mother that I had found Jesus and was going to follow Him. . . . And I said, "Mother, if I should look to myself I should fail, but I look to Jesus. I have given my life and He can hold me in the power of His might and can keep me from failing; so I can not go against your will, but I must follow Him, for you know how He has saved me from sickness so many times, and now the time has come for me to pay my vows unto Him for making me His own." I went forward in the way that He marked out for me and then to pray that she might be saved.[39]

Her faith resulted in a passion for education and her enrollment at Wayland Seminary under the leadership of G. M. P. King. The road to Wayland was not easy. Drumgoold "worked hard and long to get the means that [she] might be able to go." In the face of her peers, who mocked her pursuit of higher education, and in spite of a three- or four-year bout with smallpox that delayed her enrollment, Drumgoold's determination and faith in God did not waver, and her plans remained unbroken. During her bout with smallpox, she wrote: "I had many a hard spell of sickness since the death of this lady and the doctors said that I could not live beyond a certain time, but every time they said so Doctor Jesus said she shall live, for because I live she shall live also; and he came to me and laid his strong arm around me and raised me up by the power of His might." Drumgoold's spiritual vitality was rooted firmly in the Black hermeneutical tradition that applied exodus language to the daily life of Black people, framing their being delivered from all types of oppression as like Israel being delivered out of Egypt.[40] As a result, she was able to continually look on God's faithfulness in the past as a foretaste of what could be expected in the future.

---

[39]Drumgoold, *Slave Girl's Story*, 19.
[40]Drumgoold, *Slave Girl's Story*, 27, 21, 14-15, 3, 32, 34.

After eleven years of preparation, Drumgoold pursued her calling, even knowing it might cost her life. She recalled, "For every time that I saw the newspaper there was some one of our race in the far South getting killed for trying to teach and I made up my mind that I would die to see my people taught. I was willing to prepare for death for my people, for I could not rest till my people were educated."[41]

Drumgoold's journey as an in-class instructor began in 1887 and was marked by gratitude for the church's financial support and to God, who sustained her through her academic training. Her teaching career was the embodiment of diligence as she insisted that she kept her "hands full of work," but more importantly she exhibited Christlike love to students as an essential element of the teaching task.[42]

The onset of Reconstruction featured the ongoing development of each theological Anchor that emerges from the African American Christian story. These doctrinal truths were manifest in a more sophisticated clerical register and another befitting the laity. In addition, the Anchors framed the mission of the Black church, the vocation of Black ministers, and other saints including Fanny Jackson Coppin and Kate Drumgoold.

---

[41]Drumgoold, *Slave Girl's Story*, 24.
[42]Drumgoold, *Slave Girl's Story*, 29.

6

"ALPHA AND OMEGA OF ALL THINGS"

MINISTERS AND CHURCH FOLK ALIKE facilitated a variety of ministries throughout church life that were rooted in the theological Anchors of Black faith. The church was the most prominent place where Blacks could organize themselves, and its ministries served the full scope of the church's priestly and prophetic mission in various ways. The church's witness was multifaceted; in addition to its liberative political witness, the most visible Reconstruction ministries were education and missions, which were driven by the doctrinal commitments of the African American Christian community.

EDUCATION

After emancipation, few desires rivaled the longing for education within the African American community. A former slave acknowledged, "There is one sin that slavery committed against me which I will never forgive. It robbed me of my education."[1] Educational instruction was essential for free persons in society, especially emerging from an era when legal action was taken to quarantine Blacks in ignorance through indoctrination or illiteracy. Educational efforts emanated from the church in a variety of forms during Reconstruction. Black churches partnered with likeminded religious and nonreligious groups to establish a variety of educational institutions that implemented an array of instructive models, including Sunday school, literacy training, and vocational skills.

Sunday school. Sunday school was a principal means of promoting biblical literacy by upholding faith Anchored in the Good Book. During Reconstruction,

---

The title of this chapter comes from a quotation by popular Black intellectual and abolitionist Martin Delany, who wrote in 1849, "Among our people generally the church is the Alpha and Omega of all things."
[1]James D. Anderson, *The Education of Blacks in the South, 1860–1935* (Chapel Hill: University of North Carolina Press, 1988), 5.

denominational publishing houses produced literature to facilitate Bible knowledge among laity. Among Blacks, Richard Henry Boyd (1843–1922) established the National Baptist Publishing Board in 1896. By his death, this innovative Mississippi-born entrepreneur had engineered a means of furnishing Sunday school literature to churches nationwide. Recurring theological themes in the study guides included a Big God's miraculous engagement with his people, and self-sacrificing heroes.[2]

In his book *The Negro's God*, Benjamin Elijah Mays (1894–1984) analyzes various types of literature, including children and adult Sunday school quarterlies, to ascertain how Black Christians perceived God. During Reconstruction, Mays discerned a distinction between children (ages six through seventeen) and adult Sunday school literature. For children, God was portrayed as one who brought about spiritual and otherworldly security, which enabled Blacks to endure horrendous conditions that they should endeavor to change.[3]

By contrast, the adult literature promoted a God who comforted the soul and insisted that believers pursue Deliverance in social life. Prior to 1860, pursuing Deliverance meant the abolition of slavery, but during Reconstruction pursuing Deliverance meant securing the rights and privileges cherished by every American citizen.[4] Significant themes included a Big God who protected the righteous, God's goodness, God's fighting battles on his beloved's behalf, and God's rewarding good and destroying evil. God cared for his people holistically, and Mays captures the logic of the era, saying, "Since God alone gives life, we have no right to rob God of that which is his, neither in Manslaughter nor in suicide. We are further obligated in life to our fellow man in the same sense that Jesus felt his obligation to die to better the conditions of human life."[5] Thus Mays Anchors the Christian drive for deliverance in a Big God as portrayed in the Good Book.

Literacy. Literacy was an assumption of Sunday school literature development that must not be taken for granted. The desire to read was chief among the educational goals of freed people. The primary motivation that undergirded Black literacy was the ability to read the Bible for themselves and further Anchor their faith in the Good Book. An essential motivating factor was the hope of learning about Jesus firsthand to undo racist exegesis fabricated to justify slavery. Furthermore,

---

[2] Mark A. Noll, *God and Race in American Politics: A Short History* (Princeton, NJ: Princeton University Press, 2008), 55.
[3] Benjamin E. Mays, *The Negro's God: As Reflected in His Literature* (Eugene, OR: Wipf & Stock, 2010), 96 (originally published in 1938).
[4] Mays, *Negro's God*, 96.
[5] Mays, *Negro's God*, 95.

literacy was an essential prerequisite to becoming a full participant in society and realizing the possibilities afforded to Blacks by the Reconstruction amendments.

According to the United States Bureau of the Census, in 1860 approximately 90 percent of Southern Blacks were illiterate; by 1890 that population decreased to 57.1 percent, and by 1910 it was 30.4 percent. In 1910, the vast majority of the illiterate Black population were elderly. A parallel shift in literacy rates has never been documented in modern history. This dramatic shift altered the way Black laity and clergy related to the faith while maintaining the cultural forms of an oral people.

Clergy education and Bible centrality. The Bible-centrism that developed in the late nineteenth century was Anchored in the narrative of Scripture and assumed its divine authority. Early in the period, most Blacks did not have access to liberal arts education, which included literary classics, history, and languages. Consequently, their studies consisted of intensive exploration of Scripture itself, not extratextual background, theories of authorship, and reception history. This trend resulted in African American Christians producing few systematic theology texts and "classic" introductions to biblical books. Most written materials were exegetical in nature, with significant attention given to the biblical text's spiritual and social implications.

Evidence of Bible centrality among African American Christians is evident in one of the earliest systematic theology texts produced by former slave, Charles Octavius Boothe (1845–1924). As a slave, Boothe learned to read from the etchings on a tin plate under the legally prohibited instruction of teachers who boarded at the plantation where he was enslaved. He enhanced his reading skill and Bible literacy as a clerk at a local law firm and recounted his Conversion, saying, "In 1865 . . . I reached an experience of grace which so strengthened me as to fix me on the side of God's people."[6] Boothe went on to establish two churches, the second of which was Dexter Avenue Baptist Church in Birmingham, Alabama, now called King Memorial Baptist Church after its twentieth pastor, Martin Luther King Jr., who ignited the Montgomery Bus Boycott and the civil rights movement from its pews.

As an educator who helped found Selma University and served as its second president, Boothe desired to craft an orderly account of the faith to serve as a theological handbook for his itinerant teaching ministry. *Plain Theology for Plain People* was a Scripture-rich account of the faith that upheld the centrality of the Bible while encouraging his sharecropping audience to develop a more

---

[6]Charles Octavius Boothe, *Cyclopedia of the Colored Baptists of Alabama: Their Leaders and Their Work* (Birmingham: Alabama Publishing Company, 1895), 10.

comprehensive understanding of the faith. The need for increasingly educated clergy was heightened during Reconstruction because pastors were the chief catalyst for biblical, liberal arts, and vocational instruction in their communities.

The church and its educational partnerships. The clerical role of educational entrepreneur was especially important before the advent of public education to help Black people pursue economic liberation. The establishment of Sabbath schools was essential for providing widespread biblical and literacy instruction to the Black community. These church-sponsored schools were accessible to sharecroppers and other day laborers because they operated primarily in the evenings and on weekends. The success of these academies was astonishing; in 1869, conservative estimates from the Freedmen's Bureau approximate that there were 1,512 Sabbath schools with 6,146 teachers and 107,109 pupils throughout the country. The pace of Sabbath school growth continued through 1885, when African Methodist Episcopal Sunday and Sabbath schools alone enrolled more than 200,000 pupils.[7]

While not explicitly sponsored by the church, native schools were educational coalitions that boasted significant participation by Christians and were staffed entirely by Black teachers. Missionaries from the North were astonished to discover these schools upon their arrival in the South. Poor Southern Blacks demonstrated their devotion to education by investing more than a million dollars into their own instruction by the 1870s.[8]

The American Missionary Association hired nearly five hundred Black teachers and missionaries throughout the latter part of the nineteenth century, the majority of whom were from the South. During the post–Civil War years, American Missionary Association workers taught over 21,000 students in daytime and evening schools, and an additional 16,000 in Sabbath schools. The association's influence spread over sixteen states and two hundred distinct fields of work.[9] In addition to American Missionary Association efforts, one of the most popular aid societies for Blacks was the Freedmen's Bureau.

The Freedmen's Bureau met the needs of freed persons, including food, clothing, fuel, temporary living facilities, and medical treatment.[10] Over time the Bureau

---

[7] Anderson, *Education of Blacks*, 13. See vol. 2 for an excerpt from a work by minister and educator Lucius H. Holsey titled *Autobiography, Sermons, Addresses, and Essays of Bishop L. H. Holsey, D. D.*
[8] Nell Irvin Painter, *Creating Black Americans: African-American History and Its Meanings, 1619 to the Present* (New York: Oxford University Press, 2006), 134.
[9] Paul Harvey, *Freedom's Coming: Religious Culture and the Shaping of the South from the Civil War Through the Civil Rights Era* (Chapel Hill: University of North Carolina, 2005 Press), 30.
[10] I. A. Newby, *The South, a History* (Orlando, FL: Holt, Rinehart & Winston, 1978), 252.

expanded its efforts to include the promotion of education, job placement, and legal assistance. As time passed, it was increasingly obvious that the bureau's lasting contribution to reconstructing America was in Black education. The Freedmen's Bureau, Freedmen's Aid Societies, and northern missionary groups such as the American Missionary Association established 740 schools, serving nearly one hundred thousand students throughout the South.

By 1870, the Freedmen's Bureau educational network included more than 2,500 schools and 150,000 students, plus several colleges dedicated to developing African American teachers.[11] Training Black educators in the South was a high priority because Southern Blacks often rejected "refined" Northern African American and White instructors. Before 1870, the Freedmen's Bureau spent more than five million dollars on education, instructing nearly a quarter-million Blacks in more than four thousand schools.[12]

DEBATE ABOUT EDUCATIONAL PHILOSOPHY

The church produced schools that embodied two primary educational philosophies. The first, popularized by W. E. B. DuBois, emphasized a liberal arts approach focused on studying the classics and languages. The second approach, popularized by Booker T. Washington, promoted a skills-based approach focused on vocational readiness.

The postsecondary institutions established by American Missionary Association and the Freedmen's Bureau spanned a spectrum of educational philosophies and vocational purposes. Before the Civil War, only twenty-two Black men had graduated from college in America, but following the war that number drastically increased with the founding of thirty-six Black colleges and universities. The number of recorded baccalaureate degrees conferred to African Americans leaped from forty-four between 1860 and 1869 to 1,123 between 1890 and 1899.[13] In keeping with the centrality of the church in Black education, the majority of these colleges and universities were, and remain, affiliated with Christian denominations.

Historically Black colleges and universities established before 1870 include Shaw University, 1865; Clark Atlanta University, 1865; Bowie State University, 1865;

---

[11] Henry Louis Gates Jr., *Life upon These Shores: Looking at African American History, 1513–2008* (New York: Knopf, 2013), 145.

[12] John Hope Franklin and Alfred A. Moss Jr., *From Slavery to Freedom: A History of Negro Americans*, 6th ed. (New York: Knopf, 1988), 230-31.

[13] The increase in number of Black college graduates by decade is as follows: 44 in the 1860s, 313 in the 1870s, 738 in the 1880s, and 1,126 in the 1890s.

> Fisk University, 1866; Rust College, 1866; Edward Waters College, 1866; Lincoln University of Missouri, 1866; Howard University, 1867; Barber-Scotia College, 1867; Fayetteville State University, 1867; Johnson C. Smith University, 1867; Alabama State University, 1867; St. Augustine's University, 1867; Morgan State University, 1867; Morehouse College, 1867; Hampton University, 1868; Claflin University, 1869; Tougaloo College, 1869; and Dillard University, 1869.

As time passed, schools established for the primary purpose of biblical literacy expanded their focus to cultivating broad intellectual growth. Developments in education introduced new vistas for Blacks to elevate their social status and offered opportunities to freely create literature and culture for themselves. Elevated literacy rates and a growing command of the humanities resulted in an increasingly sophisticated theological dialectic among educated Blacks. By the close of the millennium, the rise of the Black academy accompanied the longstanding social influence of the African American church as two contexts for Blacks to engage ideas and pursue freedom. The development of Black education during Reconstruction was at the core of the Black church's witness to catalyze Blacks into spiritual maturity and social uplift.

Theological development. While the desire for well-studied clergy was not the norm among Black churches, it was a growing phenomenon approaching the turn of the century, as clergy were often the most learned representatives of the Black community. Early in Reconstruction, an unnamed African Methodist Episcopal bishop recounted,

> For it is one of the brightest pages in the history of our church, that while the Army of the Union were forcing their victorious passage through the southern land and striking down treason, the missionaries of our Church in the persons of Brown, Lynch, Cain, Handy, Stanford, Steward, and others, were following in their wake and establishing the Church and the school house.[14]

Black-run institutes of theological training provided an opportunity to think deeply about reconciling the Christian faith and the Black experience. The ecclesiastical and educational expansion during Reconstruction afforded new opportunities to foster theological development away from the watchful eye of slave masters and denominationally appointed watchmen. This freedom provided a

---

[14] Anderson, *Education of Blacks*, 45-46. Frazier does not reveal the identity of this bishop, and the source used to ascertain the quote is unclear as well.

context for creative theological exploration that forged one of the most significant yet underexplored developments in this period—the expansion of the Black theological voice. In addition to physical gathering spaces to worship and think freely, Blacks developed presses, periodicals, and Sunday school literature to disseminate their ideas.

Entrepreneurs such as Richard Henry Boyd (1843–1922) created opportunities for materials written by Blacks to be distributed via the National Baptist Publishing Board. Other periodicals, such as *The Baptist Pioneer* and *The Christian Recorder*, circulated opinions on issues ranging from social uplift to theological debates to an increasingly literate Black citizenry. At the time, much of the discussion was about scientific discoveries that challenged a literal biblical interpretation and about theological developments.

During Reconstruction, it was evident that there was not a single Black theological voice but rather a myriad of factors that forged an African American theological dialect that included various faithful expressions. The formal discourse featured theologically trained ministers and intellectuals who contributed to periodicals and produced manuscripts for sermons and addresses. Two discernible trends within the formal theological dialectic were theological hybridization and unique theological claims first asserted by African American Christians.

Theological hybridization was forged by Black clergy and scholars who were able to borrow features from Anglo theological influences. In the Black academy, theological hybridization ranged from subtle incorporation to sharp inclusion. A delicate theological fusion emerged in Charles Octavius Boothe's *Plain Theology for Plain People* and in *The Negro Baptist Pulpit* (chaps. 5–9). The theological expression of these works incorporated the systematic-theological categories common in academic theology yet remained undergirded by the Bible-centric narratival disposition toward the Good Book that marked the African American Christian tradition.[15] The hybridization was highly evident in *The Negro Baptist Pulpit* because the editor was White, and his influence helped with the book's publication in 1890 after publishers rejected the idea of a book with Black and White contributors.

In *The Negro Baptist Pulpit*, Rufus L. Perry (1834–1895) drafted a helpful essay, titled "The Scriptures," that conveys the consensus among Black Christians about the Good Book's authority, yet he executes his task by borrowing terms commonly

---

[15]E. M. Brawley, ed., *The Negro Baptist Pulpit: A Collection of Sermons and Papers on Baptist Doctrine and Missionary and Educational Work* (Philadelphia: American Baptist Publication Society, 1890).

used in theological seminaries during his time. Perry was a Baptist minister from Brooklyn, New York, and editor of *The National Monitor*.[16] Perry's essay offers three claims about Scripture's inspiration. Six of his assertions about inspiration arise from Scripture itself, demonstrating fidelity to biblical authority, which was common for the time. The remaining argument, which is not Anchored within the Bible's pages, is based on the "common conviction" that there is a Creator who has revealed himself to intelligent creatures, which builds on the African American assumption of a Big God.[17]

True to the African American theological tradition, the simple affirmation of biblical concepts is not the goal of a doctrinal statement. Perry's second section insists on the duty of studying God's Word and obedience. He stresses that Scripture's "divine authority carries with it an undeniable obligation to search them. It is there that God tells us how to review our relations and regulate our conduct toward him and each other. This knowledge can be found nowhere else. Then we should read the Bible and heed its teachings, as if God himself were present and speaking to us."[18]

Before transitioning into his final section, he admonishes readers to regularly avail themselves of Scripture by encouraging them with the story of Reformer Martin Luther and his role in inaugurating Bible publication societies as well as with the narrative of the Ethiopian eunuch. The final section of Perry's essay remains a cherished affirmation of Scripture for the vast majority of Black Christians, namely, Scripture as the supreme authority for faith and practice.[19] Together, the lay and formal discourse lays a foundation for a biblical faith that developed a Bible-centered people who looked to dramatically enact Scripture's implications in the present.

Other examples of theological hybridization caused Black scholars to adopt legitimate theological concerns from the broader academy and at times caused them to overlook the most pressing questions of the Black community. An example of this kind of assimilation is an essay by Walter H. Brooks (1851–1945) in *The Negro Baptist Pulpit*.[20] Brooks was pastor of Nineteenth Street Baptist Church in Washington, DC. In his essay, titled "The Doctrine of God: His Existence and

---

[16]Rufus L. Perry, "The Scriptures," in Brawley, *Negro Baptist Pulpit*, 28-38.
[17]Perry, "Scriptures," 29. See vol. 2 for an excerpt from this work.
[18]Perry, "Scriptures," 32.
[19]Perry, "Scriptures," 36-38.
[20]Walter H. Brooks, "The Doctrine of God: His Existence and Attributes," in Brawley, *Negro Baptist Pulpit*, 39-49.

Attributes," he pursues the apologetic task in a way that satisfies the inquiries of those beyond his primary audience. While a discussion about God's attributes was common among African Americans, Black apologetics revolved around the problem of evil and suffering, not the argument for God's existence, as Brooks put forward.[21]

Brooks's essay demonstrates the kind of theological hybridization that developed between Black theological elites and White thinkers. As evidenced via citation, famed Princeton theologian Charles Hodge (1797–1878) influenced Brooks's approach to his topic. While Hodge's theological contributions about divine existence are helpful, it is evident that the shape of Hodge's argument is in response to a discussion raging in his context—not one within Brooks's community. Thus, theological hybridization can be helpful, but biblical ideas must be communicated directly to the writer or speaker's immediate audience, not replicated without care for readers or hearers.

The budding Black theological voice was Anchored by a Big God, but the idea of God being a Negro was widespread for the first time in the 1890s. Throughout his service as the first Black chaplain in the US Army, a local church pastor, and chancellor of Morris Brown College, Henry McNeal Turner witnessed the negative moral and ethical implications of a Whitewashed God. Racialization had been part of Christianity's existence since it landed on the shores of the New World, and Turner desired to stir the affections of Black Christians by contextualizing God's pigmentation—like the Anglos of his time.

Turner was accused of "becoming demented" for his claim that God was a Negro. In *The Voice of Missions*, where he later served as editor, he responded by marshaling two arguments and drawing a conclusion from his logic. Turner argued:

> [Black people] have as much right biblically and otherwise to believe that god is a Negro, as you buckra, or White have to believe that God is a fine looking, symmetrical and ornamented White man. For the bulk of you, and all the fool Negroes of this country, believe that God is White-skinned, blue-eyed, straight-haired, projected-nose, compressed lipped and finely robed White gentlemen sitting upon a throne somewhere in the heavens. Every race of people since time began who has attempted to describe their God by words, or by paintings, or by carvings, or by any other form or

---

[21]See vol. 2 for an excerpt from Lorenzo D. Blackson's *The Rise and Progress of the Kingdoms of Light and Darkness*.

figure, have conveyed the idea that the God who made them and shaped their destinies was symbolized in themselves, why should not the Negro believe that he resembles God as much as other people? We do not believe that there is any hope for a race of people who do not believe that they look like God.[22]

Turner concluded that the assertion of a White God led "the negro [to] believe that the devil is Black, and that the Negro favors the devil, and that God is White, and that the Negro bears no resemblance to Him."[23] Turner insisted that this rhetorical move was necessary in a nation of unbridled racism and in which Black-White color symbolism had far-reaching moral and ethical implications. He asserted that the ideas that Whiteness was synonymous with godliness, while Blackness symbolized ignorance and degradation, were engrained in the subconsciousness of every American.[24]

Divinely validated color symbolism justified racial inequities from slavery to Jim Crow segregation. Black Christians such as Turner rightly analyzed the racialized undercurrents of American theology. His declaration allowed Blacks to draw nearer to God in their suffering because God symbolically joined them in it. Theological themes that affirmed Blackness and its beauty drove a reaffirmation of Black aesthetics that was later summarized as "Black is beautiful." This positive affirmation of Blackness collapsed Whiteness as the standard of beauty and morality in the generations to come. The concept of divine Blackness, although distinct from Turner's, mushroomed into popularity with the advent of Black liberation theology in the 1970s.

Overall, the elite discourse developed by the most highly trained Blacks had a more otherworldly disposition, presumably because of their interaction with thinkers from other traditions. Although their written theology did not always engage matters of justice, they intuitively applied the faith to daily trials in spite of its not often being accounted for in formal theological statements. Black theological elites engaged the struggles of Black life, but references to these struggles are most commonly found in prayers, sermons, and Sunday school literature.

International missions. Consistent with pre-emancipation Black Christians, the ever-present missionary impulse to carry the gospel to Africa (and beyond)

---

[22]Henry McNeal Turner, *The Voice of Missions*, February 1, 1898.
[23]Turner, *Voice of Missions*, February 1, 1898.
[24]Paul Harvey, *Through the Storm and Through the Night: A History of African American Christianity* (Lanham, MD: Rowman & Littlefield, 2011), 81.

marked the witness of Black believers. Anchored to a deeply held belief in Conversion, this conviction was evident in the post–Civil War missionary explosion, when the number of free Blacks increased from 68,000 to over 665,000. Among Black believers, there was a widespread conviction that African Americans were uniquely equipped to carry the gospel to Africa.[25]

Alexander Crummell (1819–1898) insisted that the African American's duty was to transmit the Christian gospel to Africa. Furthermore, he insisted that White Christians had no business proselytizing on African soil because of the common and disastrous equation of colonization and evangelism. Crummell's familial relation to Henry Highland Garnet (1815–1882), who served in Africa for two decades, intensified his passion. Crummell argued,

> The day of preparation for our race is well nigh ended; the day of duty and responsibility on our part, two suffering, be knighted, Africa, is at hand. In much sorrow, pain, in deepest anguish, God has been preparing the race, in foreign lands, for a great work of grace on this continent. The hand of God is on the Black man, in all the lands of his sojourn for the good of Africa.[26]

Crummell's sentiment harmonized with a concert of Black pastors, including Baptist minister Emmanuel K. Love (1850–1900), who insisted, "There is no doubt in my mind that Africa is our mission field of operation and that [as] Moses was sent to deliver his brethren, and as the prophets were members of the race to whom they were sent, so I am convinced that God's purposes is to redeemed Africa through us. This work is ours by employment, by inheritance, and by choice."[27]

William W. Colley (1847–1909) also shared the conviction that African Americans were uniquely equipped to carry the gospel to their kinsmen in the flesh in Africa. Colley was convinced of this fact during his first missionary appointment with the Southern Baptist Convention's Foreign Mission Board, beginning in 1875. While serving as a missionary aide in West Africa, he observed that he had fewer hurdles ministering to Africans than his White counterparts. Colley returned to the United States and traveled the country urging Blacks to minister

---

[25] See vol. 2 for an excerpt from Crummell's "The Destined Superiority of the Negro."
[26] Alexander Crummell, "Emigration, an Aid to the Evangelization of Africa. A Sermon to Barbadian Emigrants at Trinity Church, Monrovia, Liberia, West Africa, May 14th, 1865," *The African Repository* 41, no. 10 (October 1865): 421.
[27] Albert J. Raboteau, *Canaan Land: A Religious History of African Americans* (New York: Oxford University Press, 1999), 73.

internationally—especially in Africa. Colley's resolve is considered to have been an immediate catalyst for the Baptist Foreign Mission Convention in 1880. Soon after this development, the desire to send missionaries to Africa formalized again among Baptists with the Lott Carey Mission Society in 1897.

Among the cloud of African American witnesses to the nations, Louise (Lula) Celestia Fleming (1862–1899) stands out as the first African American woman appointed as a full-time missionary by the Women's American Baptist Foreign Mission Society in 1886 to serve in the Congo. She was born to slave parents on a plantation in Clay County, Florida, and was converted at the age of fifteen at Bethel Baptist Institutional Church in Jacksonville, Florida. After graduating from Shaw University in 1885, Fleming returned to Florida as a public school teacher, but soon after she began her teaching career she was invited to serve as a missionary to the Congo with the Woman's American Baptist Foreign Mission Society. After a short time abroad, she returned to the United States for further training at the Women's Medical College in Philadelphia to be a physician. After graduating in 1895, she returned to the Congo as the only known female medical doctor in the country at that time.

During this period, African American missionaries were disproportionally successful along the African coastal regions. At the end of the period, Western missionary societies settled in inland Africa because Black missionaries evangelized the coast so successfully. Furthermore, Anglo missionaries also utilized the relational infrastructure built by Black missionaries to undertake their work. This phenomenon gave rise to Anglo missions organizations with names including the Sudan Interior Mission and the African Inland Mission.[28]

DISAGREEMENT OVER "APPROPRIATE" WORSHIP

At the conclusion of the Civil War, the Black community came face to face with its diversity. Against the assumption that post–Civil War Black culture was monolithic, geographic differences, class distinctions, and educational disparities produced cultural differences that engendered tension in the Black church. Differences came to a head when goodhearted Northern Blacks relocated to the South to teach biblical literacy, foster educational opportunities, and teach former slaves refined cultural customs. Despite racial congruity, Northern and Southern Blacks encountered

---

[28] Carl F. Ellis Jr., "The Forgotten History of African American Missions" (lecture, Southeastern Baptist Theological Seminary, Center for Faith and Culture, Wake Forest, NC, February 2, 2018). See vol. 2 for an excerpt from Amanda Smith's autobiography.

significant cultural impasses as they struggled to understand each other's attitudes, speech, and traditions.

Cultural differences between Blacks coalesced in a vigorous debate about Christian worship. Whites and Blacks from the North were shocked by what they deemed to be primitive, barbaric, and heathenish worship practices in the South. Prominent Northern African American leaders were convinced that cultivating a worship style that paralleled White ecclesial practices would engender respect from White Christians. Well-known Bishop Daniel Alexander Payne was a proponent of refining Black worship practices in the South.

After the Civil War, Payne traveled throughout the South in hopes of transforming the worship practices of his newly freed kinsmen by condemning the emotionalism prominent in ring shouts and in numerous Black churches. Despite Payne's efforts, the following scene conveys the commitment of Southern Blacks to their worship practices:

> At one brush meeting, [Payne] witnessed congregants forming a ring after service, stamping their feet, clapping, swaying, and dancing "in the most ridiculous and heathenish way." When [he] asked the congregants to sit down and worship more sedately, they responded by walking away. A leader of the congregation told Payne that unless there was a ring, the sinners would never convert, but Payne refused to accept the old folkways of worship as true manifestation of the spirit of God and criticized those who encouraged them.[29]

This picture characterized Payne's travels throughout the South. Despite his efforts, Black churchgoers continued attending ring shouts and worship services with Africanisms reminiscent of the invisible institution. The worship battle during Reconstruction is often reduced to the education gap. Southern Blacks insisted they be educated, yet many persisted in their "heathenish" worship practices. This coexistence offers explanatory power to understand the nature of faith and its manifestation within the Black experience during Reconstruction.

The Christian faith encompasses more than the intellect; it captivates body and soul. The song and dance that accompanied Southern Black worship fostered an environment that holistically directed body and soul to the Savior. Beyond the immediate benefits of a holistic worship experience, these practices connected congregations to a tradition where Christ carried their forebearers through

---

[29]Harvey, *Through the Storm*, 85.

difficult times—not unlike their own. The budding intellectual life and the cultural sophistication of Reconstruction did not replace the holistic religious force that upheld generations of Black believers during difficult circumstances. Rather, its place was solidified within the African American Christian tradition as expressive worship practices grew together with theological sophistication.

The worship battles of this period raise an important dialectic in African American history, namely, the accommodationist-separatist debate. Like Payne, accommodationists contended that Black uplift was best achieved by mimicking White culture to gain cultural power; by contrast, separatists held that races should be autonomous and left to preserve their cultural heritage and organize their own affairs. Accommodationists deemed better living standards as the greatest need and made the difficult decision to relinquish part of their culture—at least in public—for the sake of uplift. By comparison, separatists equated Black flourishing with preserving Black cultural customs over all else. Since Reconstruction, both positions have thrived in the Black community, but not without friction. In the contemporary moment, it is important to realize that neither accommodationists nor separatists have a corner on the most beneficial way forward; in fact, they benefit from each other. As a result, joining forces must occur to further Black uplift in the present.

CHRISTIAN THOUGHT AND BLACK LITERATURE

During Reconstruction, the African American theological tradition continued to develop the pre-emancipation doctrinal Anchors in various expressive forms. Among the nonsermonic mediums that conveyed biblical truths, poetry generated a vigorous Christian witness. Ohio native, poet, and playwright Paul Laurence Dunbar (1872–1906) poetically captured a traditional view of a Big God during his short life, marked by the paradoxes of his poverty and fame, defeat and success. In a ninety-three-word hymn, Dunbar expresses trust in God, who is able to keep him during difficult times:

> When storms arise
> And dark'ning skies
> About me threat'ning lower,
> To Thee, O Lord, I raise mine eyes
> To Thee my tortured spirit flies
> For solace in that hour.

Thy mighty arm
Will let no harm
Come near me nor befall me
Thy voice shall quiet my alarm,
When life's great battle waxeth warm—
No foeman shall appall me.
Upon Thy breast
Secure I rest
From sorrow and vexation;
No more by sinful care oppressed,
But in Thy presence over blest,
O God of my salvation.[30]

With turmoil emitting from his words, Dunbar acknowledged the difficulties that threatened to overwhelm him but later rejoiced in the Lord, his deliverer, who was bigger than his circumstances. Characteristic of the African American theological tradition, Dunbar's declaration of divine salvation did not preclude joining with God to work toward Deliverance. These concluding stanzas from "The Warrior's Prayer" beautifully characterize the battle that marked Black social existence during Reconstruction. Dunbar poetically concedes his weakness yet asserts his willingness to press on as he relies on a Big God to grant him "strength for the fight":

When foes upon me press, let me not quail
Nor think to turn me into coward flight,
I only ask, to make mine arms prevail,
Strength for the fight!
Still let mine eyes look ever on the foe,
Still let mine armor case me strong and bright;
And grant me, as I deal each righteous blow,
Strength for the fight!
And when, at eventide, the fray is done,
My soul to death's bed chamber do Thou light,
And give me, be the field or lost or won,
Rest from the fight.[31]

---

[30]Lida Keck Wiggins, *The Life and Works of Paul Laurence Dunbar* (Washington, DC: Mulliken-Jenkins), 204.
[31]Wiggins, *Life and Works*, 160.

"The Warrior's Prayer" elevated an emphasis that was indigenous to the African American experience during Reconstruction. However, the elite theological discourse acquired elements from Anglo sources that shaped the theological dialogue.

In addition to Dunbar's Big God, who grants strength in trials, Jesus of the masses is evident in the 1890 "Mattin Hymn," written by Josephine Delphine Henderson Heard. Its four stanzas exemplify the effect of looking to the Savior, who is near during times of struggle. The first stanza begins with the depths of human experience, depicting the troubling questions of God's children amid turmoil. The vivid description of walking the arduous terrain of life "with timid and faltering feet" and "fighting with weak and failing heart" propels the reader to consider their own struggles. The second stanza features the expected pivot, where Jesus interjects himself into their despair:

> "Nay! Nay! My child," the Father saith,
> "Thou dost not walk alone—
> Gird up the loins of thy weak faith,
> And cease thy plaintive tone.
> Look thou with unbeclouded eyes
> To calvary's gory scene—
> Canst thou forget the Saviour's cries?
> Go thou, on His mercy, lean."

The third and fourth stanzas account for the change, when Jesus is identified with the contemporary human struggle. Heard captures the emboldening of the heart and the ability to carry on despite the circumstances that befall those whose gaze is on Christ. While the distinction between formal and lay Christology is evident, they are harmonious and offer a robust witness to the Jesus who carried Black Christians through the trials of Reconstruction and its aftermath.

DECONSTRUCTION

Only eight years into Reconstruction, the civil rights of Blacks were challenged when the Supreme Court reinterpreted the Fourteenth Amendment beginning with the Slaughterhouse Cases. These cases narrowed the scope of "privileges and immunities" subject to federal protection. In addition, the verdicts of two 1875 cases, namely, *United States v. Reese* and *United States v. Cruiksank*, effectively announced the federal government's intention to leave the fate of African Americans in the hands of Southern White supremacists; this began what is colloquially known as "Deconstruction."

> **The "Slaughterhouse Cases"** refer to three interrelated court cases: (1) *The Butchers' Benevolent Association of New Orleans v. The Crescent City Live-Stock Landing and Slaughter-House Company*; (2) *Paul Esteben, L. Ruch, J. P. Rouede, W. Maylie, S. Firmberg, B. Beaubay, William Fagan, J. D. Broderick, N. Seibel, M. Lannes, J. Gitzinger, J. P. Aycock, D. Verges, The Live-Stock Dealers' and Butchers' Association of New Orleans, and Charles Cavaroc v. The State of Louisiana, ex rel. S. Belden, Attorney-General;* and (3) *The Butchers' Benevolent Association of New Orleans v. The Crescent City Live-Stock Landing and Slaughter-House Company.*

Reconstruction efforts continued unraveling when Blacks were legally disenfranchised from the voting booth. This action immediately eliminated the possibility of Blacks holding public office. The fate of Southern African Americans was sealed by the Compromise of 1877, an unwritten agreement that removed federal troops from the South who were installed to enforce the Reconstruction amendments. After the Compromise, Southern Blacks endured dwindling legal rights and were increasingly subjected to localized racism that aimed to relegate Blacks to an inferior legal, social, and economic status.

As Albert Raboteau writes, "Gradually deprived of the vote, Black Southerners found themselves increasingly segregated in public places."[32] Furthermore, they were vulnerable to White supremacist violence. Government inaction on behalf of Blacks, especially after 1877, encouraged racial terrorism. The most notorious of these radical terrorist groups was called the Ku Klux Klan (KKK). Extralegal executions increased drastically in the final two decades of the nineteenth century, and incidents of violence against African Americans were commonplace.

> **LYNCHING STATISTICS**
>
> Between 1882 and 1888, 227 Black people were lynched, and that number increased to 1,240 from 1889 to 1899. In 1889 alone, White mobs seized and murdered 104 Black people.[33]

Lynching was a spectacle that reinforced White supremacy. Nell Irvin Painter describes the abhorrent act: "Special trains carried spectators to the scene, and professional photographers made picture postcards for sale. Lynching victims were often tortured, mutilated, and killed slowly to ensure the maximum amount

---

[32]Alfred J. Raboteau, *African American Religion* (Oxford: Oxford University Press, 1999), 76.
[33]Raboteau, *Canaan Land*, 72.

of pain and humiliation."[34] Ultimately, lynchings were staged for the purpose of entertaining spectators and intimidating Black people.

Lynching brought about a renewed interest in the events of Good (or Holy) Friday among Blacks. During a period of reinvigorated racial violence, Black pastors shepherded their people by preaching about Jesus' death more than any other aspect of his earthly ministry. Jesus' suffering and persecution paralleled their own encounter with lynching and racialized violence. Black Christians took comfort in identifying with their Savior. Dwelling on Jesus' sufferings and the African American experience of suffering, a twentieth-century Black theologian reflects:

> Though wonderful and beautiful, Jesus' cross was also painful and tragic. Songs and sermons about the "blood" were stark reminders of the agony of Jesus' crucifixion—the symbol of the physical and mental suffering he endured as "dey whupped him up de hill" and "crowned him wid a thorny crown." Blacks told the story of Jesus' Passion, as if they were at Golgotha suffering with him. "Where you there when de crucified my Lord?" "Dey nailed him to de cross"; "dey pierced him in de side"; and "de blood came twinklin' down."[35]

Suffering was a means for Black Christians to anchor their story to that of Jesus. Suffering and humiliation caused both Blacks and Jesus to beg the Father to let this cup pass from them but often led to the declaration "My God, my God, why have You forsaken Me?" (Matthew 27:46) before resting in death. Despite the emphasis on Jesus' suffering, Black Christians never lost sight of Christ's resurrection from the dead. In his resurrection, he conquered the injustice that laid him to rest. Jesus' vindication gave African Americans suffering under the weight of White supremacy hope that someday they too would rise in victory over their circumstances because they know the one who "made a way out of no way."

Many White Christians responded passively as the Ku Klux Klan, the Knights of the White Camellia, and other organized mobs menaced, assaulted, and murdered African Americans. The inactivity of many White Christians on behalf of the Black community was dumbfounding to Blacks. However, it was consistent with the dualistic gospel message that was proclaimed to Blacks in the pre-emancipation era, which minimized the terror and mutilation of Black bodies while preaching the gospel to their souls. This theological malformation has

---

[34] Nell Irvin Painter, *Creating Black Americans: African-American History and Its Meanings, 1619 to the Present* (New York: Oxford University Press, 2006), 167.

[35] James H. Cone, *The Cross and the Lynching Tree* (Maryknoll, NY: Orbis Books, 2011), 73-74.

carried into the twenty-first century as segments of White evangelicalism remain silent, and some antagonistic, in the face of social injustice that brings about emotional, spiritual, and at times physical death for Blacks.

By the 1880s, the national descent into Jim Crow segregation was in full swing. In 1883, the Supreme Court ruled the Civil Rights Act of 1875 unconstitutional; this legislation deemed individual acts of discrimination outside the reach of the Fourteenth Amendment. This law permitted discrimination in public accommodations by individuals, states, and localities and was challenged by Blacks, whose case was not sustained. In addition to individual acts of violence, three Black men sued their states for depriving them the right to vote. In all three cases, decided between 1895 and 1903, the Supreme Court ruled against the men and set a precedent for states to deprive Blacks their right to vote. These decisions provided the legal backing for segregation and disenfranchisement for a nation moving toward legalized segregation for the first half of the twentieth century.

> **Three failed Black voting-rights cases** were *Mills v. Green* (1895), *Williams v. Mississippi* (1898), and *Giles v. Harris* (1903).

In 1896, the landmark *Plessy v. Ferguson* case was the beginning of a new era. With Blacks already having been stripped of the vote, this case introduced the doctrine of "separate but equal" that became the bedrock of the American South during the civil rights era (1896–1968). These discriminatory customs and state laws that upheld segregation were enacted to end racial strife by separating public facilities by race, including transportation, public accommodations, schools, colleges, swimming pools, libraries, and so on. The case's stated purpose was rife with discriminatory unintended consequences. Jim Crow segregation has been described as a racial caste system:

> It was based on race in a starkly simple way. Anyone—from a pale-skinned mulatto to a very dark-skinned—who had Negroid physical characteristics was considered to be a Negro. Negros were born into their caste and could never escape it even by marriage or personal achievement. . . . Jim Crow was systemic. It involved the virtually total disfranchisement of Blacks and sweeping racial segregation in social relations and, in many instances, in economic relations.[36]

---

[36]William J. Cooper Jr. and Thomas E. Terrill, *The American South: A History* (New York: McGraw-Hill, 1991), 545.

These laws allowed White supremacists to bar African Americans from public life with the backing of the US Supreme Court. This brief look at the legal transitions within the era helps to clarify the context and the challenges that the church faced in the aftermath of Reconstruction.

CONCLUSION

The rise of Reconstruction demonstrated the centrality of the Black church within the African American community and revealed its doctrinal, ethical, and social shaping hand on Black life. Reconstruction's demise displayed the sustaining power of Black Christianity for a people through unimaginable suffering. Despite the trials of the period, the institutional development that occurred produced denominations and churches. The Black church served as a spiritual bulwark, a political outpost, and a social hub, and continues to uphold African Americans—and others—today.

In addition to the spiritual deepening that occurred in churches across the country, the proliferation of Black education in its various forms provided a context for intellectual deepening that forged unprecedented opportunities for Blacks to further explore the Anchors of the African American Christian tradition. In the years to come, the organizations forged during this period exerted a social force Anchored in a theological commitment to Deliverance and an unwavering spiritual vitality during Jim Crow segregation that ultimately caused segregation's demise. Through it all, Black Christians expressed unprecedented levels of agency in the postemancipation social and cultural context, and the institutions that emerged during this period continued to fan the flame of Black image bearing.

7

A NEW NORMAL

THE STORY OF AFRICAN AMERICAN CHRISTIANITY grew increasingly complex during Jim Crow segregation. This period featured a perplexing array of historical and intellectual movements that included two world wars, antilynching campaigns, the Great Migration, the Harlem Renaissance, and modernism. These nationwide phenomena created national movements and sparked coalitions that remain pillars of Black faith today.

> **Jim Crow segregation** began in 1896 with *Plessy v. Ferguson* and came to a gradual end that spanned two decades. The end of segregation began with several landmark decisions, beginning with President Harry Truman integrating the military (1948), the desegregation of schools (1954), the Civil Rights Act of 1964, the Voting Rights Act of 1965, and the Fair Housing Act of 1968.

This period was marked by momentous cultural change, and the Black church encountered massive social, economic, and intellectual movements of the day. This ideological soup generated by the Great Migration was perhaps the first time that Christians arriving from the South had to vie for Christianity's religious primacy in a widespread manner. The seismic shifts of this period resulted in a new normal for Black Christians in their quest for faithfulness.

HISTORICAL CONTEXT

The struggle for Black uplift characterized the civil rights era, and the largest institution in Black America—the Black church—was at the epicenter of the story. Despite the centrality of the institutional Black church, Black Christians diversified the locus of their efforts for racial justice in organizations including the National Association for the Advancement of Colored People (NAACP), the Congress of Racial Equality, eventually the Southern Christian Leadership Conference, and increasingly in academia.

> **"Black uplift"** was a term introduced by Black elites including W. E. B. DuBois and Booker T. Washington that encouraged educated African Americans to take responsibility for raising the social and economic well-being of their race.

Throughout the civil rights era, the Black church was both lauded and scrutinized. The Black church was praised for the prophetic leadership of figures such as Henry McNeal Turner (1834–1915) and Francis J. Grimke (1850–1937), who labored for equal rights based in local churches. These clerical leaders continued the Reconstruction tradition of the Black church being the near-exclusive means of pursuing racial justice within the Black community. The rise and fall of nonreligious Black advocacy groups including the Afro-American Council (1898–1907) and the Niagara movement (1905–1908) accentuated the longevity of the Black church's endeavors, so Black churches were further scrutinized because of its potential impact for the common good.

Black intellectual W. E. B. DuBois (1868–1963) critiqued the growing otherworldliness of the Black church in the early decades of the twentieth century. More pointedly, religious historian Gayraud S. Wilmore (1921–2020) insisted on the deradicalization of the Black church upon the death of Henry McNeal Turner in 1915. Wilmore insisted that there were no clergymen of Turner's stature who could, by temperament or ideology, assume the leadership position he occupied to mobilize the Black church in the social realm.[1] Regardless of Wilmore's criticism, the meteoric rise of the Black church back into a seat of social influence is scarcely contested at the emergence of the civil rights movement, beginning with the Montgomery bus boycott in 1955.

There are several factors to consider when comprehending the arc of the Black church's social influence and the embodiment of its priestly and prophetic mission during this era. Among them are the rise of Jim Crow violence, the effects of the Great Migration, internal church politics, the proliferation of the New Negro, and the rise of the NAACP. At first glance each of these factors can be skewed to uphold Wilmore's claim, but on further exploration, they problematize his deradicalization hypothesis by providing a more fully orbed telling of the story.

Jim Crow violence. At the turn of the century, individual and mob violence against Blacks was unprecedented, and energy used to fight Jim Crow segregation from within the church was diverted toward daily survival. Blacks continued to be

---

[1]Gayraud S. Wilmore, *Black Religion and Black Radicalism: An Introduction of the Religious History of African Americans* (Maryknoll, NY: Orbis Books, 1998), 165.

lynched at a staggering rate well into the twentieth century for the purpose of inciting fear in African American communities and specifically in the church, the historic hub for social advancement. Racially motivated violence continued into the 1960s, and socially engaged pastors feared for their safety and worried that their churches would be burned down. The Ku Klux Klan targeted clergy, the traditional leaders for Black social uplift, in an effort to grind efforts for Black equality to a halt.

Extralegal violence from terrorist groups, such as the Ku Klux Klan and Knights of the White Camellia, accounted for thirty-five hundred victims to mobs between 1885 and 1914, with 325 lynchings in the year 1896 alone.[a] Blacks continued to be lynched at a rate that intimidated the African American community. The following list of Blacks lynched over a five-year period is staggering: 1915–1919, 278; 1920–1924, 208; 1925–1929, 73; 1930–1934, 77; 1935–1939, 42; 1940–1944, 19; 1945–1949, 12; 1950–1954, 2; 1955–1959, 4; 1960–1964, 2.[b]

[a]Gayraud S. Wilmore, *Black Religion and Black Radicalism: An Introduction of the Religious History of African Americans* (Maryknoll, NY: Orbis Books: 1998), 167.
[b]Archives at Tuskegee Institute, http://law2.umkc.edu/faculty/projects/ftrials/shipp/lynchingyear.html (accessed July 6, 2022).

The Great Migration and economic need. The tempered social witness of the Black church is also explained by the demographic shifts that took place during the Great Migration. The dramatic shift in the African American population away from the rural South to Northern and Midwestern cities dramatically shifted the needs within the Black community and simultaneously severed meaningful ties to the rural Southern church network that historically engaged the Black population's political, social, and economic challenges. The drastic shift in the Black populace taxed Northern churches, and they were unable to meet the vast social needs of the relocated population. In an effort to do so, energy previously dedicated to social advancement was redirected toward survival.

The radical demographic shift in the African American population occurred in two distinct waves, the first beginning in the second decade of the twentieth century and the second in the 1940s.[2] The first Black exodus from the countryside

---

[2]Nell Irvin Painter, *Creating Black Americans: African-American History and Its Meanings, 1619 to the Present* (New York: Oxford University Press, 2006), 174; Hans A. Baer and Merrill Singer, *African American Religion: Varieties of Protest and Accommodation*, 2nd ed. (Knoxville: University of Tennessee Press, 2002), 44.

started in 1915 and peaked in 1917. Between 1910 and 1920, the net increase of Southern-born Blacks living in the North was 322,000, which exceeded the increase of the preceding forty years.

> **The first Great Migration wave** caused Northern and Midwestern cities to swell. Between 1910 and 1920, the Black population in Chicago increased from 44,000 to 109,000; in New York City from 92,000 to 152,000; in Detroit from 6,000 to 41,000; and in Philadelphia from 85,000 to 134,000. A less significant yet substantial migration also occurred to Southern cities, especially those with significant shipbuilding and heavy industry that created jobs.[a]
>
> [a] Harold M. Baron, "The Demand of Black Labor," in *Radical Conflict, Discrimination and Power: Historical and Contemporary Studies*, ed. William Barclay, Krishna, and Ruth P. Simms (New York: AMS, 1976), 105.

The secondary migration in the 1940s witnessed just over 1.5 million Blacks moving northward. By 1970, only 52 percent of African Americans were located in the South, and the majority of Blacks in the North and South alike were situated in urban areas.[3] The urbanization caused by the Great Migration affected the Black community dramatically. The most significant loss was the rural ecclesiastical infrastructure that undergirded life in the South and gave meaning to Black people.[4]

The striking population change during the Great Migration further contributed to the Black church's seeming departure from engaging social and economic issues. Compared to the network of Southern churches, the proportionally frail Northern church network diverted attention from the political and educational advancement that marked Reconstruction and became a receiving agency for their Southern Black kinsmen who arrived in their cities. Urbanization intensified the financial needs that plagued Blacks in the South as people left their means of feeding their families in search of a better life.

Despite the church's best efforts, the financial needs of Southern newcomers outstripped the Northern church's ability to support them. The economic strain on the Northern church network resulted in many churchgoers depending on government assistance. In Chicago's South Side, Black unemployment was over

---

[3] Baer and Singer, *African American Religion*, 44.
[4] E. Franklin Frazier, *The Negro Church in America* (New York: Schocken Books, 1974), 54; Baer and Singer, *African American Religion*, 48.

85 percent by 1931. In 1931, approximately 22,000 Black families collected welfare; a year later, the figure jumped to 48,000. By comparison, in 1933, over 26.5 percent of urban Blacks were on relief, compared to 9.5 percent of Whites in urban centers.[5] During the proliferation of federal aid, the NAACP and other non-Christian agencies gained prominence for meeting the daily needs of Blacks. Consequently, this contributed to the church losing its nearly exclusive status as the chief provider and advocate for the Black community during the Great Migration.

The religious and ideological cocktail of the Great Migration. Their numerous needs notwithstanding, Black Southerners did not arrive North emptyhanded; they came with a rich oral and liturgical tradition that forever changed corporate worship gatherings where these travelers descended. Although the emotionalism and spontaneity of Southern Black faith clashed with the decorum of Northern Black religion, the collision of church cultures that the migration initiated gave rise to the birth of modern gospel music. Southern gospel sounds fused with popular Northern genres, coupled with the emergence of radio, forever changed Black church music.

Thomas Dorsey (1899–1993) was known as the "father of gospel music." Formerly known as "Georgia Tom," upon his Conversion, he drew from his background in blues and ragtime. These styles of music paired with the soul and rhythm-and-blues musical influences of this bandmates, and modern gospel music was born. Dorsey's influence on church music is unmistakable. As a composer, he captured the musical fusion that produced his gospel sound on sheet music, and it was distributed around the country. In addition to composing musical arrangements, he embodied the genre as music director at Pilgrim Baptist Church in Chicago. He also influenced other choir directors by arranging a convention of gospel singers, whose popularity soared due to the radio and phonograph.

Although Southern Christians brought the longstanding trappings of Southern church culture with them, the Northern urban centers were religiously crowded before they arrived. Southern Blacks encountered religious diversity, including African Americans who were Catholics, Jews, and Muslims. Black Muslims (often called Nation of Islam) were known for their social separatism, which insisted on owning their own businesses and leading their own communities because they were convinced that fighting for civil rights in the courtroom was a fool's errand.

---

[5]Baer and Singer, *African American Religion*, 44.

Developing a nation within a nation, a true Black society, was the only viable avenue toward uplift for Black Muslims.

> **Nation of Islam** is a religious and political organization founded in the United States by Wallace Fard Muhammad in 1930. A Black nationalist organization, the Nation of Islam focuses its attention on the African diaspora and especially on African Americans.[a]
>
> [a]"Nation of Islam," www.noi.org (accessed July 19, 2022).

Among the most charismatic leaders in the North were Bishop Charles Manuel "Sweet Daddy" Grace (1884–1960). Sweet Daddy Grace was the founder and captivating leader of the Universal House of Prayer for All People in 1921, whose spiritual leaders were said to be able to restore peace in this world and the next. After establishing a House of Prayer in Egypt, a ministry that featured Pentecostal holiness practices, ring shouts, healings, miraculous signs, and mass baptism, the movement expanded around the world and peaked with a half million congregants internationally.

Southern Black Christians also encountered quasi-religious movements, including Garveyism. Led by its namesake, Jamaican activist Marcus Garvey (1887–1940), Garveyism sparked the most successful pan-African movement in American history. The movement upheld racial unity and pride and sparked the formation of the Universal Negro Improvement Association, whose mission was to "unite all the Negro peoples of the world into one great body to establish a country and Government absolutely their own."

> **Marcus Garvey** was born in Jamaica in 1887. Albert Raboteau reports, "As a young man he learned the trade of printing and began publishing his own newspaper in 1910. He traveled to Central America and relocated in 1912 to England, where he worked on the *African Times and Orient Review* and learned the philosophy of pan-Africanism."[a]
>
> [a]Alfred J. Raboteau, *African American Religion* (Oxford: Oxford University Press, 1999), 88.

Shifts in the religious landscape in the wake of the Great Migration cannot be overstated. In addition to expending energy meeting the economic needs of migrated peoples, for the first time historic Black denominations had to vie for their place in the religious marketplace of ideas.

PORTRAITS OF CHRISTIAN FAITHFULNESS
DURING THE GREAT MIGRATION

Amid incessant racial violence, demographic shifts, and growing religious pluralism, the theological and social witness persisted in the historic Black denominations. During the early days of the civil rights era, the vast majority of Black worshipers attended Baptist or Methodist churches, and this trend continued throughout the period, although the emergence of the Church of God in Christ diluted that near monopoly.

The Great Migration highlighted the faithful work of pastors laboring in the North, including Adam Clayton Powell Sr. (1865–1953), pastor of Abyssinian Baptist Church from 1908 to 1937. Powell was born to an African Cherokee woman and a German slave owner in Franklin County, Virginia, and his autobiography *Against the Tide* captures his journey from a sharecropping family to leading what became one of the most prominent churches in the nation. Powell's family lived in "direst poverty," and formal education was almost an afterthought to daily survival.[6] Even though Powell had minimal time to study, his stepfather was impressed with his aptitude and agreed to send him to boarding school when he could read through the entire Gospel of John. Although that promise was never fulfilled, the ability to read was life altering.

After enduring a move to West Virginia and then to Ohio in search of better wages, Powell moved to Rendville, Ohio, which he describes as a "lawless and godless place," where he received salvation. After being denied entry to Howard University's law school, he spent a year meditating on Scripture and was "seized with an unquenchable desire to preach."[7] Graduating from Wayland Seminary, Powell took a pastorate at Ebenezer Baptist Church in Philadelphia in 1892. After one year, Powell moved to New Haven, Connecticut, to pastor Immanuel Baptist Church. During his stay in New Haven, he became an internationally known orator and took additional courses at Yale University.[8]

In 1908, Powell was installed as the pastor of Abyssinian Baptist Church in New York City. Under his leadership, the church left its building in New York City and found a home in Harlem to maintain a gospel witness amid a population influx composed of Southern Blacks during the Great Migration and others captured by the ethos of the Harlem Renaissance. By Powell's retirement in 1937, Abyssinian was

---

[6]Adam Clayton Powell Sr., *Against the Tide* (New York: Little and Ives, 1938), 7.
[7]Powell, *Against the Tide*, 20.
[8]See vol. 2 for an excerpt from Adam Clayton Powell Sr.'s sermon "The Significance of the Hour."

the largest Protestant congregation in the world.⁹ Although Powell was known for providing a Christian presence in Harlem—"Black mecca"—his theological contributions should not be overlooked, including his ecclesiology of faithful action.¹⁰

DIETRICH BONHOEFFER AND ABYSSINIAN BAPTIST CHURCH

German Lutheran pastor, theologian and anti-Nazi dissident Dietrich Bonhoeffer said of his time in Harlem that it was the only time he "experienced true religion in the US."[a] During this period he was an attendee and Sunday school teacher at Abyssinian Baptist Church. While at Abyssinian, he encountered a Harlem Renaissance Christianity that featured a Christ who suffered with African Americans in their struggle against systemic injustice and racial violence. This Jesus, who stood with the oppressed, recast Bonhoeffer's understanding of how God worked on behalf of the lowly. This realization transformed the rest of Bonhoeffer's life and marked his writing and activism from that time until his death as a martyr vying for justice on behalf of the marginalized.

[a]Charles Marsh, *Strange Glory: A Life of Dietrich Bonhoeffer* (New York: Knopf Doubleday, 2014), 117.

During the Great Migration, Presbyterian pastor Francis James Grimke (1850–1937) also labored tirelessly for Black uplift in the nation's capital. A transitional figure who led powerfully during Reconstruction and into the civil rights era, Grimke was born in Charleston, South Carolina, to his master, Henry, and enslaved mother, Nancy. Henry's affection for Nancy and her three boys forced them to live within the tension of being tolerated but never accepted. Upon Henry's death, in 1855, Nancy and her children were freed. However, five years later, Grimke's Anglo half brother attempted to enslave him again. At the age of ten, Grimke escaped and ironically found sanctuary as a valet in the Confederate Army. After emancipation, Grimke was free to fulfill his academic potential. In 1870, he graduated from Lincoln University as valedictorian, and in 1875, after a year of studying law at Princeton University alongside his brother, Archibald, Grimke answered God's call into ministry and transferred to Princeton Theological Seminary.

The racial injustice Grimke experienced in his childhood compelled him to speak out against the injustice Black people endured in nineteenth- and twentieth-century

---

⁹Marvin A. McMickle, *An Encyclopedia of African American Christian Heritage* (Valley Forge, PA: Judson University Press, 2002), 77.

¹⁰Reggie L. Williams, *Bonhoeffer's Black Jesus: Harlem Renaissance Theology and an Ethic of Resistance* (Waco, TX: Baylor University Press, 2014), 94-96.

America. As the pastor of Fifteenth St. Presbyterian Church in Washington, DC, Grimke faithfully called the church to embody the Christian distinctives of brotherhood and love. In 1916, Grimke criticized the blind spots affecting many Christian churches of his day. An explicit example of this practice is that he admonished evangelist Billy Sunday for his denouncement of drunkenness and sexual immorality while leaving other sins untouched during his Washington rally, including sins that uniquely affected Blacks (including racial injustice, discrimination, and economic oppression).[11]

During Reconstruction and into the civil rights era, Grimke experienced the benefits of Christian distinctives, but with the institution of the Jim Crow laws, he noticed a great shift within the church in regard to African Americans. Theological institutions that once welcomed Black clergymen denied these men the opportunity to be equipped for the work of ministry. Pulpits that were once opened to them were now closed. In his sermon "Race Prejudice and Christianity," Grimke indicted the church for its hypocrisy and employed Scripture to call them to turn away from the partiality of Jim Crow segregation to the impartiality of Christ.[12]

DENOMINATIONAL POLITICS

Despite the faithful witness within Black denominational life, points of interdenominational tension emerged, not regarding theology but about the appropriate methods to pursue social change for Black people. The conflict over engaging oppression within the Black church reached a zenith in the National Baptist Convention in the 1950s and '60s. The National Baptist Convention represents a worthy cross section of the Black church because it is one of the two oldest and most prominent Black denominations. Ethicist Peter J. Paris insists that there were no distinct differences in the social thought among Black Baptist and Methodist denominations during this period, and similar tensions emerged in both denominations.[13]

> **Joseph H. Jackson** (1900–1990) served as the senior pastor of Olivet Baptist Church in Chicago (1941–1990), as the longest-standing president of the National Baptist Convention (1953–1982), and as a leading conservative voice during the civil rights era. He is arguably the most influential leader in the National Baptist Convention's history.

---

[11]See vol. 2 for an excerpt from Francis Grimke's *Christianity and Race Prejudice*.
[12]See vol. 2 for Mary McLeod Bethune's letter to Josephine T. Washington, 1946.
[13]Peter J. Paris, *The Social Teaching of the Black Churches* (Philadelphia: Fortress, 1985), xi.

Joseph H. Jackson, National Baptist Convention president from 1953 to 1982, was given a lifetime term when he was voted into office. Jackson represented Black ministers who grew increasingly conservative politically and became more estranged from the fight for racial equality as time progressed. Jackson thought that the Christian way of affecting the legal system was via "patronage politics." This term refers to the acceptance of favors from local politicians in exchange for illusions of power.[14] Consequently, Jackson viewed Martin Luther King Jr.'s approach of direct action as troubling because, from his perspective, King did not take seriously the importance of a Christian engagement with the US Constitution and its democratic vision for social transformation.[15] It followed that Jackson and King disagreed on the fundamental role of the preacher. For Jackson, the pastoral task was to bring the good news of the gospel to the people so that salvation might come to congregants. In turn, upon Conversion, believers would bring about change in society through exemplary conduct.[16] Jackson's convictions were shared by numerous Black church leaders of his generation, but despite his perch of influence, he did not persuade every Black clergyman of his methods for pursuing racial equality.[17]

The methodological squabbles regarding Christian social engagement climaxed in a multiyear debate about term limits for the National Baptist Convention's presidential office. In an effort to break Jackson's stronghold on the convention, in 1956 an appointed committee concluded that denominational leaders should be subject to term limits. Several prominent leaders, including Martin Luther King Jr. (1929–1968), Martin Luther King Sr. (1899–1984), Ralph Abernathy (1926–1990), and Benjamin E. Mays (1894–1984), nominated Gardner C. Taylor (1918–2015) as a candidate for the presidency during the 1960 meeting. Taylor was not considered as a candidate, and Jackson was reelected as president. Taylor's supporters held a second election that concluded with Taylor as the victor, but the convention did not recognize the vote.

---

[14] Paul Harvey, "Is There a River? Black Baptists, the Uses of History, and the Long History of the Freedom Movement," in *Through a Glass Darkly: Contested Notions of Baptist Identity*, ed. Keith Harper and James P. Byrd (Tuscaloosa: University of Alabama Press, 2012), 259.

[15] Anne H. Pinn and Anthony B. Pinn, *The Fortress Introduction to Black Church History* (Minneapolis: Fortress, 2002), 95.

[16] C. Eric Lincoln, *Race, Religion, and the Continuing American Dilemma* (New York: Hill and Wang, 1999), 100.

[17] C. Eric Lincoln, *The Black Church Since Frazier* (New York: Schocken, 1974), 119.

> **Gardner C. Taylor** (1918–2015) is often called one of the greatest preachers in the English-speaking world. He began a pastorate at Concord Baptist Church in Brooklyn, New York, at thirty years old, and nearly thirteen thousand people joined during his tenure. Taylor has been dubbed the "dean of preachers" because of his incredible pulpit ministry, which was affirmed by thirteen honorary degrees and numerous awards.[a]
>
> [a]See vol. 2 for an excerpt from Taylor's sermon "In His Own Clothes."

The denomination officially expelled Taylor's leading proponents from the convention because they had "gone against the rules of fellowship in opposition to and contrary to [its] principles and ideals."[18] With few options left, those who supported Taylor founded the Progressive National Baptist Convention in 1961. The new denomination avidly supported the direct-action strategy championed by Christians who participated in the civil rights movement, and the revolutionary stance of the historic Black church was reclaimed. This type of denominational drama is not uncharacteristic of any denomination, but the intensity was heightened because of the cultural moment of the 1960s. The importance of in-house discussions notwithstanding, these denominational clashes required time and resources that could have been dedicated to pastoral care, shepherding, or combating issues in public life.

> **The Progressive National Baptist Convention** "started as a movement which reflected the religious, social and political climate of its time. Its mission was to transform the traditional African American Baptist Convention as well as society. The formation of the convention was wrapped up in the civil rights movement and was begun by some of the same persons who were deeply involved in the freedom movement for African Americans in the United States. The need for a convention which would embrace tenure of office and leadership was a shared need among a cross section of Baptists."[a]
>
> [a]"History of PNBC," Progressive National Baptist Convention, https://pnbc.org/content/history-of-the-pnbc/ (accessed January 8, 2024).

THE NEW NEGRO

As Blacks shifted geographically and vocationally during the Great Migration, the first generation born free came of age with a new attitude toward faith, the

---

[18]Lincoln, *Black Church Since Frazier*, 119.

intellectual life, and social problems, causing the church's stronghold on Black culture to wane. This burgeoning coalition was called the "New Negro" and was closely bound with the Harlem Renaissance, which affected the reading of both secular and religious texts.

> **The Harlem Renaissance** was named after the neighborhood in New York where it emerged. Harlem was a Black cultural mecca in the early twentieth century during what is often considered the golden age of African American culture. The Harlem Renaissance produced art, music, literature, and stage performances by internationally renowned artists, including Langston Hughes (1901–1967), Countee Cullen (1903–1946), Louis Armstrong (1901–1971), Josephine Baker (1906–1975), and Aaron Douglas (1899–1979).

During the Jim Crow era, most ministers in training had a "father in the ministry" and served as an apprentice while learning the doctrine and practices of the church. This began changing in the twentieth century. As African Americans gained wealth and access to higher education, and as the mood of the New Negro proliferated, it became more common for Blacks to attend seminary or divinity schools for theological training. Having been barred from most evangelical seminaries and Bible colleges during the early and middle part of this era because of racism, Black Christians were unable to attend schools that held closely to the doctrinal Anchors of the African American Christian tradition. Instead, they attended university divinity schools that were socially progressive but often doctrinally liberal.

In the middle of the twentieth century, some African American Christian scholars began interacting with the intellectual resources of the secular academy to combat racism in society, biblical interpretation, and theological studies. Among these were a higher-critical method of reading Scripture, which ran contrary to how African Americans historically read the Good Book—especially related to biblical authority. The fruit of these ideas did not fully ripen among Black Christian intellectuals until after Martin Luther King Jr. was assassinated.

Intellectual developments from non-Christian sources and new academic horizons that spawned the New Negro solidified new ways of engaging the world. These advances encouraged a renewed interest in Black roots and culture and simultaneously invigorated their association with White thought forms and those of Marxist intellectuals. This fusion of ideas prompted a form of social criticism that was foreign to the Black church's perspective and furthered the perception of its isolation within a cocoon of pietism and "old time" religion.

> **The New Negro** was the African American who was self-confident, urban, and Northern following World War I, in contrast to the stereotype of the Southern Black who gave deference to White people.[a]
>
> [a]Nell Irvin Painter, *Creating Black Americans: African-American History and Its Meanings, 1619 to the Present* (New York: Oxford University Press, 2006).

For the New Negro, the social complexity of the new urban environment demanded a new form of social engagement, and they were not content to rest on traditional church practices to find solutions. For these budding intellectuals, NAACP activists, and the underclass hipsters of 125th Street in Harlem or South Park in Chicago, the church was simply out of style and ceased to offer solutions to contemporary problems.[19] The new Black intelligentsia and growing Black middle class began looking to alternative institutions to meet the social and activistic needs historically met by the church. These new organizations included Greek fraternities and sororities, the NAACP, Masons, Elks, Odd Fellows, and others.

W. E. B. DUBOIS (1868–1963)

The tension between the historic Black church and the New Negro was embodied by Black intellectual and activist W. E. B. DuBois. His departure from his Congregationalist upbringing and embattled ongoing partnership with Black Christianity typified the relationship of many New Negros with the Black church. DuBois was born to a family who was committed to the Congregationalist Church. As he was a young Black boy whose father was estranged and whose mother died in 1885, DuBois's financial support to attend college was nonexistent. Despite the challenges at home, DuBois flourished as a student and was recognized by his high school principal, Edward Van Lennep, as having exceptional potential. Lennep gathered funds from the Congregationalist Church and offered DuBois a scholarship to Fisk University in Nashville. After graduating with a bachelor's degree from Fisk, DuBois earned a second undergraduate degree and a Doctor of Philosophy from Harvard University. DuBois was greatly influenced by two years of study at the University of Berlin during the coursework for his

---

[19]Wilmore, *Black Religion and Black Radicalism*, 194.

doctoral degree. DuBois's formal intellectual journey begun at Fisk in 1885 and culminated in 1895 with his being the first African American to graduate with a PhD from Harvard University.

While at Fisk, an institution established with a commitment to the Christian faith, DuBois's frustration with the legalistic practices of the church grew, and he became further disenchanted with the faith when the charge of heresy was lodged against a New York Episcopal priest whose book on religion and politics was used at Fisk.[20] DuBois later admitted that until the Fisk controversy he never questioned the veracity of his religious convictions. "Its theory had presented no particular difficulties: God ruled the world, Christ loved it, and men did right, or tried to."[21] At this juncture, Christianity repelled DuBois both in theory and in practice.

DuBois's faith was not completely absent at the completion of his Fisk years in 1884, but his drift soon began to materialize. However, it has been argued that a total loss of conventional faith did not come to fruition until he was at Harvard.[22] DuBois arrived at Harvard in 1888 as a junior, frustrated with the Black church and with waning confidence in the power of Christian ideals to aid oppressed Blacks.[23] The time of DuBois's formal education featured a drastic turn away from the Christian faith and toward agnosticism and faith in the social sciences.[24]

Despite DuBois's personal frustrations with the Christian community, his writing and research intentionally engaged the Christian faith because he understood the necessity of rallying the Black church if there was any hope of galvanizing the Black community as a whole. DuBois's intentional interface with churchgoing Blacks is evident in the essays that comprise his book *The Souls of Black Folk*. Each chapter of the monograph began with what DuBois called a "sorrow song" (i.e., a Negro spiritual), and themes from these songs ran throughout the body of the essays. Most poignantly, the essay originally called "The Religion of the American Negro" was later changed to "The Faith of Our Fathers" to endear himself to the Black Christian community. The amended title included a first-person familial reference that associated DuBois with the Christian faith more

---

[20]David Levering Lewis, *W. E. B. DuBois: Biography of a Race 1868–1919* (New York: Henry Holt, 1993), 65.
[21]Lewis, *W. E. B. DuBois*, 66.
[22]Lewis, *W. E. B. DuBois*, 65-66.
[23]Harvard and Yale traditionally required African American baccalaureates to repeat a portion of their undergraduate training, a requirement frequently imposed on White graduates from undistinguished colleges (Lewis, *W. E. B. DuBois*, 82).
[24]Brian Johnson, "The Role of Higher Education in the Religious Transformation of W. E. B. DuBois," *The Journal of Blacks in Higher Education*, no. 59 (Spring 2008): 74-79, here 74.

closely and ultimately beckoned Christians to the cause of working for racial justice across religious and ideological lines.[25]

DuBois leveraged his intentional reach into the Black church for broad (i.e., religious and nonreligious) participation with the NAACP. During its first twenty years of existence, the NAACP became the primary civil rights outpost for middle class African American intellectuals, many of whom had wavering faith in the Black church.[26] DuBois had a strong hand in molding Black public opinion across the country in the struggle for human rights, and his influence was solidified as the NAACP's first elected Black officer. DuBois was also the organization's first full-time employee and editor of *The Crisis*, the NAACP's official publication. *The Crisis*'s influence was widespread, and for the first time there was a Black voice against oppression with significant organizational resources that did not pursue justice from a distinctively Christian perspective.

> **The NAACP's reach** climbed to 6,000 members in 1914, comprising 50 branches. From 1916 to 1920, membership ballooned from 9,000 to 90,000, and by 1946 membership reached approximately 600,000.[a] In November 1910 the first issue of *The Crisis* sold out of all 1,000 copies that were printed. In March 1911, 6,000 were circulated, and that number grew to 25,000 in November 1912 and to 44,000 in 1917. *The Crisis* grew stronger in 1918, boasting 50,000 subscribers and printing 100,000 copies by Easter. In 1919 and 1921 respectively, the publication sold 100,000 and 600,000 copies.
>
> [a]Langston Hughes, *Fight for Freedom: The Story of the NAACP* (New York: Norton, 1962), 11.

Beyond the NAACP's popular influence with *The Crisis*, jurisprudence advocacy and litigation were its chief means of combating racial oppression. The NAACP took on a range of issues, including voter discrimination, residential segregation, courthouse discrimination, and antilynching campaigns in the work of Ida B. Wells, which culminated with the publication of *Thirty Years of Lynching in the United States 1889–1919*. This era witnessed an enduring shift from legislation being used to disenfranchise Blacks to African Americans utilizing legislation to pursue racial equality, and the NAACP was essential to this plot twist.

---

[25]Jonathan S. Kahn, "Religion and the Binding of *The Souls of Black Folk*," *Philosophia Africana* 7, no. 2 (August 2004): 17-31, esp. 18.

[26]Wilmore, *Black Religion and Black Radicalism*, 200. A number of these individuals generally followed the intellectual and secularization pattern of DuBois.

A New Normal 119

> **Ida B. Wells** (1862–1931) was a journalist and activist who led an antilynching campaign beginning in the 1890s. Born into slavery in Holly Springs, Mississippi, she overcame all odds and began teaching in a county school by age fourteen. As an early civil rights leader, she influenced the founding of the NAACP and founded a women's suffrage organization called the National Association of Colored Women's Club.

The NAACP was committed to nonreligious methodologies that were inspired by a vision for democratic socialism that promised the American dream to foster unity spanning a variety of justice seekers.[27] The NAACP's purpose and methods of speechmaking, lobbying, and publicizing were employed broadly—beyond racial, religious, and philosophical boundaries—which resulted in ideological and religious diversity. The NAACP's broad constituency included Christians, social radicals, and Marxist intellectuals, all united by a cry for justice.[28] Collaboration between distinct social groups identified the magnitude of the problem that brought them together.

Historians C. Eric Lincoln and Lawrence H. Mamiya coined the phrase "partial differentiation" to describe the personnel overlap between the Black church and the NAACP.[29] The NAACP created an avenue for Christian and secular social advocates to pursue equal rights for African American people together. For the religious, the organization was particularly timely because it provided an opportunity to influence the political process without raising undue suspicion about the growing divide between the church and state.[30] For the nonreligious, the NAACP's orientation toward jurisprudence shifted the focus away from the Bible and to the US Constitution as the central and authoritative document. Together, the NAACP and the Black church were a two-pronged assault on social and political inequality during this period. The social and political developments also prompted a theological response that allowed the universal truths of the Christian faith to come to bear on the most pressing challenges of the day.

---

[27] Langston Hughes, *Fight for Freedom: The Story of the NAACP* (New York: Norton, 1962), 11.
[28] Wilmore, *Black Religion and Black Radicalism*, 199.
[29] C. Eric Lincoln and Lawrence H. Mamiya, *The Black Church and the African American Experience* (Durham, NC: Duke University Press, 1990), 122-23.
[30] Lincoln and Mamiya, *Black Church*, 9.

8

BUDDING THEOLOGICAL MOVEMENTS

THE INTELLECTUAL AND DENOMINATIONAL developments of the Jim Crow era resulted in new theological movements. Two of those developments were Black Pentecostalism and Black fundamentalism. These groups embodied the priestly and prophetic mission of the Black church, Anchored in the historic doctrines of African American faith, but each persuasion emphasized the doctrinal Anchors of Black Christianity in its own way.

BLACK PENTECOSTALISM

Unlike Black Methodists and Baptists, Pentecostals trace the proliferation of their movement back to an African American minister. Also distinct is that Pentecostalism began as an interracial phenomenon from which Whites later withdrew.[1] The denomination's immediate predecessor was the holiness movement, which emerged in the latter part of the nineteenth century with Charles Fox Parham (1873–1929) and was popularized as Pentecostalism by William Joseph Seymour (1870–1922) via the Azusa Street revival in Los Angeles, which began in 1906 and concluded in 1909. This move of God that sprang from a dilapidated African Methodist Episcopal Church building became the fastest-growing Christian movement in the twentieth century and remains so into the twenty-first century.

> **"Black Pentecostalism"** is a necessary nomenclature because it distinguishes the unique customs and institutions of the Black Pentecostal tradition from White denominational expressions.

---

[1] C. Eric Lincoln and Lawrence H. Mamiya, *The Black Church and the African American Experience* (Durham, NC: Duke University Press, 1990), 76.

The conclusion of the Civil War marked a heightened need for "right living" as soldiers returned home from combat with a moral compass decayed by the trauma of battle. The impact of a generation with diminished moral principles reentering society sparked a religious response among Methodists that was later named the holiness movement. This movement had its roots in the Second Great Awakening and featured notable figures such as Pheobe Palmer and Amanda Smith. Initially, holiness proponents remained within Methodist denominations, and the relationship grew tense. These reformists vigorously critiqued Methodists because it soft-pedaled worldliness expressed in immodest dress, unwholesome entertainment, and indulging in alcohol.

Holiness promoters believed themselves to be returning to the principles of Methodist founders and to the teachings of Scripture. These enthusiasts claimed additional spiritual gifts that included healing and boasted a Spirit-filled worship style that did not cohere with the order of Methodist liturgy. The theological emphasis within the holiness campaign emphasized the two-pronged Anchor of Conversion and Walking in the Spirit. The holiness movement offered a call to sanctification that was preceded by salvation. Salvation was the first act of God's grace, a gift of unmerited favor, given by God to an individual. Sanctification was a second act of God's grace, wherein believers pursued enhanced fellowship with God by removing sinful thoughts and actions that separated them from God.

In 1898, Methodist churches in the South ruled that churches could bar ministers and evangelists from their pulpits who advocated holiness doctrine. This ban on holiness teaching resulted in many leaving Methodist denominations to establish holiness churches. These new churches gave careful attention to the work of the Holy Spirit as recorded in the initial chapters of Acts. Upholding a plain reading of Scripture, some holiness ministers revisited Jesus' promise to baptize the disciples with the Holy Spirit as with fire. This interpretation of Acts resulted in speaking in tongues (glossolalia) as evidence of salvation—which constituted a third act of God's grace. Those who adopted the third act of God's grace became known as Pentecostals.

William Joseph Seymour. Holiness minister and traveling evangelist Charles Fox Parham was the theological architect for Pentecostalism. Parham established several schools, which is where he encountered William Joseph Seymour. Seymour was born to former slaves Simon and Phillis Seymour and hailed from the sleepy town of Centerville, Louisiana. The culture of this little Bayou town, nestled between the Mississippi River and the Gulf of Mexico, played a significant part in the development of a man who changed the course of contemporary religious history.

Throughout Seymour's adolescence, he became more aware of his plight as a Black man in the South. As Seymour understood the frequency and random nature of violent racial attacks, the feeling of imminent doom was overwhelming, and he moved north at the age of twenty-five. Seymour boarded a freight train in 1896, landed in Indianapolis, and remained there until 1899. During his time in Indiana, he chose to attend Simpson Chapel Methodist Episcopal Church because of its focus on basic Christian doctrine, which underscored the doctrinal Anchors of Black faith, and its interracial composition—which Seymour concluded was the outworking of his theological convictions. While a member of Simpson Chapel, Seymour aligned himself with a holiness group called the Evening Light Saints. After moving to Cincinnati in 1900, he joined the Church of God also affiliated with the Evening Light Saints. They, too, abhorred racial violence and held interracial worship services as an indicator of the church's holiness and unity. While at this church Seymour went forward to the alter and was "prayed through" to salvation, and he went a second time and prayed until he was wholly sanctified.[2]

> **William Joseph Seymour's call to ministry** occurred when he contracted smallpox that was so severe that it caused him to go blind in one eye. During his illness, he discerned a calling to divine ministry that he did not immediately express, but he surrendered to the call of becoming a minister and evangelist in time.

Seymour moved to Houston to reunite with his family, and he encountered congregant Lucy Farrow at church. She began to share seemingly strange wonders, including the possibility of a third religious experience that enabled sanctified believers to speak in tongues unknown to them. Seymour accepted this new doctrine, though he did not speak in tongues himself or profess a new experience. Time passed, and in 1905 Farrow moved to Kansas to be a governess for Parham's children. Seymour was appointed the interim pastor for the small holiness church in Houston. Later that year, Farrow returned to Houston with Parham and began a Bible school in the area. After the commencement of his studies with Parham, Seymour began teaching the third blessing of tongues to the holiness congregation in Houston. He was asked to leave the church but continued to study at the Bible school.[3]

---

[2] James S. Tinney, "William J. Seymour: Father of Modern-Day Pentecostalism," *Journal of the Interdenominational Theological Center* 4, no. 1 (Fall 1976): 38.

[3] Rufus G. W. Sanders, *William Joseph Seymour: Black Father of the Twentieth Century Pentecostal/Charismatic Movement* (n.p.: Xulon, 2003), 59; Tinney, "William J. Seymour," 38. See vol. 2 for an excerpt from William J. Seymour's "Receive Ye the Holy Ghost."

Jim Crow laws in Texas forbade Blacks and Whites to sit in the same classroom, but Parham encouraged Seymour to listen to his lectures from the hallway through a cracked door. In 1906, emboldened by his studies, Seymour took a pastorate at a small holiness church in Los Angeles. The first message he preached overflowed with passion and power from Acts 2, highlighting the gift of tongues. Seymour returned to preach the evening service and found the church door padlocked to prevent his entry. After his teaching on tongues was rejected, he returned to the home of some of his parishioners, the Asberrys, where he had dinner that afternoon. The home was located at the now famous 214 Bonnie Brae Street. There, after months of fasting and praying, the Asberry family grew sympathetic to Pentecostal teaching, and Seymour and several others spoke in tongues.[4]

The Azusa Street revival. The popularity of the nightly prayer meeting began spreading across the city. Meetings were characterized by men and women shouting, dancing, weeping, falling on the floor, and, of course, speaking in tongues.[5] The prayer gatherings grew so large that participants and hecklers filled the streets of the neighborhood. The *Los Angeles Times* described the scene as "wild" and the people as "a new sect of fanatics." Seymour was described as "an old colored exhorter" whose glass eye hypnotized believers.[6]

The crowds caused Seymour and other key leaders to search for a nonresidential location to hold the meetings. They discovered an abandoned Methodist church in the business section of Los Angeles, located at 312 Azusa Street. The building had most recently been converted into an animal stable; it featured a sawdust floor, raw wood planks fastened to empty nail kegs as pews, and a pulpit made of two old shoeboxes.[7]

Months after the mission was opened, there were reportedly thirteen hundred attendees present inside the building and another eight hundred on horseback outside. The building, which was eventually dubbed the Apostolic Faith Mission, also drew a number of hecklers, but it is reported that many came to scoff but stayed to pray. Seymour's lifelong dream of racial unity came to fruition amid this revival, which was unheard of in the early twentieth century. Though Blacks were still predominant, there were Whites, Mexicans, Jews, Chinese, Germans, and

---

[4]Vinson Synan, "William Seymour," *Church History* 56 (2000): 18, 40.
[5]Sanders, *William Joseph Seymour*, 87.
[6]*Los Angeles Times*, April 18, 1906, 1.
[7]Robert R. Owens, *Speak to the Rock: The Azusa Street Revival, Its Roots and Its Message* (Lanham, MD: University Press of America, 1998), 62.

Russians in attendance.[8] The revival in Los Angeles had a global footprint. The building on Azusa Street was dubbed "American Jerusalem" because of the vast number of missionaries who were sent throughout the world relying on the power of the Spirit.[9]

The nightly meetings consisted of a traditional Black worship style, which included shouting, trances, and holy dancing, yet the central attraction was tongues. There was often no order of service because the Holy Spirit was in charge. Though meetings were Spirit led, at times Seymour sensed Christ becoming secondary to the phenomena of tongues, and he shouted, "Don't go out of here talking about tongues; talk about Jesus."[10]

The Azusa Street revival featured a cast of leaders who ministered to worshipers and facilitated an environment where sojourners from around the world experienced the Holy Spirit's power. In addition to having interracial roots, the Pentecostal movement was also countercultural because women had a profound shaping hand on the revival. Black and White women ministered side by side, leading corporate worship, preaching, and interpreting tongues. The distinctiveness of the revival captured media attention. The regular sight of a prominent White clergyman or community leader on bended knee before a Black woman who was praying for him to receive Holy Spirit baptism was commonplace.[11]

Seymour's revolutionary incorporation of women in the revival is epitomized when he said at the beginning of the movement,

> Before Jesus ascended to heaven, holy anointing oil had never been poured on a woman's head; but before He organized His church, he called them all into the upper room, those men and women, come on and anointed them with the oil of the Holy Ghost, but this qualifying them all to minister in this Gospel. On the day of Pentecost they all preached through the power of the Holy Ghost. In Christ Jesus there is neither male nor female, all are one.[12]

Despite the movement's egalitarian beginnings, Seymour did not maintain thoroughly egalitarian commitments as the mission gained more structure. This was

---

[8]Larry E. Martin, *The Life and Ministry of William J. Seymour and a History of the Azusa Street Revival* (n.p.: Christian Life Books, 2006), 177, 96; Tinney, "William J. Seymour," 42.

[9]Gary B. McGee, "The Azusa Street Revival and Twentieth-Century Missions," *International Bulletin of Missionary Research* 12, no. 2 (April 1988): 58.

[10]Syana, "William Seymour," 18-19.

[11]Estrelda Y. Alexander, *Black Fire: One Hundred Years of African American Pentecostalism* (Downers Grove, IL: InterVarsity Press, 2011), 295.

[12]Untitled article, *Apostolic Faith* 1, no. 10 (1907): 4.

evident in *The Doctrines and Discipline of the Azusa Street Apostolic Faith Mission of Los Angeles, California*, Seymour's most thorough theological statement. Seymour makes a distinction between men and women and their roles in worship and ministry, most clearly by determining, "All ordination must be done by men not women. Women may be ministers but not . . . baptized or ordained in this work."[13]

Seymour's doctrinal statements were not adopted around the country, and Lucy Turner Smith (1874–1952) emerged as a pillar of the Pentecostal tradition in the Midwest. Smith typified many who arrived in Chicago during the Great Migration. Born on a plantation in rural Georgia, as a single mother she and her nine children moved from Atlanta to Chicago to find the subdued worship style of large Black churches sterile and uninviting.[14] After worshiping at Stone Church, in 1916 Smith established All Nations Pentecostal Church as a result of hosting prayer and faith healings in her one-room apartment on Chicago's South Side. The ministry grew, and the church blessed Blacks and Whites with regular food distributions throughout the Great Depression of the 1920s. The impact of her ministry was widespread in the city, and her funeral was one of the largest the city held, boasting sixty thousand mourners viewing her body and fifty thousand lining the streets for a processional.[15]

In addition to churches, Black Pentecostal women established new denominations. A small outpouring of the Spirit occurred among Blacks on the East Coast. In 1903, Mary Magdalena Tate (1871–1930) traveled as a missionary and evangelist throughout the Midwest and the South, proclaiming the baptism of the Holy Ghost evidenced by glossolalia. Unaware of the revival in Southern California, her followers claimed that this was "the first great Pentecostal revival" and that she "had never seen such manifestation of the power of God in such manner upon anyone except herself." Tate organized two holiness movements into the first congregation of the Church of the Living God the Pillar and Ground of the Truth. As the bishop of this body of churches, she became the first female presiding bishop of a Protestant Christian denomination.[16]

While smaller Pentecostal bodies emerged, the most recognizable was the Church of God in Christ, cofounded by Charles P. Jones and Charles Mason,

---

[13] William J. Seymour, *The Doctrines and Discipline of the Azusa Street Apostolic Faith Mission of Los Angeles, California* (Joplin, MO: Christian Life Books, 2000), 110.
[14] Alexander, *Black Fire*, 304.
[15] Alexander, *Black Fire*, 305.
[16] Alexander, *Black Fire*, 301.

though Mason emerged as its longstanding leader. Mason was licensed as a Baptist minister but was dismissed in 1895 because of his belief in the holiness manifestation of sanctification. Not compelled to silence, Mason gathered a convention after a Baptist association meeting in Jackson, Mississippi, to explore holiness teachings in 1 Corinthians 12. Mason continued to preach as an evangelist and joined Jones, who was also expelled from his state Baptist association.

After being disfellowshipped, Mason and Jones opened a church in 1897 that met in a dilapidated cotton gin, which they called the Church of God. In 1906, it was renamed the Church of God in Christ. Soon after hearing about the Azusa Street revival, Mason, Jones, and two others traveled to Los Angeles to participate in the services. Mason received the gift of tongues while in Southern California. He recalled,

> It seemed that I heard the groaning of Christ on the cross dying for me. All of the work was in me until I died out of the old man. The sound stopped for a little while. My soul cried, "Oh, God, finish your work in me." Then the sound broke out in me again. Then I felt something raising me out of my seat without any effort of my own. I said, "It may be imagination." Then I looked down to see if it was really so. I saw that I was rising. Then I gave up for the Lord to have his way with me. So there came a wave of glory into me, and all of my being was filled with the glory of the Lord. So when I had gotten myself straight on my feet there came a light which enveloped my entire being above the brightness of the sun. When I opened my mouth to say glory, a flame touched my tongue which ran down to me. My language changed and no word could I speak in my own tongue.[17]

After this experience, Mason's life was never the same. Pentecostal themes including glossolalia, deliverance from demons, and healing characterized his teaching. During an upcoming Church of God in Christ general assembly, Mason moved that Pentecostal doctrine be adopted, and it was not well received. Most notably, Jones broke away from the Church of God in Christ with the majority of the churches to form the Church of God in Christ (Holiness), USA, and Mason remained as the leader of the Church of God in Christ.

The Church of God in Christ was the only incorporated Pentecostal body from 1907 to 1914. As a result, independent Pentecostal churches appealed to its

---

[17]Elsie W. Mason, "Bishop C. H. Mason, Church of God in Christ," in *Afro-American Religious History: A Documentary Witness*, ed. Milton C. Sernett (Durham, NC: Duke University Press, 1999), 286.

authority, and one of the Church of God in Christ's primary functions was to serve as an ordination body for Black and White Pentecostal ministers who, upon ordination, were all officially designated Church of God in Christ clergymen. In the second decade of the twentieth century, White Pentecostal ministers ordained by Mason capitulated to segregation mandates and established the Assemblies of God in 1914. With the establishment of a White Pentecostal denomination, the denomination's interracial beginnings stalled almost completely by 1924.[18]

Amid the denominational turbulence, Mason remained innovative in his methods of expanding the Church of God in Christ's reach. Taking a page from the Great Awakenings and capitalizing on the displacement caused by the Great Migration, Mason sent out evangelists on horseback, who made converts and formed new churches. These and other methods caused the denomination to grow to over four hundred thousand by Mason's death in the early 1960s, making it the second largest African American Christian body, second to the National Baptist Convention.

The women of the Church of God in Christ. True to its Pentecostal roots, the Church of God in Christ historically ordained men, but the influence of women was unmistakable. Despite the denomination's affirmation of complementary gender roles, its disposition toward women serving in the local church and as missionaries was distinct from longstanding Black denominations. As Baptist and Methodist women experienced increasing ministry restrictions, they sought a place to serve in Church of God in Christ churches. Recognizing this trend, Mason appointed Arkansas native Lizzie Woods Roberson (1860–1945) to establish a women's department to serve Church of God in Christ women and to facilitate discipleship throughout the churches.

THE CHURCH OF GOD IN CHRIST ON WOMEN IN MINISTRY

While recognizing women's talents more readily than other denominations, the Church of God in Christ's leadership stated in 1973 that the New Testament gave no strong indication that women should serve as elders, bishops, or pastors. Rather, they were to play support roles, through which they could help men fulfill their responsibilities as church leaders.

Roberson typified many women affiliated with the Church of God in Christ. She was Baptist affiliated but received the indwelling of the Holy Spirit during a

---

[18]Lincoln and Mamiya, *Black Church*, 81.

service led by Charles Mason while she was a student at the Baptist Missionary Society School. Roberson catalyzed women throughout the denomination and led in their missionary efforts.[19]

Among Church of God in Christ women, Amanda Berry Smith (1837–1915) was a Methodist who encountered holiness teaching through Phoebe Palmer (1807–1874) and her evangelistic ministry. Smith garnered national name recognition during her travels as she preached at revivals to both Blacks and Whites associated with the National Camp Meeting Association for the Promotion of Holiness. As time passed, women continued to positively affect the denomination. While not being ordained for the express purpose of leading a church, a growing number of seminary-trained Church of God in Christ women were ordained to serve as military chaplains, to lead churches during a pastoral transition (without the title of pastor), and to serve as missionaries who were able to "speak" but not preach.

The post-Mason years. The Church of God in Christ experienced unprecedented growth under the leadership of Bishop Mason, who died in November 1961. The denomination's growth is particularly impressive in light of the national racial turmoil that characterized his tenure. The death of a founder and charismatic leader is often difficult for an organization, and this was also true of the Church of God in Christ. Often called the denomination's "wilderness wanderings," the period following Mason's death was characterized by passionate conflict and litigation by those seeking to chart a constructive path forward. The period of conflict resulted in Bishop James Patterson (Tennessee's overseer and Mason's son-in-law) being elected as presiding bishop. This office replaced that of senior bishop that Mason occupied. The denomination's wilderness wanderings caused several of its churches to create their own denomination in 1969, most significantly the Church of God in Christ, International.

In the second half of the 1960s, the Church of God in Christ regrouped and continued to nurture its churches with the establishment of the Charles H. Mason Theological Seminary, the Church of God in Christ's official institution of theological education. Preliminary planning for the seminary was conducted by Senior Bishop Ozro Thurston Jones Sr. in 1965, and the plans were approved by the general assembly in 1968. The administration was headed by Presiding Bishop James Patterson Sr.

---

[19] Anne H. Pinn and Anthony B. Pinn, *The Fortress Introduction to Black Church History* (Minneapolis: Fortress, 2002), 115.

Budding Theological Movements 129

> **Charles H. Mason Theological Seminary** is part of the Interdenominational Theological Center. The Interdenominational Theological Center is a cooperative ecumenical initiative for theological education that features five Protestant denominational seminaries for several historically Black denominations.

The Church of God in Christ and other Pentecostal movements represent a resurgence of spiritualized faith among Blacks in the first half of the twentieth century. This movement's doctrinal convictions upheld the Anchors of the African American Christian tradition but emphasized the third Anchor, with a particular emphasis on Walking in the Spirit with renewed fervor manifested in speaking in tongues. This emphasis on Conversion and Walking in the Spirit was coupled with a deemphasis of the fifth Anchor, Deliverance. While Black Pentecostals did not turn a blind eye toward social challenges, Black Pentecostalism's emphasis on the individual's spirituality was a greater cause of theological reflection among Pentecostals. This new, Spirit-filled movement developed alongside another spiritually oriented movement known as Black fundamentalism. These new movements contest assumptions that Black Christianity has maintained an exclusive focus on social issues rather than spiritual formation.

BLACK FUNDAMENTALISM

The changing intellectual climate of the early twentieth century featured Darwinian evolution and modern biblical criticism, which encouraged a rationalist and naturalistic reading of Scripture. These adaptations to Christian doctrine caused many modernized Christians to abandon or revise central Christian beliefs, including the virgin birth of Christ, the divine inspiration of Scripture, and the resurrection of Jesus.[20]

In the face of these cultural developments, which mushroomed in the 1920s, fundamentalism emerged as an antimodern Christian movement that championed theological notions that accord with several of the doctrinal Anchors of Black faith. Most pronounced was biblical inerrancy, which affirmed the authority of the biblical text that is common throughout the African American Christian story. In addition, the deity of Christ, Jesus' virgin birth, and the literal (bodily) return of Christ were emphasized, which was a new way of emphasizing existing doctrinal commitments within the second Anchor of the tradition.

---

[20]See vol. 2 for an excerpt from William L. Banks's "Cults and the Negro."

There was also an insistence on holy living that accords with the third Anchor (Walking in the Spirit), but this persuasion of the faith had a tendency to veer into legalism. Like Black Pentecostals, however, Black fundamentalists were concerned about the social and economic realities that affected the Black community, but lengthy theological reflection on Deliverance was not a central concern for the movement. Fundamentalists battled for theological commitments in a world that they saw as having turned its back on God and his saving power.[21] Despite these doctrinal commitments, Black fundamentalism's defining feature was not theology but its militantly antimodern ethos, which set it apart from other forms of Christianity.[22]

Black fundamentalists shared similar concerns to what was often summarized as the "old-time religion" that transformed the nation during the Great Awakenings, which marked the first documented explosion of Christianity among Blacks in America. This included a commitment to biblical literalism—especially regarding supernaturalism—and a stalwart insistence on a Big God as Creator to undercut the theory of Darwinism. These theological commitments were often articulated in the language of *The Fundamentals*. Yet, despite agreement on these core theological issues, African Americans in historically Black denominations—especially Baptists and Methodists—did not regularly self-identify as fundamentalists because of the overt racism that festered within its institutions.

> **The Fundamentals: A Testimony to the Truth** is a set of ninety essays that were originally published in quarterly volumes spanning 1910 to 1915 and later bound into a four-volume set addressing threats to Christian doctrine by modernism and Darwinism. These volumes are considered the founding documents of Christian fundamentalism.

Moreover, despite the shared doctrinal commitments between Black and White fundamentalists, Blacks intentionally chose not to align themselves with White fundamentalists because of their segregationist heritage and failure to acknowledge the social problems that plagued Black life in America. Likewise, Black fundamentalists resisted association with modernists, despite their commitment to

---

[21] Mary Beth Swetnam Matthews, *Doctrine and Race: African American Evangelicals and Fundamentalism Between the Wars* (Tuscaloosa: University of Alabama Press, 2017), 3-4.
[22] Daniel R. Bare, *Black Fundamentalists: Conservative Christianity and Racial Identity in the Segregation Era* (New York: New York University Press, 2021), 12.

ameliorating Black social challenges, because many lacked commitment to historic Christian doctrines and the biblical text they held dear.[23] Throughout the 1920s and '30s, the social and theological tightrope that Black fundamentalists walked was on display in denominational publications that offered extended coverage of the fundamentalist-modernist controversy and included some Blacks affirming arguments against modernism made by Whites.

Many Black fundamentalists insisted that White Christians were weak of mind because modernism was invented by White people and disproportionately caused many to leave the faith behind in their own communities. In addition, Black fundamentalists critiqued White fundamentalists who accepted segregationist social policies. Due to these failings, some Blacks considered themselves to be the guardians of orthodoxy.

Jonathan H. Frank, editor of the *National Baptist Union Review*, described the United States' dual struggle as the Great War followed by the fundamentalist-modernist controversy. He insisted, "Thus far colored folks are not engaging in the unholy task of explaining away the scriptures because of scientific thought, so called." Frank also wrote that Black Christians did not engage in atheism, biology, philosophy, and sociology as attempts to understand the world. However, White people might rely on "the spirit of modern progress," and they might not fear "a new religion" but, he assured his readers, "colored folks are not ready as yet to discard Christianity for civilization. Thank God."[24]

> **MODERNISM IN BLACK THOUGHT**
>
> Despite some Blacks insisting that modernism was a White problem, it would be disingenuous not to acknowledge the modern influence on Black intellectuals. The most prominent Black intellectual of the early and mid-twentieth century, W. E. B. DuBois, was deeply influenced by rationalism during his doctoral studies in Germany and enthusiastically substituted old-time religion with the social sciences for discovering truth about the world.

Black fundamentalists existed within historically Black denominations, which necessitated a distinctively less separatist tendency than their White counterparts. White fundamentalists severed associational and denominational ties to any manifestation of modernism and liberalism, but Blacks often existed side by side with

---

[23] Matthews, *Doctrine and Race*, 2, 69.
[24] Matthews, *Doctrine and Race*, 42.

a broader swath of believers.[25] Black fundamentalists resisted splintering from longstanding affiliations because the racial context complicated establishing new entities, but most significantly Black Christians affirmed the need to address social ills that negatively affected the Black community, a task for which doctrinal uniformity was not prerequisite.

> **Doctrinal uniformity** was not the norm within Black denominations; however, individual churches organically typify strict theological unity.

Consistent with the Deliverance ethos of African American faith, social action was an enduring hallmark of Black fundamentalism, but the focus contrasted with what was often associated with the broader fundamentalist movement. Consistent with the African American Christian tradition, Black fundamentalists focused their collective social energy on opposing segregation, promoting equality for all, and seeking social uplift for marginalized people regardless of their ethnic background. This contrasted with other fundamentalists, who devoted their social energy to opposing the teaching of evolution in public schools and resisting the proliferation of modernism from the universities into the public square.

The social expression of Black fundamentalism highlights yet another reason that there was no overt association with White fundamentalism. Among White fundamentalists, affinity constituted more than just agreement on the theological commitments summarized in *The Fundamentals*; it required an antagonistic disposition toward specific social problems from the institutions of their making. As a result, White fundamentalism marginalized "those who might have been theologically aligned with the movement but whose cultural context and social circumstances prohibited overt participation in the movement's institutional structures."[26]

Black fundamentalists fused two traditions that are often assumed to be mutually exclusive, namely, theological conservatism and social progressivism. Black fundamentalists, along with countless faithful saints in the African American Christian story, transcend the labels liberal and conservative. While some Black Christians fit the binary, the bulk of Black Christians find their home outside this spectrum. The term *conservative* assumes opposition to the social status quo, which did not befit Black Christians—including fundamentalists. Likewise, the

---

[25]Bare, *Black Fundamentalists*, 8.
[26]Bare, *Black Fundamentalists*, 7-8.

nomenclature *liberal* presupposes opposition to the old-time religion that Black Christians endeavored to preserve.[27]

> **FALSE ASSOCIATIONS**
> Conflating social conservatism and theological orthodoxy, on the one hand, and fusing social progressivism and theological liberalism, on the other hand, are false constructs. This wrongheaded synthesis causes those outside the Black Christian community—who see only its social activity—to more eastly mistake Black Christians as theological liberals. This non sequitur puts an inappropriate burden on Black Christians to prove their orthodoxy among believers of other ethnicities.

These new movements, Black Pentecostalism and Black fundamentalism, combined with the strain on African American congregations during and after the years of the Great Migration, multiplied the complexities of shepherding a Black congregation during this period. These two theological movements continue to exert their force on the theological landscape of Black Christianity in the United States. The theological Anchors of the tradition find their unique emphasis within these movements, and each Anchor persists in its own way among Black Pentecostals and Black fundamentalists.

---

[27] Matthews, *Doctrine and Race*, 7.

9

THE ROAD TO THE CIVIL RIGHTS MOVEMENT

THE THEOLOGICAL DIVERSITY THAT EMERGED within the Jim Crow era is astounding compared to the previous periods of Black Christianity in the United States. From the Great Migration encounter with other faiths to the priestly emphasis of Black Pentecostalism and Black fundamentalism, Black Christians were not left without a faith expression that had a keen interest in the Deliverance Anchor of African American Christianity. The Black social gospel tradition emerged from faithful pastors, including figures such as Cesar Blackwell (1769–1845), Adam Daniel Williams (1863–1931), and Martin Luther King Sr. (1897–1984), who insisted that a pastor was responsible for the holistic well-being of their parishioners. They preached a gospel with social implications, anchored in a belief in personal salvation and the need to apply the gospel of Jesus to the daily problems of their congregants.[1]

Distinct from the social gospel of Walter Rauschenbusch (1861–1918), this tradition was rooted in the long-held doctrinal Anchors of African American faith and expressed in the priestly and prophetic mission of the Black church. In the early decades of the twentieth century, sons of this movement began matriculating into university divinity schools, which served as an incubator for the theological foundations that sustained the civil rights movement.

The theologically motivated response to Black inequality during the Jim Crow era cannot be divorced from its foundations. The African American Christian story follows a discernible pattern that is common throughout church history—namely, a three-generation cycle beginning with *institutional creativity*, followed by a time of *intellectual deepening*, and concluding with a phase of *public impact*.[2]

---

[1] "King, Martin Luther, Sr.," The Martin Luther King, Jr. Research and Education Institute, Stanford University, https://kinginstitute.stanford.edu/king-martin-luther-sr (accessed October 28, 2023).
[2] Mark Noll, *God and Race in American Politics: A Short History* (Princeton, NJ: Princeton University Press, 2008), 57.

For Black Christians, institutional creativity occurred with the boom of ecclesial and academic institutions during Reconstruction. The often-overlooked first half of the twentieth century constituted a period of intellectual deepening, and the civil rights movement was its public impact.

THE BLACK SOCIAL GOSPEL

Amid the struggle for equality, the civil rights era was a significant time of African American intellectual deepening. Gayraud Wilmore's lament of a lull in activist radicalism notwithstanding (see chap. 7), the reclamation of social impact in the Black church under Martin Luther King Jr. would have been impossible without the theological development that required quiet moments in libraries around the country and intellectually stimulating pilgrimages around the world. King's sophisticated theological framework was built on a foundation laid by Black religious intellectuals in the 1930s and '40s. The Black intellectual awakening that provided the theological groundwork for King and the civil rights movement was in part the result of Blacks obtaining important academic positions and creating scholastic environments that provided the intellectual freedom to theologize a religiously based assault on segregation.[3]

As African Americans secured significant positions in the academy, Black Christianity came of age. While there were numerous Black religious intellectuals in the academy, this account focuses on developments that directly influenced the theological maturation of King and ultimately the civil rights movement (1955–1968). Mordecai Wyatt Johnson (1891–1976) was a centerpiece in the formation of the Black religious intellectual. Johnson served as the first Black president of Howard University, from 1926 until 1960. Johnson was the son of former slaves and was compelled to formalize the insights of the Black social gospel in light of the parallel work of Walter Rauschenbusch and its ability to provide theological answers to the struggles that plagued poor people.[4] While at Howard, Johnson recruited the brightest Black scholars in the nation to an environment that fostered a unique interplay of ideas to combat segregation.

Johnson's band of scholars was essential to cultivating King's theological paradigm, which energized the civil rights movement. Most significantly, Johnson

---

[3]Dennis C. Dickerson, "African American Religious Intellectuals and the Theological Foundations of the Civil Rights Movement, 1930–55," *American Society of Church History* 74, no. 2 (June 2005): 218.
[4]Jessie Carney Smith, ed., "Mordecai W. Johnson," in *Notable Black American Men* (Detroit: Gale, 1998), book 2.

hired Benjamin E. Mays (1894–1984) as dean of the School of Religion, who went on to serve as president of Morehouse College and was a mentor to the young King during his studies. Mays's desire for theological education was to produce clergy who were distinguished intellectually, applied Scripture to contemporary social and economic challenges, and were committed to challenging the social caste and ending legalized segregation.[5]

> **Benjamin E. Mays** (1894–1984) was often called "the schoolmaster of the [civil rights] movement." In 1921, Mays took a pastorate at Shiloh Baptist Church in Atlanta for two years, later joining the faculty at Morehouse College. Mays earned a master's degree and was appointed dean of the Howard University School of Religion in 1934, a year before completing his PhD at the University of Chicago. He was appointed the sixth president of Morehouse College in 1940, where he enjoyed a twenty-seven-year tenure.[a]
>
> [a]See vol. 2 for an excerpt from Mays's autobiography, *Born to Rebel*.

In addition to Mays, Johnson hired Howard Thurman to the faculty to assist in developing theological answers to social problems. Thurman's fingerprints are all over the theological framework that drove the civil rights movement—despite his becoming a mystic later in life. Thurman also influenced King directly when he was appointed dean of Marsh Chapel in his final year of doctoral residency. Despite only having a year together in Boston, Thurman and King shared fond personal memories of watching the World Series on television together. Their relationship was reaffirmed when Thurman traveled to comfort King and offer advice after King was stabbed in New York. Beyond their friendship, Thurman formed King's theological moorings, as journalist Lerone Bennett claimed that King traveled with a well-worn copy of Thurman's *Jesus and the Disinherited*.[6]

> **Howard Thurman** (1899–1981) was installed as professor of religion at Howard University in 1932, where he also served as the first dean of Rankin Chapel. In 1936, he was the first person to lead a delegation of African Americans to India to meet with Mahatma Gandhi, which directly affected his mentorship of Martin Luther

---

[5]Dickerson, "African American Religious Intellectuals," 223-24.
[6]Edward Crowther, "'I Am Fundamentally a Baptist Clergyman,' Martin Luther King Jr., Social Christianity, and the Baptist Faith in the Era of Civil Rights," in *Through a Glass Darkly: Contested Notions of Baptist Identity*, ed. Keith Harper (Tuscaloosa: University of Alabama Press, 2012), 180.

> King Jr. In 1944, Thurman accepted an invitation to be copastor of Fellowship of All People (Fellowship Church) in San Francisco—the first interracial, interfaith church in the United States. In 1953, Thurman departed California to serve as dean of Marsh Chapel at Boston University.

George Kelsey also exerted a profound impact on King and the civil rights movement from his professorate at Morehouse College. Despite never having taught at Howard, Kelsey delivered lectures and contributed to a volume with Thurman and Mays titled *The Christian Way in Race Relations*, edited by William Stuart Nelson, in 1948. Kelsey had a profound impact on King as he completed his PhD in philosophy from Yale as he taught King during his studies at Morehouse. King admired Kelsey's philosophical rigor and his conviction that Christianity was essential to addressing racial issues in society. King also credited Kelsey with helping him to reconcile the biblical text with his doubts about its literal usefulness. King found that his intellect could be used to uncover God's deep moral truths for daily life.[7]

> **George Kelsey** (1910–1996) was a renowned Christian intellectual and pastor. After graduating from Morehouse College in 1934, he was valedictorian at Andover Newton Theological School and matriculated into a Doctor of Philosophy program at Yale University. During his doctoral studies, he took a teaching post at Morehouse University and simultaneously served as a minister at Providence Baptist Church. During his time at Morehouse, Kelsey shaped the minds of many, including Martin Luther King Jr. Their relationship extended beyond the classroom, and when King was writing *Stride Towards Freedom*, where he clarified his stance on nonviolence, he sent his manuscript to Kelsey requesting his critique.

Black religious intellectuals such as Johnson, Mays, Thurman, and Kelsey—all ordained Baptist ministers—wrote multiple books, lectured around the world, and preached numerous sermons that condemned segregation as sinful. These scholars theologized direct action techniques and advocated nonviolent strategies that contested Jim Crow segregation. In doing so, they laid a theological foundation for Martin Luther King Jr. and the civil rights movement.[8]

---

[7]Crowther, "I Am Fundamentally," 180, 190. See vol. 2 for an excerpt from George D. Kelsey's "The Christian Way in Race Relations."
[8]Dickerson, "African American Religious Intellectuals," 219.

The echoes of Mays, Thurman, and Kelsey in King's theological formulation come into sharper focus in light of the historical faith of the Black church. The themes of justice, hope, and love, which ground King's thought, are rooted in the Black church's faith in Jesus Christ. The importance of Scripture as the means of revealing Christ in Black Christianity cannot be overstated. After King's widely known doubts about biblical literalism, his rejuvenated trust in Scripture situated him to understand Christ and therefore justice, hope, and love.

The Jesus that Anchored the Black social gospel movement stands in contrast to the dominant christological formulations of the day. Thurman's *Jesus and the Disinherited* explores who Christ is for those whose "backs are against the wall."[9] Thurman advocates for a Christ at the center who sides with the poor, oppressed, and depressed. It follows that Christ stands against unjust systems and is intensely present with those who "stand up for righteousness," as Thurman reassured King in his kitchen during a sleepless night in the early days of the civil rights movement.

In addition to the person of Christ, Black religious intellectuals and King alike rooted their pursuit of justice in a robust kingdom theology with implications for the current moment. Mays writes:

> The Christian is a citizen of two worlds: the world that now is and the world that ought to be. He is a part of the existing order with all of its imperfections, shortcomings, and brutality. Yet he can never accept the present order.... The Christian's allegiance is to the God of Jesus Christ and not to any particular economic, political, national, racial, or denominational order.... If a man really believes in God, in Jesus, and in man, there will be, and there must be, tension between him and the world in which he lives. And this tension can never be completely resolved unless he accepts the world as it is—which the true Christian can never do.[10]

Mays's kingdom vision and its contemporary ramifications offered a divinely established imperative for justice and a renewed hope for unity, which bolstered his pursuit of Deliverance. Kelsey further illuminates the nature of the kingdom and the hope for an abiding unification of humanity:

> The Kingdom is now present; but it is present in only a small way, it is not here "in fullness of power." It is here as a little more than a "mustard

---

[9]Howard Thurman, *Jesus and the Disinherited* (Boston: Beacon, 1996), 11. See vol. 2 for an excerpt from this work.

[10]Benjamin E. Mays, "The Obligations of the Individual Christian," in *The Christian Way in Race Relations* (New York: Harper, 1948), 209-10.

seed." It is yet to become a full tree. We recognize the presence of the Kingdom means union. It is the most thoroughgoing expression of universalism, for the principle of its union is God. All other types of union—institutions, clubs, and societies of all sorts—are oriented around some one or more particulars.[11]

The love necessary for supernatural unity has its origins outside humanity—in a Big God himself. Kelsey rightly argues, "All men are sinners. . . . Christianity does not know of two [human] camps, the one constituted of saints and the other of sinners. There is only one camp; it is mankind standing before God in sin and in need of redemption."[12] Kelsey explains how, after a person is transformed into one who is capable of the love required for unity, union with Christ and Walking in the Spirit have far-reaching implications that include race relations:

> In its highest expression, the Christian ethic is not an ethic of race relations. It is an ethic of the individual and mankind; it is not an ethic of a nation, class, or race. It is the theory of the Christian life, which issues from the union of the soul with God. . . . It means the abandonment of the self to Christ, so that it is no longer the self which thinks, feels, speaks, or acts, but Christ.[13]

The love that is the product of Christian transformation stands in stark contrast with human-centered attempts to love the "other." Kelsey admonishes Christian leaders that the hope of a just society comes only through divinely imparted love. He argues,

> In an effort to improve the attitudes of one racial group toward another, Christian teachers commonly point to the contributions of literature, arts, and sciences of the group of poorer reputation. From what has been said above, it can be seen that such emphasis is irrelevant to essential Christian teaching. The worth of the individual does not lie in his writing a poem or making a scientific discovery. A human being or a group has value because he or it is valuable for God. Any other valuation is based entirely on human judgment and is, therefore, both selfish and from a particularistic point of view.[14]

---

[11] George D. Kelsey, "The Christian Way in Race Relations," in *Christian Way in Race Relations*, 34.
[12] Kelsey, "Christian Way in Race Relations," 32.
[13] Kelsey, "The Christian Way in Race Relations," 29-30.
[14] Kelsey, "Christian Way in Race Relations," 35.

Mays explicitly roots the brotherhood in humanity's common source of life, the Creator God. True to the methodology of the Black religious intellectuals and King, Mays asserts his logic in the realm of public life. He says:

> The Christian is also committed to a belief in man. This involves a belief in the intrinsic worth of each individual and, since God is the author of life, a belief in the kinship of all humanity, in the fatherhood of God, and in the brotherhood of man. Though living all the time in the imperfect world, the Christian is obligated in all social relations to strive to square his life with the best there is in the Christian tradition.[15]

Mays's argument concludes with the daily social coexistence of humanity. His transition from theological anthropology to social ethics was a step that numerous Christians disavowed because, as Kelsey writes, "Many Americans need to believe that they can meet the requirements of Christian love by loving the souls of members of another race while holding their bodies in contempt."[16] The Christian faith embraces whole persons, both soul and body, and assumes a robust Christian ethic.

Thurman agrees, asserting: "Implicit in the Christian message is a profoundly revolutionary ethic. This ethic appears as the binding relationship between men, conceived as children of a common Father, God. The ethic is revolutionary because the norms it establishes are in direct conflict with the relationship that obtains between men in the modern world."[17] The blessed hope of God, the author of life, and a kingdom vision that necessitates justice, hope, and love results in an ethic that transforms communities and churches. Mays insists that "separate churches for people may not be un-Christian but segregated churches are un-Christian."[18]

Constrained by these theological convictions, although he spent time chiding Whites, Mays boldly encourages Blacks not to hate Whites:

> Despite jim crow, segregation, and discrimination, which he meets almost incessantly, the Negro Christian does not have to hate white people. Even when he piles up evidence to prove that efforts are being made to keep him a second-class citizen, it is not foreordained of God that he has to nurture rancor in his heart and hate in his soul. He can rise above hate.[19]

---

[15] Mays, "Obligations of the Individual Christian," 209.
[16] Kelsey, "Christian Way in Race Relations," 229.
[17] Howard Thurman, "Judgment and Hope in the Christian Message," in *Christian Way*, 229.
[18] Mays, "Obligations of the Individual Christian," 223.
[19] Mays, "Obligations of the Individual Christian," 224. King's emphasis on loving the oppressor parallels Mays and is similar to Thurman's idea of transformative and redemptive love. Thurman writes:

Firmly Anchored in the Black faith tradition, Mays, Kelsey, and Thurman lovingly and prophetically engaged racism and segregation with overtly theological language. Their theological convictions highlighted a Big God who was the ground of their theological ethic and the father of all humanity, forging a transracial brotherhood. The emphasis on Jesus accentuated his identification with Blacks whose "backs are against the wall" but also made a way for Conversion and empowered Blacks to Walk in the Spirit and treat others as brothers. Finally, the Deliverance imperative was highlighted by insistence on a coming kingdom, which has clear implications for action in the present. Resonance with Anchors of the African American tradition in the struggle for Black equality was passed along to the students of Mays, Kelsey, and Thurman, most notably King, and others who led the civil rights movement.

THE KINDLING OF THE CIVIL RIGHTS MOVEMENT

One stride toward freedom after another had been taken by Blacks since the mysterious cargo arrived on the Dutch man-of-war in 1619. Like thunder follows lightning, each heroic step toward Black uplift was met with a racist backlash intended to keep Blacks in their place. In the mid-1950s, those strides and their reactions reached a fever pitch that sparked a movement unlike any the nation had ever seen. The shock waves that caused the civil rights movement were the aftermath of the *Brown v. Board* decision, the infamous murder of Emmitt Till, the arrest of Rosa Parks, and the ensuing Montgomery bus boycott. The nation was at a breaking point. These nationally televised events in close succession served as a catalyst for the Black church's unmistakable surge back into the center of the public drama of race relations.

The most iconic court case the NAACP Legal Defense and Education Fund won was the 1954 *Brown v. Board of Education* suit, which deemed racially segregated schools unconstitutional.[20] The aftermath of the *Brown* decision revealed the true character of race relations in America. The juxtaposition between the legal victories celebrated by the NAACP and the response of average White Americans was glaring. In the South, public-opinion polls demonstrated that 80 percent of White Southerners opposed school desegregation. Consequently, actualizing school

---

"The religion of Jesus says to the disinherited: 'Love your enemy. Take the initiative in seeking ways by which you can have the experience of a common sharing of mutual worth and value. It may be hazardous, but you must do it.' For the Negro it means that he must see the individual white man in the context of a common humanity" (quoted in Crowther, "I Am Fundamentally," 180).

[20]The Legal Defense and Education Fund was established in 1940 under the leadership of Thurgood Marshall as the legal arm of the NAACP.

desegregation was a long and difficult process that caused grassroots African Americans to grow weary of the NAACP's method of jurisprudence, especially since the organization became less of a protest agency and focused almost exclusively on litigation and lobbying after World War II.[21]

> **The attack on the NAACP** by White supremacist groups was vicious after its victory, which legally toppled school segregation. The NAACP lost 246 branches in the South by 1958, and NAACP membership in the South dropped from nearly 50 percent to approximately 25 percent of the organization's registrants.[a] Much of the NAACP's attention was diverted from legal advocacy for the race toward freedom to vying for its own existence.
>
> [a]Harvard Sitkoff, *The Struggle for Black Equality* (New York: Hill and Wang, 2008), 27.

The ongoing difficulty of implementing the *Brown* ruling was exacerbated by the heinous murder of Emmett Till (1941–1955), a fourteen-year-old African American boy who lived in Chicago. While visiting relatives in Money, Mississippi, he was murdered for allegedly flirting with a White cashier at a grocery store. Till's killers beat him in a barn, gouged out his eyes, shot him in the head, and threw him in to the Tallahatchie River with a cotton gin fan tied to his neck. Emmett's mother elected to have an open-casket funeral to show the world what hate looked like. The nation was gripped by this story, and the two men accused were acquitted after being tried before an all-White jury.

With the brokenness of the justice system on full display after the September 23, 1955, verdict of the Till trial, the nation soon witnessed the December 1, 1955, arrest of Rosa Parks (1913–2005). After a long day of work in Montgomery, Alabama, Parks was instructed by a bus driver to give up her seat for a White passenger. She refused and was detained by police.

The news of Parks's arrest spread around the city with the help of many, but especially JoAnn Robinson (1912–1992). She led the Women's Political Council and distributed leaflets to Blacks in Montgomery urging them to attend a mass meeting. The meeting's location was a point of serious deliberation because the host site needed to transcend any factions to encourage broad participation. Against the host minister's desires, the meeting was held at his church because he had not been in town long enough to make either many friends or many enemies. The church

---

[21]Harvard Sitkoff, *The Struggle for Black Equality* (New York: Hill and Wang, 2008), 24, 17-18. Also see Risa Guluboff, *The Promise of Civil Rights* (Cambridge, MA: Harvard University Press, 2010).

was Dexter Avenue Baptist Church, and the minister was Reverend Martin Luther King Jr., a newly appointed pastor.

Several ministers sought to rally the crowd to no avail, so Reverend King mounted the pulpit and delivered an extemporaneous plea to the people of Montgomery that mobilized the Montgomery Improvement Association on December 5, 1955. Under the leadership of King, Black ministers and community leaders coordinated a bus boycott that challenged segregation laws in the state and brought national attention to racism in the South. The 381-day boycott (December 1, 1955, to December 20, 1956) sidestepped the NAACP's pattern of using the courtroom alone to dismantle White supremacy. The ideological shift toward nonviolent direct action commanded immediate attention, which directly influenced the Supreme Court's *Browder v. Gayle* decision in 1956, the case that successfully ended segregation in Montgomery's city bus system.

King recognized the need to capitalize on the momentum generated by the success of the boycott in Montgomery, so on January 10-11, 1957, he gathered sixty Black civil rights–minded clergy from ten states to discuss the coordination of efforts against racism throughout the South.[22] From this meeting the Southern Conference on Transportation and Nonviolent Integration was born. At the first meeting of the conference, in Montgomery in August 1957, the leaders adopted a new name, the Southern Christian Leadership Conference.[23]

With activists no longer waiting for the NAACP to plead their case in court, the development of the Southern Christian Leadership Conference ushered in a new chapter in the fight for civil rights that activated grassroots Blacks weary of their daily struggle against racism. Now the Southern Black church once again became the foremost leader in the fight against White oppression—transferring the mantel from Northern Black elites who focused on legal action in courtrooms. In short, the struggle for Black equality was taken from the courthouse to the church house and spilled out into the streets.

Examples of nonviolent direct action during the civil rights movement include the sit-in movement (beginning in February 1960), freedom rides (beginning in May 1961), the Albany movement (October 1961–August 1962), "Project C" in Birmingham (beginning in 1963), "Freedom Summer" in Mississippi (1964), and the Chicago freedom movement (mid-1965 to early 1967), among others.

---

[22] Sitkoff, *Struggle for Black Equality*, 56.
[23] See vol. 2 for Fred Shuttlesworth's letter to Martin Luther King Jr. in 1959.

The ministerial leadership of the Southern Christian Leadership Conference asserted theologically derived convictions for a just society and catalyzed the masses to nonviolent demonstrations to exact strategic pressure on unjust laws throughout the South. These protests were often organized by conference leadership in conjunction with local clergy. Mass demonstrations were preceded by failed attempts to unravel a particular unjust law (or laws) in private meetings with local government leaders. The goal of protests was to draw attention to unjust legislation through media and to cause lawmakers to pursue a just course of action.[24]

During their many days of protest, demonstrators met in churches, sang hymns (often spirituals), and prayed in preparation to meet the violence of racist mobs with nonviolence. This church-led movement climaxed on August 28, 1963—the eighth anniversary of Emmett Till's murder—with an estimated 200,000–300,000 people participating in the March on Washington, punctuated by Martin Luther King Jr.'s famous "I Have a Dream" speech.

> **Non-Christian influences in the civil rights movement** cannot be ignored. The leadership and resources of the Black church notwithstanding, the contributions of non-Christian Black leaders were a vital part of the movement. Most notable are W. E. B. DuBois (1868–1963), A. Phillip Randolph (1889–1979), Zora Neale Hurston (1891–1960), Richard Wright (1908–1960), and James Baldwin (1924–1987).

The foot soldiers. There would have been no civil rights movement without the foot soldiers—the faceless masses who organized rallies, marched, suffered violence, and were arrested. Many of these laypeople were following the lead of their pastors into nonviolent direct action Anchored by the doctrines of historic African American Christianity. Black Christians' "experience of miracles and dramatic conversions made an essential contribution in transforming" the faith into the "imperative of civil rights reform." In essence, once these Christians "had been galvanized into social action, they exerted the same force in the public square as they had experienced" in their prayer closets as they dramatized the continuation of Deliverance chronicled in the biblical witness.[25]

The theological formulation of the foot soldiers during the civil rights movement was far less complex than that of their leaders, but it still drove them to engage racial prejudice in society. Fannie Lou Hamer (1917–1977) stated, "If Christ were

---

[24]See vol. 2 for an excerpt from King's "Letter from Birmingham Jail."
[25]Noll, *God and Race*, 115.

here today, he would be branded a radical, a militant, and would probably be branded as 'red.'" Christ, she said, was a "revolutionary person, out there where it was happening. That's what God is all about, and that's where I get my strength."[26] Foot soldiers focused on a God who helped them traverse the chasm from what was to what should be.

Songs were a means of reinforcing the Anchors of the Christian faith in the face of clubs, water hoses, and dog attacks. In the 1950s, grassroots protesters began transforming spirituals and gospels into freedom songs that became the soundtrack for the movement. The renowned Mahalia Jackson (1911–1972) declared, "I sing God's music because it makes me feel free. It gives me hope." The communal roots of African ceremonial life were channeled during the civil rights movement as spirituals and gospel music were embedded into the movement's daily tasks. Music focused the foot soldiers on the mission and allowed them to overcome the fear of beatings and abuse, giving them boldness to respond to their abusers in love, consistent with a nonviolent ethic.[27]

The student movement. The Black student movement began quietly in 1942 with the Congress of Racial Equality. This organization was founded as the Committee on Racial Equality by a group of interracial students in Chicago who were committed to nonviolence.[28] Student efforts against racial oppression did not receive national attention until four freshmen from a Black college nonviolently demanded service at a Woolworth lunch counter in Greensboro, North Carolina, in February 1960. In April 1960 approximately two hundred students met at Shaw University in Raleigh, North Carolina, to form a new organization called the Student Nonviolent Coordinating Committee. Civil rights veteran Ella Baker (1903–1986), having served with both the Southern Christian Leadership Conference and the NAACP as a field secretary in the 1940s, organized the Student Nonviolent Coordinating Committee to capture the spirit of the student movement and mold it into a formal body.

Ideologically, students affirmed the nonviolent methods popularized by Martin Luther King Jr. at its founding conference.[29] The first stanza of the Student

---

[26]Paul Harvey, "Is There a River? Black Baptists, the Uses of History, and the Long History of the Freedom Movement," in Harper and Byrd, *Through a Glass Darkly*, 262. See vol. 2 for the lyrics to "Keep Your Eye on the Prize" and an excerpt from Fannie Lou Hamer's autobiography.

[27]See vol. 2 for the lyrics to "Keep Your Hand on the Plow," "We Shall Overcome," and "Go Down Moses."

[28]The Congress of Racial Equality served as a forerunner for similar groups. For more, see August Meier and Elliott Rudwick, *CORE: A Study in the Civil Rights Movement, 1942-1968* (New York: Oxford University Press, 1973).

[29]Clayborne Carson, *In Struggle: SNCC and the Black Awakening in the 1960s* (Cambridge, MA: Harvard University Press, 1995), 19.

Nonviolent Coordinating Committee's original purpose statement is a faithful summary of their commitments:

> We affirm the philosophical or religious ideal of nonviolence as the foundation of our purpose, the presupposition of our faith, and the manner of our action. Nonviolence as it grows from the Judaic-Christian tradition seeks a social order of justice permeated by love. Integration of human endeavor represents the crucial first step towards such a society.[30]

In concert with the Southern Christian Leadership Conference, which sponsored the event, the motifs of love and nonviolence, as emphasized in the Christian tradition, were central at the establishment of the Student Nonviolent Coordinating Committee.

Thirty-one-year-old King was the primary attraction for the attendees of the inaugural conference. While in Raleigh, King gave specific recommendations to the budding student movement to express their nonviolent convictions. First, King called the students to develop some type of continuing organization to unify the sit-in movement. Second, he encouraged the assembly to initiate a nationwide selective-buying campaign. Third, the students needed to galvanize an army of volunteers willing to go to jail rather than pay bail or fines. Fourth, the youth had to take the freedom struggle into every community of the South. Last and most vitally, King called the students to delve deeper into the philosophy of nonviolence as the means of pursuing reconciliation and cultivating the beloved community.[31]

The ideological banner over the meeting was nonviolence, but the spirit of the gathering stood in contrast to meetings held by their elders who were also committed to nonviolent direct action. To capture the attention of his young listeners, King concluded his address for the youth assembly with a distinct edge contextualized for his audience. King exclaimed, "The tactics of nonviolence without the spirit of nonviolence may indeed become a new kind of violence."[32]

Over time, some Student Nonviolent Coordinating Committee proponents moved away from nonviolent tactics because they were pragmatic, not convictional on a doctrinal level. The complicated intersection of the Christian faith and the student movements notwithstanding, not all young people jettisoned an explicitly Christian ideology during this period. A significant number of youth

---

[30]Student Nonviolent Coordinating Committee, *Constitution* (Raleigh: SNCC, 1960).
[31]Martin Luther King Jr., *The Papers of Martin Luther King, Jr.*, ed. Cayborne Carson et al. (Berkeley: University of California Press, 2005), 5:427.
[32]King, *Papers of Martin Luther King, Jr.* 5:427.

The Road to the Civil Rights Movement   147

and college students, as well as young professionals, were theologically bound to a nonviolent approach to Black uplift. Many of these young people began working directly with the Southern Christian Leadership Conference as Student Nonviolent Coordinating Committee became more radical.

Rev. Dr. Martin Luther King Jr. The tragically short life of Martin Luther King has drawn a tsunami of attention from scholars assessing his accomplishments as a political figure, the leader of a social movement, and a figurehead for justice and racial equality. The methods associated with those explorations, however, do not always account for what King identified as the wellspring of his efforts: his Christian heritage. King said, "In the quiet recesses of my heart, I'm fundamentally a clergyman, a Baptist preacher. This is my being and my heritage for I am also the son of a Baptist preacher, the grandson of a Baptist preacher and the great-grandson of a Baptist preacher."[33] King's self-consciously Christian engagement with social power structures was theologically Anchored in prophetic evangelical biblicism interfaced with orthodox, neo-orthodox, and liberal scholars during his formal education.[34]

King was the product of a successive line of preachers and was nurtured in the Black Baptist tradition from his infancy. The Christian activism of his father and grandfather's ministerial leadership made an enduring impact on the young King. Despite his appreciation for the thoughtful engagement of his immediate Black Baptist role models, in his early years King was put off by their emotionalism and what he saw as their overly wooden reading of Scripture.

> **Michael King** was the name originally submitted on the birth certificate of the man renowned as Martin Luther King Jr. In the summer of 1934, Reverend Michael King Sr. was sent by his church, Ebenezer Baptist Church in Atlanta, to important biblical sites and significant locations in church history, including the Wittenberg castle church where Protestant Reformer Martin Luther nailed his Ninety-Five Theses to the door. In an act of identification with Martin Luther's theological commitments and rebellious ethos, Reverend King renamed himself and his son Martin Luther King.

During King's academic studies, he read liberal theologians and he was intrigued by their intellectual sophistication. Many of King's professors were schooled in predominantly White educational institutions where familiarity with

---

[33] King, *Papers of Martin Luther King, Jr.* 1:1.
[34] Noll, *God and Race*, 107. See vol. 2 for an excerpt from King's sermon "Our God Is Able."

liberal theological scholarship was prerequisite for graduation. King's time at Morehouse College, where he matriculated as a fifteen-year-old freshman, and his time at Crozer Theological Seminary were marked by a broad exploration of the theological universe beyond his Black Baptist upbringing. During these exploratory years is when King penned his theological papers questioning the bodily resurrection of Jesus and the veracity of Scripture.

Rather than pitting his evangelical Baptist heritage against his new liberal explorations, King admitted that he became "a victim of eclecticism" as he sought to "synthesize the best of liberal theology with the best of neo-orthodox theology."[35] However, further exposure to theological liberalism alerted him to its shortcomings. King insisted, "Liberalism's superficial optimism concerning human nature caused it to overlook the fact that reason is darkened by sin. . . . Liberalism failed to see that reason by itself is little more than an instrument to justify man's defensive ways of thinking."[36]

> **Neo-orthodoxy** (commonly also called "dialectical theology" or "crisis theology") is a term that was never used by its proponents but was given by others who argued that they brought orthodoxy back up to date. It involved a broad coalition of theologians, including Karl Barth (1886–1968), Rudolf Bultmann (1884–1976), Emil Brunner (1889–1966), and Friedrich Gogarten (1887–1967). Despite the theological diversity among neo-orthodoxy's proponents, they (1) shared revelation as their starting point for faith, with a strong emphasis placed on Scripture; (2) emphasized a definite historical consciousness, moving away from German theological liberalism with a reformational mood; (3) fostered an ecumenism between Lutheran and Calvinist thinkers; (4) drew on divine transcendence in the thought of Søren Kierkegaard (1813–1855) and a surprising, uncanny, and often paradoxical in-breaking of revelation; and (5) held a generally negative assessment of Fredrich Schleiermacher (1768–1834), the father of classical liberal theology.[a]
>
> [a]Christopher Ben Simpson, *Modern Theology* (London: Bloomsbury T&T Clark, 2016), 22-230.

King's seminary years reflected a young man whose appreciation for his religious roots was eventually energized by his academic study, though he did not leave the findings of his formal education behind. After becoming skilled at

---

[35]Clayborne Carson, "Martin Luther King, Jr., and the African-American Social Gospel," in *African-American Religion: Interpretative Essays in History in Culture*, ed. Timothy E. Fulop and Albert J. Raboteau (New York: Routledge, 1997), 351.

[36]Martin Luther King Jr., "My Pilgrimage to Nonviolence," in *Papers of Martin Luther King, Jr.* 5:420.

juxtaposing his father's religious emotionalism and activist orientation with the complexity of White academic theologians, King concluded that orthodox Christianity was not necessarily anti-intellectual, and academic theology did not contain all the answers. As such, King's theological maturation was marked by a growing capacity to synthesize the best elements of theological alternatives, which has made him a bewildering subject for subsequent theologians and religious scholars.

Among the influences in King's theological maturation was theologian Walter Rauschenbusch. Regarding his intellectual development, King insisted,

> I was immediately influenced by the social gospel. In the early '50s I read Rauschenbusch's *Christianity and the Social Crisis*, a book which left an indelible imprint on my thinking. Of course there are points at which I differed with Rauschenbusch.... He came perilously close to identifying the kingdom of God with a particular social and economic system—a temptation which the church should never give in to.[37]

While at Boston University, King encountered the writings of Reinhold Niebuhr and utilized them to critique the extreme optimism found in the social gospel.[38] King reflected, "It seems to me that one of the great services of neo-orthodoxy, notwithstanding its extremes, is its revolt against all forms of humanistic perfectionism. They call us back to a deeper faith in God. Is not this the need of the hour? Has modern man placed too much faith in himself and to little faith in God?"[39] For King, Niebuhr's Christian realism allowed him to account for the complexity of life, which included acknowledging human evil while still allowing for human morality.[40]

King's intellectual journey during his studies was marked by his enthusiastic exploration of Protestant liberalism guided by professors who were positively predisposed to the African American Christian tradition. His subsequent years were marked by a demonstrable move away from bona fide theological liberalism and toward his father's faith. In particular, he rejected the optimism of liberal theology and the pessimism of Niebuhr's neo-orthodoxy. King's student papers "demonstrate that he adopted European American theological ideas that ultimately reinforced, rather than undermined, the African American social gospel tradition

---

[37]King, "My Pilgrimage to Nonviolence," 422.
[38]Crowther, "I Am Fundamentally," 182.
[39]Matin Luther King Jr., "Notecards on Books of the Old Testament," in *Papers of Martin Luther King Jr.* 2:166.
[40]Noll, *God and Race*, 108.

epitomized by his father and grandfather."[41] This conclusion directed him toward the personalism of Boston University professor Edgar S. Brightman (1884–1953).

King said that philosophical personalism provided him the "metaphysical and philosophical grounding for the idea of a personal God, and it gave me a metaphysical basis for the dignity and worth of all human personality," a longstanding feature of a Big God in African American Christianity.[42] Personalism helped King synthesize intellectual reflection and religious belief. In particular, it helped him solve the quandary of how an omnipotent God could oversee a world full of evil. "God's power is finite, but his goodness is infinite," that is, there could be no real goodness if God simply compelled morally good behavior. This "is the only adequate explanation for the existence of evil. . . . It establishes the Christian idea of sacrificial love on metaphysical grounds. . . . Theistic absolutism fails."[43]

As King's theological commitments crystallized, he sought methods of social action that were consistent with his Christian commitments. True to his propensity for synthesizing various thought forms, King borrowed concepts of grassroots mobilization from secular socialist A. Philip Randolph. In addition, King found an example of nonviolence that sparked social change embodied by Indian lawyer Mahatma Gandhi (1869–1948). King insisted that *"Christ furnished the spirit and motivation while Gandhi furnished the method."*[44] The centrality of Christian nonviolence embodied by Gandhi peppered King's speeches and publications. The conviction that the unearned suffering of Blacks was redemptive appeared early in his theology and remained dominant throughout his life. When his home was bombed and Blacks were prompted to respond violently, King took an opportunity to send a clear message about nonviolence: "We must not return violence under any condition. I know this is difficult advice to follow, especially since we have been the victims of no less than ten bombings. But this is the way of Christ; it is the way of the cross. We must somehow believe that unearned suffering is redemptive."[45] By the time King graduated from Boston University with his Doctor of Philosophy, he was decidedly a preacher, not a scholar. Forging an oftenunwieldy synthesis from diverse (and at times divergent) theological streams, King

---

[41] Carson, "Martin Luther King, Jr.," 344.
[42] Martin Luther King Jr., *Stride toward Freedom: The Montgomery Story* (New York, Harper, 1958), 100.
[43] Martin Luther King Jr., "Final Examination Answers Philosophy of Religion," January 9, 1952, in *Papers of Martin Luther King Jr.* 2:109.
[44] Martin Luther King Jr., *The Autobiography of Martin Luther King, Jr.*, ed. Clayborne Carson (New York: Warner Books, 1998), 67.
[45] King, *Autobiography of Martin Luther King, Jr.*, 103.

"affirmed his abiding faith in a God who was both a comforting personal presence and a powerful spiritual force acting in history for righteousness."[46]

As a pastor thrust onto the international scene, his faith in a personal God who called people to action was undeniable, even in his theological basis for diagnosing and mending social problems. King referred to segregation as immoral. The modernists of his day relegated this evil to the realm of unjust social policy (labeling it a sociological disorder), but King insisted that segregation was a sin and an evil that was contrary to God's perfect plan for humankind. Racist systems treated people in ways not intended by the Creator.

"The problem of race and color prejudice," King declared, "remains America's greatest moral dilemma." He added, "There must be a recognition of the sacredness of human personality." He noted that "segregation stands diametrically opposed to (this) principle." Instead, "the tragedy of segregation is that it treats men as means rather than ends, and thereby reduces them to things rather than persons."[47]

As King was the preeminent leader of the Southern Christian Leadership Conference, continued references to Christianity marked the methods that many relied on during the tumultuous days of the civil rights movement. For King, nonviolence was not a methodology that he pragmatically adopted; it was demanded by the Christian faith he embraced. Framing his fight for racial justice as a battle between light and darkness (Acts 26:18), not Black and White, King situated biblical *agapē* love as the cornerstone of his logic.[48] Concerning the love that motivates nonviolence, King said in an address to the Young Men's (and Women's) Christian Association at the University of California at Berkeley,

> *Agape* is understanding, creative, redemptive good will for all men. Biblical theologians would say it is the love of God working in the minds of men. It is an overflowing love which seeks nothing in return. And when you come to love on this level you begin to love men not because they are likable, not because they do things that attract us, but because God loves them and here we love the person who does the evil deed while hating the deed that the person does.[49]

In the same address, King countered his critics by affirming, "Nonviolent resistance is not a method of cowardice. . . . The nonviolent resister is just as opposed to the

---

[46]Carson, "Martin Luther King, Jr.," 357-58.
[47]Martin Luther King Jr., *A Testament of Hope: The Essential Writings of Martin Luther King, Jr.*, ed. James M. Washington (New York: Harper & Row, 1986), 117-19.
[48]Martin Luther King Jr., "The Power of Nonviolence," in *Testament of Hope*, 13.
[49]King, "Power of Nonviolence," 13.

evil that he is standing against as the violent register but he resists without violence. This method is nonaggressive physically but strongly aggressive spiritually."[50]

While not all Black Christians followed King's methods, numerous Blacks and their allies followed King in a self-consciously Christian approach to dismantling racism in society. King's complex theological formulation was translated to audiences filled with foot soldiers by his charismatic and sermonic communication style, which drew heavily on the biblical imagery that marked the Black preaching tradition. The stories and images of Scripture were vivid illustrations of good overcoming evil and endless examples of God's love for all people to leverage in the race toward justice.

---

[50] King, "Power of Nonviolence," 12.

Interlude

THEOLOGIZING BLACK CONSCIOUSNESS

THE HISTORIC BLACK CHURCH continued to be a pillar of the African American community after the civil rights movement. From within its midst, two movements—Black evangelicalism and Black (liberation) theology—emerged and formed the ongoing story of African American faith. Both movements have roots in the 1960s but did not crystallize into their most enduring forms until after the assassination of Martin Luther King Jr. Understanding these two theological movements requires insight into the social dynamics to which they responded.

The movements for civil rights, Black power, and Black consciousness set the agenda to which Black Christianity responded. On the one hand, King's primary aim for the civil rights movement was combating social and economic oppression. Fanning the flame of Black cultural development was secondary for civil rights leaders during the 1950s and '60s. King's method for pursuing social and political uplift was paired with theologically motivated nonviolence because, as King argued, it was a morally appropriate approach to translate Christian love into social action.[1]

After the initial success of nonviolent direct action, foot soldiers grew weary of frequent sit-ins, marches, and imprisonments, leading to a frustrated band of demonstrators who desired more immediate results from their sacrifice. The widespread faith in the method of nonviolent direct action began dissolving after the excitement of the 1963 March on Washington, when four young girls were killed by a bomb that erupted at Sixteenth Street Baptist Church in Birmingham, Alabama, only weeks after Dr. King delivered his "I Have a Dream" speech.

---

[1]Martin Luther King Jr., *The Autobiography of Martin Luther King, Jr.*, ed. Clayborne Carson (New York: Warner Books, 1998), 102-4.

The 1964 murder of three civil rights workers at the hands of White supremacists during "Freedom Summer" in Mississippi continued to crumble the resolve of the foot soldiers. In the wake of this tragedy, organizations such as the Student Nonviolent Coordinating Committee and Congress of Racial Equality abandoned their theologically motivated nonviolent approaches in favor of methods embodied by the more militant ideology of the Black power movement.[2] King's focus on pursuing social and political uplift with nonviolence left a felt need unengaged in the Black community, which Malcolm X seized.

Malcolm X insisted on the dignity of Black culture and fanned the flame of what became the Black power movement. Keenly aware of the self-hatred often internalized by Blacks, which resulted from unjust and inhumane treatment in society, Malcolm declared, "The worst crime the White man has ever committed has been to teach us (Blacks) to hate ourselves."[3] Malcolm's intense affection for his people drove him to demand liberation "by any means necessary," which stood in stark contrast to the nonviolent, faith-based methods of King.

The move toward cultural awareness, led by Malcolm X and others, manifested with a Black nationalist ethos under the mantra of "Black power." The term "Black power" arose during the "march against fear" in Mississippi, which was organized by Martin Luther King, Stokley Carmichael (1941–1998), and other civil rights activists. On June 5, 1966, James Meredith (1933–), who in 1962 was the first African American to enroll at the University of Mississippi, was (nonfatally) shot while participating in a nonviolent march from Memphis to Jackson, Mississippi. As Carmichael and fellow civil rights leader Floyd McKissick conversed during the march, they concluded that not much had changed in recent decades despite federal legislation modifications. At a rally in Greenwood, Mississippi, Carmichael cried, "What we need is Black power," and the phrase sparked a movement. This turning point occurred in the summer of 1966, shortly after the assassination of Malcom X in February 1965.

The Black power movement asserted the need for Black self-identity and Black self-determination because for so long African Americans were defined and governed by those outside their community. In their 1967 volume, titled *Black Power: The Politics of Liberation in America*, Carmichael and Charles V. Hamilton define Black power as "a call for Black people in this country to unite, to recognize their

---

[2]Harvard Sitkoff, *The Struggle for Black Equality* (New York: Hill and Wang, 2008), 164-66.
[3]Cited in James H. Cone, *For My People: Black Theology and the Black Church* (Maryknoll, NY: Orbis Books, 1984), 159.

heritage, to build a sense of community. It is a call for Black people to begin to define their own goals, to lead their own organizations. It is a call to reject the racist institutions and values of this society."[4]

> **Political modernization** was the primary means that Carmichael and Hamilton insisted on to assert Black power. Political modernization was upheld by three concepts: "1) questioning old values and institutions of the society, 2) searching for new and different forms of political structure to solve political and economic problems, and 3) broadening the base of political participation to include more people in the decision-making process."[a] For Carmichael, this required fundamental shifts away from King's nonviolent direct action.
>
> [a]Stokley Carmichael and Charles V. Hamilton, *Black Power: The Politics of Liberation in America* (New York: Random House, 1967), 39.

Black power meant full participation in the decision-making processes affecting the lives of Black communities. While groups asserted this desire in various ways; some were directed by Scripture and others by other means. Black power's original intent was to offer Blacks dignity by granting them authority to be self-determining in their communities, to affirm the beauty of their culture, and to include their skin tone and hair type within the bounds of what Americans defined as beautiful. The move away from being determined to a self-determined people (toward the assertion of full citizenship) was signified in the transition in terminology from *Negro* to *Black*.

The term *Negro* was given to Blacks by Whites and carried the negative connotations of being dumb, lazy, apathetic, and shiftless.[5] Consequently, animosity began growing against the term in the mid-1960s because that persona was given to Blacks to oppress them. Black power supporters also began calling themselves *African American, Afro-Americans*, or *Black* because these terms represented an image constructed by Blacks for Blacks.[6] Emerging from this struggle was a word that serves to summarize Black identity, namely, *Blackness*. This is not a simple reference to skin color; it identifies the joys, fears, hopes, and sorrows of Black life. Being Black, or Blackness, abounds with new meaning and continues to be a point of solidarity for many African Americans.

[4]Stokley Carmichael and Charles V. Hamilton, *Black Power: The Politics of Liberation in America* (New York: Random House, 1967), 44.
[5]Carmichael and Hamilton, *Black Power*, 37.
[6]Carmichael and Hamilton, *Black Power*, 37.

The insistence on Black consciousness, which incorporated justice and self-determination, was so pervasive among African Americans that individuals and professionals throughout the Black community had to define their interaction with these concepts—and pastors and theologians were no exception. This movement caused Black ministers and religious scholars to rethink conventional theology to imagine a way of being Christian without consciously or subconsciously wondering whether there was something in their belief system that was intended to pacify them into subservience or inhumanity.

VIOLENT DIRECT ACTION

The emergence of the Black power movement was accompanied with alternative means of asserting its ideals that stood in contrast to nonviolence. Carmichael insisted that the civil rights movement intentionally adopted a tone tailored to appease the White middle class and to mislead some into believing that "the Black minority could bow its head and get whipped into a meaningful position of power in society." As a result, Carmichael vehemently opposed nonviolent methods as weak and passive. According to leading proponents of Black power, nonviolent tactics ran contrary to human nature. Carmichael asked, "What man would not defend his family and home from attack?" He said that nonviolent civil rights workers had nothing to offer except to go out and be beaten again in the face of Klan and police brutality. In essence, Carmichael boldly communicated that White people must "stop messing with Black people or Blacks will fight back."[7]

The Black Panther Party, established in 1966 by students Huey P. Newton and Bobby Seale, embodied Carmichael's militant ethos. The Panthers' formation was in response to police brutality, including the shooting of a fifteen-year-old boy by an off-duty police lieutenant in Harlem, the curious speeding arrest of a young driver by the highway patrol in Watts, California, and the killing of a fifteen-year-old who was shot in the back by a police officer in San Francisco. By late 1968, there were Black Panther Party "champions" in twenty-five cities, with membership reaching over one thousand nationwide.[8] True to the Black power ideal of violence combating violence, Seale said, "Brothers and sisters, it is time to get our guns organized, forget the sit-ins and shoot it out."

---

[7]Carmichael and Hamilton, *Black Power*, 50-51, 53.
[8]Henry Hampton and Steve Fayer, *Voices of Freedom: An Oral History of the Civil Rights Movement from the 1950s Through the 1980s* (New York: Bantam Books, 1990), 349, 512.

The Black power movement appealed to battle-weary adherents of nonviolent direct action and mobilized many at the grassroots level whom the legislative advocacy of the NAACP and the nonviolent movement failed to rally.[9] In addition, the 1968 assassination of Martin Luther King Jr.—the apostle of nonviolence and symbol of belief in the fundamental goodness of American democracy—shocked the nation into a different type of action. With the bullet that killed King, "the movement for peace, nonviolence and racial fellowship ground to a halt."[10] The frustration of ongoing Black social inequality resulted in riots by African Americans in 125 cities within weeks of King's murder.[11]

Numerical data indicating how many Blacks adopted Black power ideology is difficult to generate, but longstanding civil rights organizations such as the Student Nonviolent Coordinating Committee and the Congress of Racial Equality made definitive shifts away from nonviolent direct action. Student groups were a microcosm of the frustrations held by the larger Black populace, frustrations that led some Blacks to move from nonviolence to the methods of the Black power movement.

In the years leading up to 1964, the Student Nonviolent Coordinating Committee felt increasingly alienated from other civil rights organizations and especially from King.[12] In the summer of 1964, the organization concentrated its civil rights efforts in Mississippi, and this project was nicknamed "Freedom Summer." It constituted a crucial advancement toward radicalism in the struggle for civil rights. A climactic event of the summer was the disappearance of three of the organization's workers, James Chaney, Michael Schwerner, and Andrew Goodman, the latter two of whom were White. Their disappearance made national news. In response to the national press, Student Nonviolent Coordinating Committee chairman John Lewis lamented, "It is a shame that national concern is aroused only after two White boys are missing."[13] Following the August 4 discovery of the three bodies in an earthen dam, the organization was never the same.

---

[9] Hampton and Fayer, *Voices of Freedom*, 201.

[10] Dwight N. Hopkins, *Black Theology USA and South Africa: Politics, Culture, and Liberation* (Maryknoll, NY: Orbis Books, 1989), 42.

[11] Nell Irvin Painter, *African-American History and Its Meanings, 1619 to the Present* (New York: Oxford University Press, 2006), 284. The most significant riots included those in Baltimore; Chicago; Louisville, Kentucky; and Washington, DC.

[12] Allen J. Matusow, "From Civil Rights to Black Power: The Case of SNCC, 1960–1966," in *Twentieth-Century America: Recent Interpretations*, ed. Barton J. Bernstein and Allen J. Matusow (New York: Harcourt, Brace & World, 1969), 370.

[13] Cited in Clayborne Carson, *In Struggle: SNCC and the Black Awakening in the 1960s* (Cambridge, MA: Harvard University Press, 1995), 115.

At the funeral for Chaney, Black Mississippians gathered and anticipated a standard eulogy from Congress of Racial Equality leader David Dennis. Instead, they heard the heart of a young man who was overcome with pain and emotion as he struggled with the plight of Blacks in America. Throughout Dennis's speech, the tension between working within the parameters of biased governmental, judicial, and political structures and his disdain and mistrust of these structures was on display. On the one hand, Dennis encouraged Mississippi Blacks to organize and register to vote, saying, "All these people here who are not registered voters should be in line Monday morning from one corner of this country to the next, demanding, don't ask if I can become a registered voter. Demand!"[14] On the other hand, Dennis blamed the government for the murders of Chaney, Schwerner, Goodman, and others:

> In my opinion as I stand here, I not only blame the people who pulled the trigger or did the beating or dug the hole with the shovel.... I blame the people in Washington, D. C. and on down in the state of Mississippi for what happened just as much as I blame those who pulled the trigger. Because I feel that a hundred years ago, if the proper thing had been done by the federal government of this particular country and by the other people.... We wouldn't be here today to mourn the death of a brave man like James Chaney, you see.

Dennis was also outraged at the pattern of injustice in American courthouses, declaring,

> See, I know what's going to happen. I feel it deep in my heart! When they find the people who killed those guys in Neshoba County, you've got to come back to the state of Mississippi and have a jury of their cousins, their aunts and their uncles. And I know what they're going to say, not guilty because no one saw them pulling the trigger. I'm tired of that![15]

By the end of the summer, the fraying cords that bound the Student Nonviolent Coordinating Committee to the method of nonviolence had snapped. In a sense, integration of the Black power ethos was merely an epilogue to the organization's ill-fated summer project.[16] By the end of the year, the Student Nonviolent

---

[14]Dave Dennis, "An Address at the Funeral Service for James Chaney," in *Rhetoric, Religion and the Civil Rights Movement, 1954-1965*, ed. Davis W. Houck and David E. Dixon (Waco, TX: Baylor University Press, 2006), 775.
[15]Dennis, "Address at the Funeral Service," 776.
[16]Matusow, "From Civil Rights to Black Power," 372.

Coordinating Committee officially defended the right for their field secretaries to carry weapons, and Congress of Racial Equality units in Louisiana openly defended the Deacons of Defense and Justice.[17] The Deacons of Defense and Justice were a Louisiana-based vigilante group who vowed to defend those whom law enforcement agencies would not protect. Carmichael argued that the Deacons of Defense should be immune to litigation because, "If a nation fails to protect its citizens, then that nation cannot condemn those who take up the task themselves."[18]

The contrast between the self-consciously Christian social reformers and Black power proponents was stark. Martin Luther King Jr. had a visceral reaction to the Black power movement and its political party, the Black Panthers. King sympathized with the emotion behind the movement, saying, "For people who had been crushed so long by White power and who had been taught that Black was degrading, it had a ready appeal." Despite his empathy, King held to his convictions by maintaining that "Black Power is a nihilistic philosophy born out of the conviction that the Negro can't win . . . the view that American society is so hopelessly corrupt and enmeshed in evil that there is no possibility of salvation from within."[19]

Not only did King assert that Black power was unhealthy for African Americans, but he also proposed that it was detrimental for social progress because Blacks could not achieve political and economic power in isolation from the White majority. Thus, Black violence would bring more harm to themselves than to Whites.[20] While the political tactics of the Black power movement were heavily scrutinized by Black ministers and theologians, its cultural affirmation was broadly affirmed.

The Black power movement gave African American theologians the ability to affirm Blackness as beautiful and fostered the courage to incorporate the Black experience into the theological task. A healthy Afrocentrism recovers African cultural forms from their troubled cultural connotations. This characteristic of Afrocentrism is helpful because it urges Blacks to do what the broader American culture disallowed, namely, to have a healthy pride in Africanisms that were deemed something to depart from. The affirmation of African heritage encouraged a theology that spoke directly to the Black experience, which had been underappreciated in North America.

---

[17]Sitkoff, *Struggle for Black Equality*, 165.
[18]Carmichael and Hamilton, *Black Power*, 52-53.
[19]Martin Luther King Jr., *Where Do We Go from Here: Chaos or Community?* (Boston: Beacon, 2010), 196.
[20]Sitkoff, *Struggle for Black Equality*, 199.

In the 1960s, African Americans began insisting that they not turn away from their collective experience as they undertook theological formation and ministry practice. This theological pressure resulted in two movements that self-consciously engaged what it meant to be Black and Christian. The movements are so distinct that the chronological narrative that was carried from chapters two through nine will be interrupted by depicting two movements with overlapping chronologies. The first movement is Black evangelicalism (chaps. 10-12) and the second Black liberation theology (chaps. 13-14). Despite the different number of chapters dedicated to each movement, they are given a relatively similar word count. These movements share this common history, but they responded by charting distinct trajectories marked by contrasting emphases and ways of engaging the doctrinal Anchors of Black faith and methods of social engagement. The final chapter of this book features recent developments in Black Christianity that are still taking shape but were forged in the racial, political, and cultural tension experienced nationally with the killing of Trayvon Martin through the presidency of Donald J. Trump.

10

BLACK EVANGELICAL IDENTITY

BLACK EVANGELICALISM FORMALIZED during the civil rights movement beginning in 1963, with the establishment of the National Negro Evangelical Association. The National Negro Evangelical Association was the first formal body where African Americans self-identified as evangelical. While Black evangelicals exist beyond those involved with this organization, it is the best single body for quantifying the composition of and early trends within the movement.

A quick survey of the literature produced by Black evangelicals reveals a dearth of literary witnesses. The contrast is especially stark compared to Black liberation theology, which boasts a host of trained scholars who produced theological literature, including articles, books, and academic presentations, in the 1960s and '70s. The founders of the National Negro Evangelical Association were largely pastors looking for camaraderie as ministry practitioners, so their literary footprint is much smaller and more obscured than that of Black liberationists. Due to the lack of primary and secondary sources, theological scholarship and historical accounts have largely overlooked this movement, which was an important forerunner for many Black Christians whose maturation has included engagement with evangelical institutions.

The shortage of literature notwithstanding, the history of Black Christianity in the United States is an evangelical story, from the multitudes of Blacks converting to Christianity during the Great Awakenings to the widespread affirmation of the doctrinal Anchors of African American faith. Each theological Anchor has maintained its integrity within the Black evangelical movement, with an emphasis on the work of Jesus on the cross and the Conversion made possible by his resurrection. Despite the united emphasis on Christ and the shared conviction of the Good Book as God's authoritative word, the Deliverance Anchor has manifested in real but disparate ways throughout this movement.

> **David Bebbington's quadrilateral** is a commonly used means of defining evangelicalism. The quadrilateral includes (1) conversionism, an emphasis on a personal decision to follow Jesus Christ as Lord and Savior; (2) biblicism, an understanding of the Bible as God's divinely inspired word, including the supernatural; (3) crucicentrism, which emphasizes the atonement of Christ on the cross to save sinners; and (4) activism, a conviction that the gospel should be spread "to the ends of the earth" by engaging the broader culture.[a] On the whole, Black Christianity fits comfortably within this definition.
>
> [a] David Bebbington, *Evangelicalism in Modern Britain: A History from the 1730s to the 1980s* (London: Routledge, 1989), 2-3.

Much like the Black fundamentalists of the Jim Crow era who resisted the label despite affirming many of the fundamentals, many African Americans were apprehensive about donning the label "evangelical" despite the story of African American Christianity fitting one of the most widely recognized definitions of evangelicalism, David Bebbington's quadrilateral.[1] The label has been problematized among many Black Christians because the term has become broadly synonymous with the partisan politics of White evangelicalism—rather than Christ and his kingdom. Moreover, because the term *evangelical* has been so conflated with an Anglo expression of Christianity, African American Christians—especially since the 1960s—have balked at the idea of being defined by a movement shaped by White cultural preferences. This is why many Black Christians prefer the term *Bible-believing* over *evangelical*. These concerns notwithstanding, *Black evangelical* is a self-designation used to describe a movement that is worthy of careful consideration.

THE FORMATION OF THE NATIONAL NEGRO EVANGELICAL ASSOCIATION

The progenitors of National Negro Evangelical Association were formed amid the fundamentalist-modernist controversy of the 1920s. These forerunners differentiated themselves from White liberals who adopted modernist tendencies and from some in historically Black denominations who in their view lacked an explicit doctrinal emphasis. These predecessors caused tension within some Black churches

---

[1] See Jemar Tisby, "Are Black Christians Evangelicals," in *Evangelicals: Who They Have Been, Are Now, and Could Be*, ed. Mark A. Noll, David W. Bebbington, and George M. Marsden (Grand Rapids, MI: Eerdmans, 2019).

because of their continual insistence on right doctrine, personal salvation, and propositional truth. Black fundamentalists were often branded as overly critical, which led several National Negro Evangelical Association forebears to attend the few White fundamentalist Bible colleges that accepted African American students during the 1940s and '50s.

Fundamentalists from various ethnicities interested in coalition building gathered to form the National Association of Evangelicals in 1942. This alliance included Calvinists, Pentecostals, charismatics, dispensationalists, and others from the Protestant tradition. Throughout its early history, however, minority members, and Blacks in particular, felt as if the body were conceived to pursue the ideals and concerns of the majority and invited minorities to attend—rather than charting the organization's course together.

James Earl Massey (1930–) recalled the gathering of the World Congress on Evangelism in Berlin in 1966. The theme of the meeting was "One Race, One Gospel, One Task."[2] After ten days of meetings and position papers, none of them had addressed the first portion of the theme. For non-White delegates, this was highly problematic, especially because it was a gathering of evangelicals assembled from around the globe.

When the concern was brought to the chairman, Carl F. H. Henry, he apologized for the omission and insisted that the "one race" subtheme was taken for granted by the planning committee and therefore nobody was assigned to address the matter. Massey later found that delegates from Africa, India, and South America grieved the omission as well—which made it abundantly clear that the planning committee was composed of those with exclusively White concerns. This characterized the early development of the National Association of Evangelicals.

It is highly unlikely that, at an event including "One Race" in the title, the topic would have gone unaddressed if an African diasporic representative had been on the planning committee, given that the event occurred during South African apartheid and the struggle for Black equality in America. In evangelicalism, paternalism loomed large, and Blacks were assumed to be happy for a mere invitation to participate in the National Association of Evangelicals without a voice. This was cold comfort for Black Christians who sought training and resources to minister to their parishioners amid trying social times and theological diversification.

---

[2]James Earl Massey, "African Americans and Evangelicalism," *Fuller Studio* 2 (2015), https://fullerstudio.fuller.edu/african-americans-evangelicalism/.

Massey and his counterparts were given an opportunity to include a statement on "one race" in the event's final report, but this concession was a microcosm of Black existence within the National Association of Evangelicals—being seen but rarely considered and given a token contribution after self-advocacy. Within the National Association of Evangelicals, Black leaders continued requesting that the burdens in their community be borne within the association, as it did for others, but that opportunity was denied. The indifference of White evangelicals and their lack of compassion for the evangelistic and social needs in African American communities was initially assumed to be a cordial absentmindedness, but the persistence of the sentiment eventually led some to insist on the more serious charge of racism.[3]

It was clear that Black evangelicals needed an environment to fellowship with one another and forge an evangelical theology that directly applied to the needs of the African American community. The association's inaugural gathering met in Los Angeles with an insistence that it was not a separatist association but a context focused on cultivating an evangelicalism that met the needs of the Black community and developed leaders of the next generation. In addition, due to the group's tumultuous past within Black denominations, a significant amount of energy was dedicated to communicating their brand of evangelicalism to the broader African American community.

> **Marvin Levy Prentis** served as the first chairman of the board and first president of the National Negro Evangelical Association. The association was his brainchild, especially its emphasis on addressing concerns in African American communities in distinctively Christian ways.

In the early days of the National Negro Evangelical Association, belonging was predicated on theological convictions that aligned with the doctrinal Anchors of Black faith, with varying emphasis on Deliverance. These convictions included a genuine Conversion experience through Christ alone and the reliability of the Scriptures and their final authority for matters of faith and practice. These foundations were coupled with the essential practices of evangelism and international missions, and a desire to address the kinds of suffering that were pronounced in Black communities. Among those who embodied these characteristics, three primary streams formed the early membership of the association. The first is a

---

[3] Albert G. Miller, "The Rise of African-American Evangelicalism in American Culture," in *Perspectives on American Religion and Culture*, ed. Peter W. Williams (Malden, MA: Blackwell, 1999), 265.

fundamentalist stream embodied by the Nottage brothers, Whitefield Talbot Nottage (ca. 1860–?) and Berlin Martin Nottage (1889–1966).[4]

The brothers converted to Christianity in their native Eleuthera in the Bahamas and migrated to the United States in 1910. These stalwart evangelists traveled to urban African American communities and formed new churches in St. Louis; Muskegon, Michigan; Terre Haute, Indiana; Birmingham, Alabama; Philadelphia; Richmond; and Chicago. The brothers later established and pastored churches separately in Cleveland and Detroit. These churches formed a cluster of fellowships that were characterized by premillennial dispensationalist theology. The "Black Brethren" remained markedly detached from the larger Plymouth Brethren movement, which nurtured the likes of Marvin Printis, Howard Jones, John Davis, and William Pannell.

> **Premillennial dispensationalism** is a system of doctrine based on literal biblical interpretation. The premise is that Jesus will return to the earth bodily to inaugurate the millennial kingdom and reign over it. Dispensational premillennialism also insists on a pretribulation rapture over against their historic premillennial counterparts, who affirm a posttribulation rapture.

The Nottage brothers' evangelistic zeal and conservative views on the Good Book shaped the initial ethos of the National Negro Evangelical Association.[5] The fundamentalist stream of Black Brethren that heavily influenced the beginning of the association complicated its relationship with the historic Black church because of its Caribbean roots, stringent theological parameters, and existence outside historic Black denominations.

African American Pentecostalism comprised a second stream of the National Negro Evangelical Association.[6] This theological disposition is most pronounced in the Church of God in Christ. William H. Bentley, the most prominent, clear, and consensus-building voice in the association's history, emerged from this tributary of Black Christianity. Bentley served as the association's president from 1970 to 1976. Black Pentecostal churches comprised those who had departed primarily from Black Methodist and Baptist churches and those in the

---

[4]Soong-Chan Rah, "African American Evangelicals," in *T&T Clark Handbook of African American Theology*, ed. Antonia Michelle Daymond, Frederic L. Ware, and Eric Lewis Williams (New York: T&T Clark, 2019), 76.
[5]Rah, "African American Evangelicals," 76.
[6]Rah, "African American Evangelicals," 77.

holiness tradition, and were a middle ground between Brethren fellowships and the other historic Black denominations.[7]

The pronounced autonomy of Caribbean Black Pentecostals from their White counterparts influenced the early days of National Negro Evangelical Association as they insisted on independence from White evangelicals for the movement's vitality. Confidence in Black ecclesiastical efforts emerged from the ability of Bentley's denomination, the United Pentecostal Council of the Assemblies of God, to send missionaries around the globe. The United Pentecostal Council of the Assemblies of God's missionary ethos resulted in successfully sending their founder to Liberia and extending their denominational footprint to Aruba, Barbados, Trinidad, and the West Indies.[8] The denomination's missiological independence from White influence was especially exhibited among its churches in the Caribbean, which led Christians in the United States by their example of cultivating unique methods of reaching their communities. Through the influence of Bentley, this stream exerted significant shaping effect during the second half of the National Negro Evangelical Association's first decade.

The final stream that supplied the early members of the National Negro Evangelical Association were Blacks who graduated from or worked in predominantly White institutions, namely, evangelical seminaries and parachurch organizations.[9] By the mid-twentieth century, some White educational institutions, including Fuller Theological Seminary, Dallas Theological Seminary, Nyack College, Wheaton College, Westminster Theological Seminary, and others, began admitting greater numbers of Black students. For example, the National Negro Evangelical Association's first president, Marvin Prentis, graduated from Fuller, and its second president, Howard Jones, graduated from Nyack College. Influential members Tony Evans and Carl Ellis graduated from Dallas Theological Seminary and Westminster Theological Seminary, respectively.

Graduates did not just receive diplomas for their studies; they were tacitly introduced to the institutions that comprised evangelicalism. Despite the rising number of African Americans attending evangelical institutions, their presence underscored the cultural chasm between Black and White evangelicals. As Black graduates began serving with evangelical ministries, including InterVarsity, Youth

---

[7]See vol. 2 for a transcript of an interview with Pastor Alton R. Williams.
[8]United Pentecostal Council of the Assemblies of God, "Our History," UPCAG.org, www.upcag.org/history/ (accessed July 28, 2022).
[9]United Pentecostal Council of the Assemblies of God, "Our History."

Black Evangelical Identity

for Christ, Campus Crusade, and the Billy Graham Evangelistic Association, disheartening treatment necessitated the emergence of the National Negro Evangelical Association to foster fellowship among African Americans who lamented strained relationships within traditionally Black denominations.

> **Howard O. Jones** (1921–2010) was an associate evangelist with the Billy Graham Evangelistic Association for thirty-five years. He was well-known because of his award-winning radio show and his book *White Questions to a Black Christian*, composed of inquiries about race posed to him at evangelistic events, at Bible colleges and seminaries, and during missions conferences.

PHASE 1—SEARCHING FOR IDENTITY: 1963–1969

The first phase of Black evangelicalism began with the National Negro Evangelical Association's establishment and concluded with its 1969 meeting in Atlanta. The association was a refuge for Blacks who were othered from White evangelicalism because of racial insensitivity and from Black denominations because of their meticulous doctrinal convictions. In short, the association provided fellowship for a band of theological and ecclesiological misfits who maintained a sense of spiritual homelessness because of the social and political issues to which they sought to apply their faith. The new association provided the hope of a new home and new horizons.

> **The National Negro Evangelical Association changed its name** to the National Black Evangelical Association in 1973. The name change was indicative of an ideological shift that characterized the second phase of Black evangelicalism. For this reason, this book refers to the association as the National Negro Evangelical Association until its name change.

In addition to those trained in White evangelical seminaries and others who served in White-led ministries, the majority of the National Negro Evangelical Association's early membership pastored churches within Black denominations or shepherded congregations that belonged to a minority caucus within an Anglo denomination. This pastor-led movement comprised both Black fundamentalist and Black militant evangelicals, but their differences were overshadowed by their shared insistence of the gospel's primacy.

At its inception, the National Negro Evangelical Association's leadership was characterized by priorities that mirrored their White evangelical counterparts. Bentley celebrated the confidence-inspiring leadership of the association's inaugural president, Marvin Prentis, and the robust evangelistic and expository preaching emphasis of second president, Howard Jones.[10] Embodying healthy ministry practices modeled by their seminary professors was typical, but it was also common for Black leaders to lack the ability to break free of the cultural trappings of their mentors. Bentley even described Black pastors in urban contexts rolling their r's to mimic master Scottish pulpiteers revered in their seminary training.[11] The combination of formal ministry training in evangelical seminaries and the association's early leadership having been raised in small towns (which contrasted urban Black existence after the Great Migration) conjured condescending attitudes among Black evangelicals toward traditional Black worship styles, music, and preaching.[12]

FELLOWSHIP AND MINISTRY

As time progressed, members discussed the distinct needs in their communities over against the standard ministry practices they were taught during their evangelical seminary training. Bentley and others began suggesting that the models for ministering in Black neighborhoods should differ from those in White evangelical contexts because indigenous methods needed to be developed with African American communities in mind.[13]

Along with Bentley, Ronald Potter questioned the ability of evangelical Bible colleges and seminaries to equip pastors serving in Black communities because they did not understand their own cultural captivity:

> Christianity, as it is expressed in American society, has been neocolonialist, oppressive, and racist. This has taken its most blatant form on evangelical Christian campuses. We talk a lot about peace on our Christian campuses, we talk a lot about the bringing together of people, Black people and White people, on evangelical Christian campuses; yet, many times this has been primarily based upon the norms of White evangelicals. . . . We have associated

---

[10]William H. Bentley, *The National Black Evangelical Association: Reflections on the Evolution of a Concept of Ministry* (Chicago: self-published, 1979), 18.
[11]Bentley, *National Black Evangelical Association*, 16.
[12]Bentley, *National Black Evangelical Association*, 16-17.
[13]Bentley, *National Black Evangelical Association*, 13.

Biblical Christianity with the norms and mores of evangelical subculture. We have had a wedding between Christianity as expressed in the Bible and cultural evangelicalism and the two have been so closely knit together that one can hardly differentiate them. Therefore, a student in his junior and senior year at these institutions will say, "If that is Christianity, I want no part of it."[14]

When this rebuke of Wheaton College, where Potter was studying, was published in *Inside* magazine, he was expelled for his attempt to uncover the cultural insensitivity he explained. This experience further hardened Potter's insistence that methods learned at evangelical educational institutions were ineffective in African American ministry environments and led him down the path of mainline Christianity. He finished his bachelor's degree at Rutgers University and attended seminary at the Interdenominational Theological Center in Atlanta. Potter later recalled that it was Bentley's influence that strengthened his evangelical convictions.

As National Negro Evangelical Association members affirmed the need to explore new ministry models, there was a simultaneous call to utilize the intellectual and monetary resources from within the Black community more intentionally, rather than being dependent on funds from White evangelicals. Bentley insisted,

> We were seeking to reach people, our people, but with little awareness of the resources to be found within our own religious tradition, resources that had been forged in the fires of affliction and had not been exhausted by the mere passage of time. We could not draw on these because we hardly recognized their existence. . . . The resulting cycle of dependence is so complete that those caught in its coils are virtually unable to escape. The wheel to self discovery is paralyzed and lights caught in this situation are doomed to look at themselves through the eyes of others. It is no wonder that appreciation for Black institutions and Black resources are so seldom, and even then—so inadequately appreciated. And even less frequently drawn upon![15]

The papers delivered at the earliest annual gatherings, as well as ensuing conversations, indicated a necessary and natural expansion of the association's original purpose from fellowship to intentionally exploring ministry methods. "Fellowship and ministry—these are the poles around which the Association revolves."[16]

---

[14]Ron Potter, quoted in "The Panel Discussion," *Inside* (September 1970): 60-61.
[15]Bentley, *National Black Evangelical Association*, 12.
[16]William H. Bentley, "Factors in the Origins in Focus of the National Black Evangelical Association," in *Black Theology: A Documentary Witness, 1966-1979*, ed. Gayraud S. Wilmore and James H. Cone (Maryknoll, NY: Orbis Books, 1979), 310. See vol. 2 for an excerpt from this work.

The existence of a new association did not mean that its members were uniform in their engagement with the challenges of Black life in the 1960s. During the civil rights movement, many Black evangelicals were torn in their efforts to appropriately distribute energy between engaging social ills and promoting the verbal proclamation of the gospel. As a result, the development of indigenous ministry methods and a heightened focus on issues plaguing the Black community were not met without suspicion in the association. Within the membership, there were those whose spiritual disposition prompted them to look past social issues and focus exclusively on saving souls, others who sought to engage social and intellectual movements apologetically, and still other Black activists who desired to engage in social transformation and community development as committed Christians. These subtle factions within the association became pronounced beginning with the election of George Perry as the association's third president.

THE RISE OF BLACK EVANGELICAL MILITANCE

In addition to the focus on evangelism and community ministry in phase-one leadership, others coming of age in the association insisted on the necessity of addressing current social and cultural issues—especially those associated with racial injustice. The debate about contextualized ministry was intensified because of the racial climate of the late 1960s. In short, the rising tide of social consciousness among Black evangelicals was not a move away from the doctrinal Anchors of African American Christianity but a debate about the emphasis on Deliverance within the National Negro Evangelical Association.

Howard Jones, the association's second president, embodied the fundamentalist stream of the association, which vied for an emphasis on personal evangelism in ministry philosophy. He resigned from his presidency after two years because the internal tensions mounted.[17] Jones recalled,

> The Black Power movement emerged as a dominant voice in the Black community. I had always been a strong supporter of civil rights in the vein of Dr. King; however, the Black Power movement demanded a more aggressive and nationalistic stand on issues of racial justice—and a Black man who worked for Billy Graham clearly seemed out of step with the direction the movement was going. Not everyone in the NBEA looked down upon my

---

[17]Soong-Chan Rah, "In Whose Image: The Emergence, Development, and Challenge of African American Evangelicalism" (PhD diss., Duke University, 2016), 202.

affiliation with Graham. But the small number of folks who *did* made a lot of noise, and I decided to leave that post in 1967.[18]

Jones's departure gave rise to new leaders, who were distinctly evangelical in their theology but mourned the social apathy of leading Black evangelicals amid the cultural crisis of the civil rights movement. This transition marked the rise of an emerging evangelical voice that insisted that non-Christians should not be the only ones to speak directly to issues facing the Black community. These new evangelical voices answered the lament of Ronald Potter, who was grieved by the overwhelming silence of Black evangelicals during the early 1960s. He later wrote,

> During most of the turbulent sixties, Black evangelicals remained conspicuously quiet. While Malcolm X, Stokely Carmichael, H. Rap Brown, and the Black Panthers attempted to define and defend Black personhood, most evangelicals mounted "pious irrelevancies and sanctimonious trivialities." Before the close of the decade, however, a vocal minority of militant Black evangelicals came on the scene.[19]

The National Negro Evangelical Association's third president, George Perry, broke the mold of the previous presidents with his sophisticated, urbane demeanor, sensitive to the challenges of ministering in his native New York. Perry brought a renewed commitment to caring for the whole person—both spiritually and physically. Jones's priority was "Get the gospel out!" Perry's emphasis was "Get it out to the whole man!"[20] Perry's two-year presidency was the context for the rise of the Black militant evangelical voice. The intensity of Perry's presidency was punctuated by three key events: the assassination of Dr. Martin Luther King Jr. in 1968, the ensuing conventions in Chicago and Atlanta, and the rise of the Young Turks.

KING, CHICAGO, AND ATLANTA

The debates about Black awareness hit a fever pitch after the assassination of Martin Luther King Jr. in 1968. Pastors gave extended thought to the civil rights and Black consciousness movements in an effort to shepherd their respective

---

[18]Howard O. Jones with Edward Gilbreath, *Gospel Trailblazer: An African American Preacher's Historic Journey Across Racial Lines* (Chicago: Moody, 2003), 216.
[19]Ronald C. Potter, "The New Black Evangelicals," in Wilmore and Cone, *Black Theology*, 304.
[20]Bentley, *National Black Evangelical Association*, 18.

flocks from a proactively Christian perspective. However, association members did not always agree on the proper disposition toward these movements, and debates about an appropriate Black evangelical social engagement were held in a string of the National Negro Evangelical Association's national conferences through the mid-1970s.

The 1968 convention was held in Chicago during the height of rioting sparked by King's assassination. This convention featured a presentation by the chairman of the Commission on Social Action—an initiative of the association—that further elevated the prominence of the debate. Bentley recounted that issues of Black identity swirled out of the meeting in Chicago and spilled out into unmistakable tensions during the 1969 convention, held in Atlanta.[21]

During the Atlanta gathering, matters of ethnic consciousness were central in the event's programming, and clear lines were drawn between those who held a more socially conservative bent and those who insisted that more conscious efforts be made to uphold Black culture and carefully relate the gospel within that context.[22] Voices that were previously unrepresented in the association's leadership joined with younger members to chart a new course for the Black evangelical movement.

The proceedings at the Atlanta convention were also a source of contention. This gathering marked the sixth anniversary of the association, and for the first time reports unequivocally expressed that the ministry methods honed within White evangelical seminaries were less effective in African American contexts. These reports continually asserted the need for indigenous ministry methods, yet another source of contention within the young association.[23]

THE YOUNG TURKS

A crew dubbed the "Young Turks" emerged after King's assassination, and the group's justice emphasis was a source of controversy within the National Negro Evangelical Association. While these younger Black evangelical militants were trying to understand why Black youth were rioting in the streets, traditional evangelicals, including faithful Bible expositor Edward Victor Hill (1933–2003), criticized rioters, preached law and order, and insisted on salvation as the primary means to address the challenges within the Black community. The leaders of the

---

[21]Bentley, *National Black Evangelical Association*, 19.
[22]Bentley, *National Black Evangelical Association*, 19-20.
[23]Bentley, *National Black Evangelical Association*, 20.

Young Turks included Tom Skinner (1942–1994), William (Bill) Pannell (1929–), Ron Potter, Columbus Salley (1943–), and others who sought a more holistic evangelical approach to cultural engagement and ministry.

> The term **Young Turk** emerged from the Turkish reformist and nationalist party formed in the waning years of the 1800s. Its continued use describes the ethos of the Turkish reform group as a person or group who aggressively and impatiently advocates for reform within an organization.

The rallying cries of the Young Turks were summarized in two books, both published in 1968: *Black and Free* by Tom Skinner and *My Friend, the Enemy* by William Pannell. *Black and Free* is Skinner's memoir chronicling his journey from being a gang leader in Harlem to becoming a renowned Christian leader and evangelist. Throughout his story, he conveys the brutalities of racism and White supremacy in society and recounts specific instances of overt racism while working within evangelical ministries.[24]

Like Skinner's book, Pannell's work gives a biographical sketch and speaks to the overarching challenges of pursuing racial reconciliation as a minority in predominantly White churches and organizations. The book's nearly self-contradictory title represented the growing apprehension of many young Blacks within evangelical institutions. The unadulterated honesty of the book was shocking, even to Pannell's friends, who insisted that the book was written by an outside agitator because "That's just not the Bill Pannell that I knew," having grown up in the same small town in Michigan. Pannell's response was, "That's because you didn't know Bill Pannell, or the world I lived in."[25]

Pannell's writings are clear in affirming that he believed many of his evangelical friends had good intentions toward him as an individual, but he conveys several examples of willful ignorance about the systemic racism that plagued his life story. He admits that his early evangelical experience was marked by naiveté, but his accommodation of White supremacy, both overt and covert, was transformed into a "righteous discontent" as the 1960s progressed.[26] With these prophetic volumes, Skinner and Pannell rallied an up-and-coming generation of Black evangelicals

---

[24]See vol. 2 for an excerpt from Skinner's *Black and Free*.
[25]William E. Pannell, "This Is Then, That Was Now," *Fuller Studio* 1 (2014), https://fullerstudio.fuller.edu/this-is-then-that-was-now/.
[26]Tejai Beulah, "Soul Salvation, Social Liberation: Race and Evangelical Christianity in the Black Power Era, 1969–1979" (PhD diss., Drew University), 71.

whose influence within the National Negro Evangelical Association became undeniable during the coming years.[27]

The 1969 convention marked the first exodus of conservative Black and White members from the association. Some White members sincerely believed that the association was developing into a group of White-baiting reverse racists. Less radical Black members who focused on the verbal proclamation of the gospel—through missions and evangelism—also felt betrayed by the emerging radical emphasis. The shift in leadership and convention programming left these members feeling pushed aside, so they departed.[28]

Despite the mounting tension within the association concerning Black social consciousness, a consensus remained that championed the evangelical theology that characterized the association's inception. This unanimity was clear upon the invitation to partner with the National Committee of Negro Churchmen (later named the National Committee of Black Churchmen). This coalition of Black ministers consisted of a broader swath of doctrinal convictions than the those of the National Negro Evangelical Association. Members of the National Negro Evangelical Association, on both sides of their internal skirmish, resisted the partnership because they valued theological uniformity over a common pursuit of social issues. Few within the association desired to open the door to a broader set of disagreements than those internally generated from members who held to similar theological convictions with distinct social postures. Bentley recalled,

> Had we even agreed to enter dialogue just to get better acquainted, the split in the NBEA would have swiftly escalated into a full rupture, and the NBEA would have lost virtually all its "conservative" contingent, many of its moderates, and could not have continued to exist in the gifts and commitments of the remaining radical element—for radicals are notorious for their critical propensities and not necessarily for their ironical ones. Even radicals within the association as a group were not as advanced as were the leadership of the NCBC.[29]

The refusal to entertain a partnership with the National Council of Black Churchmen is a continuous reminder that National Negro Evangelical Association members prioritized unity forged by doctrinal fidelity over uniformity of social concern. This vignette notwithstanding, the association launched into a new phase of Black consciousness with Bentley's presidency.

---

[27]See vol. 2 for an excerpt from Pannell's *My Friend, the Enemy*.
[28]Bentley, *National Black Evangelical Association*, 20-21.
[29]Bentley, *National Black Evangelical Association*, 22, 25-26.

11

BLACK EVANGELICAL CONSCIOUSNESS

THE NEXT PHASE OF BLACK EVANGELICALISM is a powerful reminder that Black Christianity, even among self-identified Black evangelicals, is not monolithic. While the feuding factions of Black evangelicals maintained the historic Anchors of African American Christianity, the battle raged over the role and emphasis of Deliverance in theological formation and ministry practice.

PHASE 2—BLACK CONSCIOUSNESS: 1970-1989

The cleavage that erupted at the 1969 gathering in Atlanta between older, traditional evangelicals and younger evangelical militants was intensified at the following year's annual meeting, held in New York.[1] This was the beginning of a new era for the National Negro Evangelical Association. This transition was accentuated by the departure of second president Howard Jones and the inauguration of William H. Bentley. Ronald Potter later insisted, "Dr. William H. Bentley, the 'godfather' of militant Black Evangelicals, was attempting to raise the social and ethnic consciousness of Black Christians years before Black Power was in vogue. Bentley, perhaps more than anyone else, has contributed to a distinct Black Evangelical school of thought."[2] This came to a head when younger members, as Potter puts it, "forced the convention to address the 'unholy' Graham-Nixon alliance and to support John Perkins, a Black Evangelical social activist who was jailed and severely beaten for his involvement in social issues in Mississippi."[3]

---

[1]Ronald C. Potter, "The New Black Evangelicals," *Black Theology: A Documentary Witness, 1966–1979*, ed. Gayraud S. Wilmore and James H. Cone (Maryknoll, NY: Orbis Books, 1979), 304.
[2]Potter, "New Black Evangelicals," 305.
[3]Potter, "New Black Evangelicals," 304.

The gathering was punctuated by Columbus Salley delivering a plenary address adapted from his coauthored book *Your God Is Too White* (1970).[4] Salley's address inspired the Young Turks because, more than Skinner's *Black and Free*, Salley's book was an explicit expression of their passion for elevating social justice issues alongside the association's existing evangelistic emphasis. Salley offered strong critiques of evangelicalism that challenged its assumptions about race relations and the difficulties facing African Americans. He insisted that Black Christians could learn from the Black power movement instead of just critiquing it, and the cadre of his peers agreed:

> The tragedy of the Black experience in relation to "Christianity" is that "Christianity" (as manifested through its association with dehumanizing institutions and their values) was and is unable to provide Blacks with the necessary basis to free themselves from White oppression and a sense of inferiority. Thus, there has crystallized within the Black community a Black consciousness and sensitivity to their own humanity and to their own past and future. This new awareness and its social expression is called Black Power.[5]

After emphasizing the absence of resources to affirm Black humanity within evangelicalism, Salley insisted on the psychological necessity to affirm Black power:

> Black Power is the bold assertion of the fact that the humanity of Blacks is a non-negotiable, indisputable, non-compromising reality. . . . Black Power is initially the psychological realization that White oppressive, dehumanizing institutions are only capable of making Blacks insensitive to their humanity; that no man or institutional form has the power to destroy the basic humming of Black people.[6]

By asserting that God is present amid the particular sufferings of the African American community, not just in the "sweet by and by," Salley illustrated his nearness by saying that God became Black.[7] At this point, Ronald Potter discerned that "the lid was blown off many previously Negro evangelicals." He identified this

---

[4]Columbus Salley and Ronald Behm, *Your God Is Too White* (Downers Grove, IL: InterVarsity Press, 1970). Behm was a White pastor of South Shore Bible Church in Chicago.
[5]Salley and Behm, *Your God Is Too White*, 63-64.
[6]Salley and Behm, *Your God Is Too White*, 65.
[7]Salley and Behm, *Your God Is Too White*, 73.

as the time when "this new form of Black consciousness began permeating Black evangelical thinking."[8]

In addition to Salley's speech in 1970, Tom Skinner's rise to prominence was yet another source of momentum for the Young Turks. Skinner's ability to proclaim his personal conversion story and highlight the importance of individual salvation seized the attention of both Black and White evangelical communities. Skinner's revivals featured alter calls that were familiar to evangelicals, but with a distinctive Afrocentric disposition. Between the success of *Black and Free* and his well-attended crusades, his global platform gave rise to his 1970 address at the Urbana student missions conference, which shook evangelicalism to its core. During this time, Skinner had become the most prominent voice among Black evangelicals. Despite his momentary rise to prominence, his life is a parable of the tensions that Black evangelicals face within the broader evangelical landscape. When he began actively applying the message of Christ to racial injustice in his speeches and books, he lost large swaths of his White evangelical following.

TOM SKINNER

Skinner was the son of a Baptist minister from Harlem, New York. His parents, Alester Jerry Skinner and Georgia Skinner, moved from South Carolina and arrived in New York during World War II among the population swell of the Great Migration. As a preacher's kid, Skinner was disenchanted by the Black church throughout his youth because of the highly emotional services driven by charismatic preaching and the apparent lack of spiritual formation among some ministers and congregants. These grievances from his childhood were carried into adulthood, and he demonstrated little appreciation for congregations such as Abyssinian Baptist Church, which worked diligently to be a spiritual oasis and to advocate for poor Blacks in Harlem.[9] Despite these grievances, Skinner regularly attended church and performed well in school.

Rev. Alester Skinner educated his children in the faith but also provided loving insight into social inequities facing African Americans to help his children thrive in a world where Black youth had to go the extra mile to succeed. Tom was an excellent student who loved to read and expand his knowledge base. He recalled

---

[8]Ronald C. Potter, "Race, Theological Discourse and the Continuing American Dilemma," in *The Gospel in Black and White*, ed. Dennis L. O'Kholm (Downers Grove, IL: InterVarsity Press, 1997), 33. See vol. 2 for an excerpt from this work.
[9]Beulah, "Soul Salvation, Social Liberation," 84-85.

that while he was growing up, he was enthralled by a Black nationalist bookstore on 122nd Street and Seventh Avenue in Harlem, owned by a Pentecostal bishop. He frequented the bookstore after school, and it was not uncommon to find men such as Malcom X, Louis Farrakhan, and Rev. Adam Clayton Powell debating politics and faith, which shaped Skinner as a young man.[10] However, like other youth in Harlem, he was drawn toward mischief and joined a street gang.

While Skinner was excelling in school, he became a leader of a notorious New York City gang, the Harlem Lords. A few months after his initiation, he challenged the leader and succeeded. Gang life granted a sense of intense camaraderie and protection that he longed for. One evening in 1956, before a gang fight, Skinner tuned in to listen to his favorite disk jockey and was caught off guard by an unscheduled radio broadcast. The preacher captivated Skinner with the words of 2 Corinthians 5:17, and for the first time he was moved to a prayer of repentance for sin in his life. He met the gang at the fight location and announced his conversion and departure from the gang, declaring that he was dedicating his passion for reading and education to serve God and his people.

In 1959, Skinner enrolled at Wagoner College on Staten Island. After studying history and philosophy during his undergraduate years, he continued his education at Manhattan Bible Institute, where he was influenced by professor Edward H. Boyce. Skinner described Boyce, an immigrant from Barbados and graduate from Moody Bible Institute and the Bible Institute of Los Angeles (now commonly called BIOLA), as a staunchly conservative Pentecostal who approached Scripture from within the Dutch Reformed tradition.[11]

As he finished his master's degree at Manhattan Theological Seminary, Skinner preached in the streets of Harlem and attracted crowds, and many placed their faith in Christ for salvation. During his final year in college, Skinner helped form the Harlem Evangelistic Association. The Harlem Evangelistic Association is often remembered for organizing an evangelistic crusade at the Apollo Theater.

> Harlem's **Apollo Theater** was a world-renowned entertainment venue that hosted legendary acts from the African American community and played a significant role in promoting little-known talent during the Harlem Renaissance.

---

[10]Soong-Chan Rah, "In Whose Image: The Emergence, Development, and Challenge of African American Evangelicalism" (PhD diss., Duke University, 2016), 211.
[11]Rah, "In Whose Image," 215-16.

According to the Harlem Evangelistic Association's head count, there were ten thousand people in attendance at the Apollo Theater for the crusade. "By the crusade's end, more than 2,200 people had responded to Skinner's presentation of the gospel, and the 20-year-old evangelist was hailed as a preaching phenomenon."[12] After his success at the Apollo, in 1963, Skinner's ministry expanded to Africa with his first set of crusades in Guyana, with an audience of over twenty-five thousand people. Throughout the 1960s, Skinner's impact continued to grow as he delivered addresses at Drew University, Grand Valley State College, and Howard University.[13]

Throughout the 1960s, Skinner's emphasis began with personal evangelism and Conversion, which broadly appealed to White evangelicals. His revivalistic emphasis afforded him the opportunity to address the National Association of Evangelicals (for the first time) in 1967, and he was introduced by Billy Graham when he addressed the National Congress on Evangelicalism in 1969. Skinner's 1970 talk at the Urbana missions conference, however, was the initiation of a new register that included racial issues, emphasizing his commitment to the Deliverance anchor of his theological commitments—for which White evangelicalism had no parallel. As a result, he was ostracized and assumed to have lost his evangelical theological moorings. While Skinner never jettisoned his commitment to writing and speaking about Conversion, his 1970 speech indicated a deepened understanding of racism and a commitment to addressing it as a Christian.

Skinner began his remarks by establishing that Black identity became synonymous with chattel slavery, and he continued by insisting that slavery was upheld by political, economic, and religious systems. He concluded by critiquing "Bible-believing" Christians who were "stringently silent" in the face of the Black plight in America. Then Skinner borrowed from Pannell's *My Friend, the Enemy* and critiqued White evangelicals for preaching a message of "love your enemy" and "do good to them who hurt you" without a decisive message that challenged the oppressive actions of Whites.

The 1970 Urbana missions conference was a watershed within the Black and White evangelical communities. The breach widened between those who insisted on an exclusive emphasis on missions and evangelism and those who affirmed the need for gospel proclamation and insisted on applying its truths to race relations. After Skinner's landmark address, many Black evangelicals who felt like orphans

---

[12]Edward Gilbreath, "A Prophet Out of Harlem," *Christianity Today*, September 16, 1996, www.christianitytoday.com/ct/1996/september16/6ta036.html.
[13]Rah, "In Whose Image," 216.

within evangelicalism flocked to Tom Skinner Associates, which was established in 1964. Tom Skinner Associates provided an opportunity for young men to be trained in ministry. Skinner and his first associate, William Pannell, promoted a pro-Black and pro-evangelical ethos that they sought to pass down to the next generation.

WILLIAM PANNELL

Pannell is from Sturgis, Michigan, a small, predominantly White town. In an interview, Pannell explained that though racism was seldom blatant in Sturgis, there was a social hierarchy established around race and class.[14] As a star athlete, Pannell experienced a kind of social privilege to which nonathletic Black men were not privy. However, he admits that while on the court, he was seen to be a "real" person, but after the game was over, he was viewed as "something else."[15]

As a young man, Pannell's greatest ambition was not to push a broom like many of the other Black men in his community. After placing his faith in Jesus Christ during his junior year of college, his goal was to discover God's will for his life. In 1951, Pannell graduated with a Bachelor of Arts from Fort Wayne Bible College. He went on to study Black history at Wayne State University and later to earn a Master of Arts in social ethics from the University of Southern California.

Pannell's perspective on theology, evangelism, and race relations was shaped by his time in the classroom and serving in the community. During the civil rights era, Pannell served as an assistant youth pastor in Detroit and an area youth director for the Brethren Assemblies. From 1964 to 1968, he served as an assistant director of leadership with Youth for Christ. After years with Youth for Christ, he transitioned to work at Tom Skinner Associates as its vice president.

After Tom Skinner Associates' heyday, beginning in the late 1960s, the organization began to decline in the late 1970s. Pannell attributes the loss of financial support for Tom Skinner Associates to Skinner's ongoing engagement with White racism within evangelicalism. A second challenge, noted by Edward Gilbreath, was that the young people mentored by Skinner and Pannell departed Tom Skinner Associates to establish their own ministries.[16] The third challenge, which the organization never recovered from, was the loss of William Pannell to Fuller Theological Seminary. Due to Skinner's heavy travel schedule, the administrative responsibilities

---

[14]Robert Schuster, "Oral History Interviews with William E. Pannell," May 25, 1995, https://archives.wheaton.edu/repositories/4/resources/448.
[15]William E. Pannell, *My Friend, The Enemy* (Waco, TX: Word Books, 1968), 18.
[16]Beulah, "Soul Salvation, Social Liberation," 101.

rested squarely on Pannell. In hopes of pursuing his passion to teach students, Pannell departed for Fuller Seminary in 1974, where he was a longtime professor and was later granted the prestigious status of professor emeritus.

> **Fuller Theological Seminary honored Pannell** in 2015 by renaming its Center for Black Church Studies the William E. Pannell Center for African American Church Studies. This honor was bestowed after forty years of service. Pannell began teaching at Fuller in 1974 and received emeritus status in 2014.

For Skinner and Pannell, both power and community were defined by a person's orientation toward Jesus Christ. Neither Skinner nor Pannell left any ambiguity about their understanding of Jesus; he was well defined in Skinner's Urbana speech and in his subsequent works, including *How Black Is The Gospel* and *Words of Revolution* (both published in 1970).[17] Together, Skinner and Pannell deployed Black power language to express their theologically rooted concepts of liberation, revolution, and radicalism. Their influence on broader evangelicalism is undeniable, and their presence within the National Negro Evangelical Association insisted that the Young Turks could no longer be ignored.

> **A debate on Black consciousness** was hosted in Boston and included Michael Haynes, Ron Potter, Carl Ellis, and others soon after the 1972 annual meeting in Jackson, Mississippi. The proceedings of this event, which was not sponsored by the National Negro Evangelical Association, were transcribed and featured as articles for an issue of *Freedom Now*, a periodical later renamed *The Other Side*.

THE SPREAD OF CONSCIOUS BLACK EVANGELICALISM

With the Bentley presidency alongside the ongoing disruption of Columbus Salley's book, the skyrocketing popularity of Skinner, and the impact of Pannell, the Young Turks were no longer fringe; they were represented in leadership and increasingly in the literature. In addition to the significant 1971 Zondervan publication *When God Was Black* (1971), written by James Montgomery and Bob Harrison, Urban Ministries was established in 1970. This organization, directed by Melvin Banks Sr., produced Sunday school and other literature for African American churches that carried evangelical Black consciousness into churches.

---

[17]Beulah, "Soul Salvation, Social Liberation," 101.

The increased Black awareness of the National Negro Evangelical Association triggered a name change at the 1973 annual convention in Pittsburgh, from the National Negro Evangelical Association to the National Black Evangelical Association. Despite the name change and the ongoing debate about developing a "Black evangelical Black theology," according to Bentley, neither of the factions was able to take command of the association with unchallenged primacy. The stability of the association during this season of self-definition was not incidental. Along with healthy organizational structures, Bentley notes the "moderate" contingent, who held the association together during a season of turbulence. Bentley specifically praises Betty Quimby, Aaron Hamblin, Ruth Lewis Bentley, Daniel and Dessie Webster, and Theodore Banks as stabilizing forces who preserved the association against polarization. Through it all, "The touchtone of whether or not a view was allowed expression, along with all others, was its willingness to submit to the lordship of Jesus Christ."[18]

> **The shift from *Negro* to *Black*** signaled an assertion of autonomy from a designation given by White people (i.e., Negro) to a Black self-designation that embodied the beauty and inherent worth of Black people and culture.

Bentley also celebrated the internal checks and balances that existed within the National Negro Evangelical Association, which allowed for a robust debate about important issues. One of those measures was the adoption of the umbrella concept of ministry. Although it was a borrowed concept, its primary framer within the National Black Evangelical Association was George Perry, alongside other officers, including Aaron Hamblin, Melvin Banks, and Bentley. The umbrella concept affirmed an intentional desire to promote leaders who represented various approaches, emphases in the Black-White dialogue, and ministry philosophies, with an irrevocable prerequisite of total commitment to Jesus Christ as Lord. This affirmed that the association was a family over whom God was Father. Bentley insists, "This required recognition and meaningful acceptance of the unity of the brethren along both racial and cultural lines accompanied by a strong emphasis on the ministry of reconciliation."[19]

---

[18]William H. Bentley, *The National Black Evangelical Association: Reflections on the Evolution of a Concept of Ministry* (Chicago: self-published, 1979), 21.
[19]Bentley, *National Black Evangelical Association*, 21, 27.

> **The National Black Christian Student Conference** was cofounded by Ruth Lewis Bentley and Wyn Wright-Potter in 1973 as the student arm of the National Black Evangelical Association. They produced a text called *Handbook for Black Christian Students: How to Remain Sane and Grow in a White College Setting*, which was celebrated and widely circulated.

After Bentley's presidency, the discussion about a Black evangelical approach to Black consciousness, ministry philosophies, and a Black evangelical Black theology continued in good spirits. Within the National Black Evangelical Association, two predominant schools of thought vied for a more socially engaged ministry philosophy against a more traditional evangelical approach. One was a Chicago-based, Bentley-led band that held Black nationalist sympathies, and the other group was based in Dallas and led by Tony Evans with the help of Ruben S. Connor, who later served as National Black Evangelical Association president. Despite the clash, the two camps had ongoing cordial interactions.[20]

"BLACK EVANGELICAL BLACK THEOLOGY"

The 1976 Chicago convention, referred to as Chicago II, took on the form of a theological workshop and took up issues associated with developing a Black evangelical Black theology. Interlocutors in the discussion were three younger association members who were not associated with the initial band of Young Turks: Anthony (Tony) Evans of Dallas Theological Seminary, Ronald Potter of Rutgers University, and John Skinner, who was studying at Union Theological Seminary in New York at the time. This was the highlight of the convention, attracting overflow crowds and producing insightful dialogue among the participants.

> **"Down with the Honky Christ—Up with the Funky Jesus"** by Clarence Hilliard was a popular article published in the January 30, 1976, edition of *Christianity Today*. This provocative article represented the ongoing struggle to undo racialization from a Christian perspective. In the article, Hilliard describes a "honky" as affirming the status quo (either Black or White), and he describes Jesus as "funky," someone who moves apart from the ruling religious system and stands with the poor, oppressed, and disinherited.

---

[20]Jamal-Dominique Hopkins, "Black Evangelicalism and the Reforming Influence of William H. Bentley," *Faithfully Magazine*, April 14, 2022, https://faithfullymagazine.com/william-bentley-Black-evangelicalis/.

The productive dialogue format that produced inroads toward understanding within the association was repeated in San Francisco in 1977 under the oversight of Tony Evans, who served as chairman of the Commission on Theology. The format was repeated and expanded at the Atlanta II convention with the addition of a formal paper read by professor Noel Erskine of Emory University. This event concluded with a newfound like-mindedness within the association. Participants agreed that the meeting took a crucial step that cleared the ground necessary to commence laying the foundation for a viable Black evangelical Black theology.[21]

Proponents of a Black evangelical Black theology resolved to retain the evangelical fundamentals of the faith, including commitments to the inerrancy and verbal plenary inspiration of the Bible, which is the sole authority of life and faith. Central to the National Black Evangelical Association statement of faith is also an affirmation of the divine Trinity and salvation, which comes through belief in Christ's substitutionary death on the cross and subsequent resurrection. However, much like the need to explore ministry models, the National Black Evangelical Association insisted on examining evangelical theological assumptions to engage the Black experience theologically and pastorally. Bentley asserted,

> We are, therefore, proclaiming our Declaration of Independence from uncritical dependence upon White evangelical theologians who would attempt to tell us what the content of our efforts at liberation should be. . . . We see no necessity of freeing ourselves from our own evangelicalism. We do see to free ourselves from the implied norms of White theologians exclusivisms![22]

Bentley decried a fatal misstep of American theology, namely that it had a "chronic myopia in matters pertaining to the interaction of the American social context with the development of theology." In short, it assumed a "normal" theological context, which was not contextless but White. Thus, "there has been next to nothing done to recognize the existence of Black Theology as a viable contribution, or even a critique to American Evangelical theology."[23] Despite Bentley's insistence on acknowledging Black theology's existence, by no means did he insist on full affirmation of the movement but rather the need to develop an evangelical approach to Black theology. Specifically, this was a theology that affirmed the full humanity of African Americans by theologizing about the full

---

[21] William H. Bentley, "Factors in the Origin and Focus of the National Black Evangelical Association," in Wilmore and Cone, *Black Theology*, 317.
[22] Bentley, "Factors in the Origin," 314.
[23] Bentley, "Factors in the Origin," 313.

scope of the Black experience—not just agreeing that African Americans are made in God's image.

Bentley asserted that one task of a Black evangelical Black theology was to come to grips with the helpful contributions of both White evangelicalism and Black liberationists while finding a distinct place to stand theologically while affirming the association's doctrinal essentials. One area where distancing from both camps needed to take place was the interface between the sacred and secular. On the one hand, Bentley argued,

> Because an historical and contemporary characteristic evangelicalism is to dichotomize too artificially "social" and "sacred"—we Blacks who have come to be called "evangelicals" (and so identify ourselves), having been nurtured under this worldview from which the dichotomy comes, have need to be more critical of the extent to which the dichotomy is valid and actively reflective of biblical truth.[24]

Having critiqued the artificial separation between sacred and secular that ran through evangelicalism, he also criticized the opposite problem, prevalent in Black theology, which uncritically accepts Black cultural forms without the need to assess them with Scripture:

> A very important part of our [i.e., Black] cultural heritage is a tendency which may be regarded as the very opposite of the dichotomy. Unchecked, and uncritically accepted, it can lead us to that other extreme—which is just as incomplete and only partially reflective of Gospel truth. Our tendency to social perception, carried to the extreme, can lead to an equally unbiblically blurring of distinctions, where distinctions ought to and do exist. In either case, we will be left with a truncated Gospel. Either it will be so severely individualistic, that it is for all practical purposes socially blind. Or, and this is the other horn of the dilemma, we can be so blinded by some elements of our cultural heritage, that we in effect identify the Gospel with our Black culture.[25]

Then Bentley continued by declaring the position a Black evangelical Black theology must take: "Caring for the whole, we must not minimize care of the soul! Our escape from the dilemma consists in our critical adoption of a more realistic 'Both-And!' All this boils down to the fact that we must be anchored to the Rock

---

[24]Bentley, "Factors in the Origin," 318.
[25]Bentley, "Factors in the Origin," 318.

even while geared to the times! Both extremes must be carefully avoided, in the interest of the truth."[26]

Bentley's vision for a Black evangelical Black theology was a sincere effort to reorder the emphasis on the theological Anchors—thereby situating the place of Deliverance—over against three groups. First, unstated in his assessment was his Black evangelical forerunners, who thoughtfully elevated the need for Deliverance with a keen understanding of the cultural context—where deliverance is pursued—without minimizing the other Anchors. Second, Bentley's stated foil consisted of White evangelicals who, much like their phase-one Black evangelical counterparts, emphasized Conversion at the cost of Deliverance. Finally, Bentley distanced himself from Black liberationists (namely, James Cone and Gayraud Wilmore), who centered Deliverance at the cost of de-emphasizing Jesus' atonement and the Anchor of Conversion, thus making them culturally captive.

A vision for a Black evangelical Black theology that does not fall into the ruts of the extremes is Carl F. Ellis Jr's. *Free at Last: The Gospel in the African American Experience* (1983). *Free at Last* assumes the biblical premise that God works through culture, and Ellis biblically analyzed the African American cultural experience as a case study. Though Ellis applies his method of cultural criticism to African American life, his approach to cultural analysis could be applied to people of any background. Ellis himself has long ties to the evangelical movement. He was among the Black students present at InterVarsity's Urbana student missions conference in 1967 who were disappointed by its exclusive overseas emphasis, which included no discussion about ministry needs in America's urban centers. Despite being recruited by InterVarsity, Ellis joined Tom Skinner Associates in 1969 as the director of campus ministries because Skinner and Pannell's ministry emphasis was more applicable for his ministry context. After decades of faithful ministry, teaching, and writing, Ellis is rightly heralded as the "father of Black Reformed theology."[27]

The notion of a Black evangelical Black theology started strong but did not persist. One reason for its lack of longevity was that many of its primary proponents were ministry practitioners, not academics. This distinction is relevant because ministers write second and minister first, as opposed to scholars in academic institutions, for whom writing is an essential part of academic life. Due to this state of affairs, the primary sources for a Black evangelical Black theology are hard to find, and the little in existence is not seriously engaged by Black liberationists.

---

[26]Bentley, "Factors in the Origin," 318.
[27]See vol. 2 for an excerpt from Ellis's *Beyond Liberation*, which was renamed *Free at Last* in a later edition.

An example of Black evangelicalism's rejection from the academy are articles by Bentley and Potter in the first edition of *Black Theology: A Documentary Witness, 1966–1979*, edited by James Cone and Gayraud Wilmore. Their essays, which critiqued Black liberation theology and attempted to chart a new theological course for African Americans, were excluded from the revised version, published in 1993. Ironically, Black liberationists and Black evangelicals have some shared concerns about the state of evangelical theology, but they rarely occupy the same conversational spaces. Black liberationists often insist that Black evangelicals are unaware of the Whiteness that is intrinsic to evangelical theology. Conversely, with the exception of a few academically minded African American evangelicals, many have not seriously engaged the written literature produced by Black liberationists because of differences in fundamental theological presuppositions. It is the exception, not the rule, that Black liberationists and evangelical scholars have serious engagement, especially because the former are commonly educated in university divinity schools and the latter are often trained in evangelical Bible colleges and seminaries.

THE NATIONAL BLACK EVANGELICAL ASSOCIATION TODAY

Longtime National Black Evangelical Association president Walter Arthur McCray (1952–) is one of the prolific contemporary embodiments of Black evangelical Black theology. His written corpus does not receive the attention it deserves because of a proactive choice to publish with his own publishing house, Black Light Fellowship, which limits distribution and marketing. Despite the ongoing efforts of McCray and others, the National Black Evangelical Association has suffered a gradual decline. After the initial decade of interest and enthusiasm, the association never recovered from the initial departure of conservative Blacks and White members at the beginning of the 1970s, and the Afrocentric Christianity that surfaced from the theological sparring of the 1970s did not entice subsequent generations of Black evangelicals to join the association.

Walter Arthur McCray is a self-proclaimed "gospelizer"—a holistic "good news messenger" of the resurrected Lord Jesus Christ. This Chicago native is a graduate of Trinity College (now Trinity International University) with a Bachelor of Arts in biblical studies. He began serving as National Black Evangelical Association president in 1999. In his four decades of ministry, he has pastored churches, has written multiple books, and maintains an ongoing itinerant ministry.

In light of the large numbers of African American Christians of evangelical persuasion and declining engagement with the National Black Evangelical Association, the 1990 convention assessed whether its relationship with the broader evangelical movement was a hindrance to greater participation. This concern emerged in a debate about dropping "evangelical" from the association's name because it evokes notions of political conservatism, which alienates them from the historically Black church. However, even self-designated Black militant evangelicals, including McCray, vied not to jettison the name because it would allow the gospel (and the associated doctrinal commitments) to become the property of Whiteness by default.[28]

> **The evangelical left** is largely misunderstood because it remains a generally underexplored phenomenon. Despite the lack of written exploration, "evangelical left" describes the political ethos of large swaths of Black Christians. The evangelical left confidently affirms Christian orthodoxy and simultaneously critiques the social status quo.

Historically, the National Black Evangelical Association served as a place where self-consciously orthodox African American Christians could have honest dialogue and reach compromise under the umbrella concept of ministry. But the tensions that mark Black evangelical existence were the association's undoing. Despite the association's ongoing decline, Black Christians of evangelical persuasion abound, and the association is an ongoing reference point for understanding Christ-centered faith and Black identity that is unfortunately well-hidden. Those involved in early twenty-first-century developments, which include an exodus of Blacks from White evangelical churches, would be well served to reference those who engaged in an eerily similar dialogue decades before.

---

[28]Walter McCray, *Pro-Black, Pro-Christ, Pro-cross: African-Descended Evangelical Identity* (Chicago: Black Light Fellowship, 2012), 1, 3.

12

BLACK EVANGELICAL DIASPORA

BLACK EVANGELICALISM'S FIRST TWO PHASES are essential to assess because they illustrate the various tensions embodied within the Black evangelical family. Phase three features a diasporic reality that spans diverse denominations, institutions, and associations. Despite occupying diverse contexts, on the whole Black evangelicals hold tightly to doctrinal Anchors highlighting a Big God, Jesus, and the Good Book. Every Black evangelical also insists that Conversion and Walking in the Spirit are essential to the Christian life, and Deliverance is a direct outworking of individual conversion.

PHASE 3—BLACK EVANGELICALISM BEYOND THE NATIONAL BLACK EVANGELICAL ASSOCIATION: 1990S–PRESENT

The third phase of Black evangelicalism highlights the varied environments that African American evangelicals call home. While some remain loyal to the National Black Evangelical Association, this phase describes the various contexts of worship and service where Black evangelicals exist into the present. Heartbreakingly, even though the majority of Black Christians can be described as evangelical (in a theological sense), the quest to find an environment of theological and social belonging remains. The sense of being without a place of their own explains the diaspora of Black evangelicals across America's Christian landscape. Interestingly, phase three demonstrates how the tensions and struggles of the previous phases were carried into the next and emerged with unique struggles in different contexts.[1]

EVANGELICALS IN HISTORIC BLACK DENOMINATIONS

The 2014 Religious Landscape Study by Pew Research indicates that African Americans read the Bible more regularly than any ethnic group in the United

---
[1] See vol. 2 for an excerpt from Robert Smith Jr.'s "The Neglected God."

States.[2] While the study did not assess the respondents' assumptions about Scripture, as a people African Americans hold the Bible in comparatively high regard. Since Scripture is alive and active (see Hebrews 4:12), it follows that when the Bible is opened, often belief is kindled or the flame of faith is fanned.[3]

Pastoral training in Black churches nurtured an abiding trust in Scripture because the lion's share of Black ministers took apprenticeships under seasoned local ministers. This model of ministry training allowed many budding African American ministers to sidestep the battle over the Bible that raged in seminaries and divinity schools throughout the twentieth century. Consequently, among Blacks, the Good Book's authority was not described with technical terms such as "inerrancy" or "verbal plenary inspiration," formulated as an apologetic to combat theological liberalism in the academy. Among Black Christians, the mark of a high view of Scripture is acknowledging its authority and yielding to it. Scriptural engagement among Black Christians insists that biblical authority is not an intellectual ascent to specific doctrines but an embodied experience of practicing God's Word in faith.

> **Bible-believing African Americans** are often required to affirm inerrancy or verbal plenary inspiration to work in evangelical institutions. For those born and reared in Black churches, terms such as *inerrancy* and *verbal plenary inspiration* are alien to their faith experience, while a full-throated affirmation of the Bible's divine authority is often without question. While it is prudent for evangelical institutions to have a statement on Scripture in the twenty-first century, the language that emerged from the battle over the Bible has cost Bible-believing African Americans countless ministry opportunities because they were unaware of the technical language but maintained an unwavering devotion to Scripture.

The history of widespread trust in the Bible resulted in many historically Black denominations having theologically evangelical doctrinal statements while rejecting the cultural and political assumptions of White evangelicalism. Since widespread orthodoxy marked the lion's share of Black churches, and the people of these denominations were often embroiled in a struggle for Black existence and freedom, there was little inherent motivation to doggedly defend their orthodox

---

[2] "2014 Religious Landscape Study: Frequency of Reading Scripture," Pew Research Center, www.pewresearch.org/religion/religious-landscape-study/frequency-of-reading-scripture/ (accessed September 10, 2022).
[3] See vol. 2 for an excerpt from Ronald V. Myers Sr.'s "Jazz Improvisation in Amos."

theological positions—they were assumed. However, some Blacks gradually donned the evangelical label to emphasize doctrinal intentionality for fear that what is assumed is often forgotten.[4]

A survey of doctrinal statements from the three largest African American denominations testifies to the evangelical heritage of Black Christianity, rooted in the African church fathers and running through the Great Awakenings. One example of a hub that trained Black ministers within the historic evangelical faith is Bishop College. Established in 1881, Bishop College was a Baptist college for African Americans established by the American Baptist Home Mission Society. Located in Marshall, Texas, Bishop was founded with a grammar and high school that offered trades including woodworking and carpentry, but its primary purpose was to educate teachers and pastors. In 1929 Joseph J. Rhodes was hired as Bishop's first Black president. A Marshall native and Bishop graduate, Rhoads led the school through a time of considerable growth. During this period, he discontinued the secondary school, and in 1931 he introduced an institute for ministers that attracted several hundred clergy.

After Rhodes's death in 1951, the United Negro College Fund and some of the school's board supported moving the campus from Marshall to Dallas. Dallas lacked a historically Black college or university, while Marshall was home to both Bishop and Wiley College. The last class to graduate on the Marshall campus was in the spring of 1961, and the school reopened in Dallas later that year. Despite Bishop's initial success in Dallas, the school lost its accreditation, faced dire financial problems, and closed in 1988. Bishop's 107-year legacy produced graduates who transformed the Christian landscape with the power of the gospel and an entrepreneurial spirit. A seminal example is Richard Henry Boyd (1843–1922), who founded both the National Baptist Publishing Board and the National Baptist Convention of America.

During the school's stint in Dallas, Bishop College trained some of America's most prolific and doctrinally sound ministers. E. K. Bailey graduated from Bishop College in 1969 and began his first pastorate at Mount Carmel Baptist Church in Dallas. During Bailey's master's and doctoral study at Southwestern Baptist Theological Seminary, he founded Concord Missionary Baptist Church, which soon became one of the fastest-growing churches in America. Bailey was known for brilliantly pairing biblical exposition with the traditional style of African American

---

[4]See vol. 2 for an excerpt from Charles E. Booth's sermon "When a Hunch Pays Off."

preaching. In 1989, in partnership with his wife, Shelia, he founded E. K. Bailey Ministries to train African American pastors and revitalize Black churches. A seminal event is the E. K. Bailey Expository Preaching Conference, which has trained both Black and White ministers to preach the gospel of Jesus Christ for decades.[5]

Pastor James T. Meeks also embodies the gospel-focused and entrepreneurial spirit of the Bishop tradition. After his graduation, Meeks founded Salem Baptist Church in 1985 with 193 members in Chicagoland. Meeks led the church, rooted in the historic confession of the Apostles' Creed, for nearly four decades until his retirement. Salem has served as a beacon of hope in the greater Chicago area and is home to over nine thousand members.

In addition to doctrinally evangelical African Americans, other Black church and denominational leaders have had direct ties to evangelical institutions. Among denominational leaders, beloved National Baptist Convention president Jerry Young earned his master's and doctoral degrees from Reformed Theological Seminary. Renowned Pastor Tony Evans, founder and pastor of the ninety-five-hundred-member Oak Cliff Bible Fellowship in Dallas, is a two-time graduate of Dallas Theological Seminary. Evans was the first African American doctoral graduate from Dallas in 1982, and he continues to set precedents, authoring several books, including the first study Bible edited by an African American minister.

Notable in this discussion of evangelical leaders is the rise of the Black megachurch. A megachurch is commonly defined as a church having at least two thousand people in attendance on a weekly basis. Pew Research estimates that there are 120 to 150 megachurches in the United States where attendees are predominantly Black.[6] While many megachurches draw large crowds because they are spreading the gospel, others, including T. D. Jakes and Creflo Dollar, have received criticism for promoting a prosperity gospel that resulted in the exponential growth of their ministries.

The essence of the term *evangelical*, which has its roots in the Greek word *euangelion*, meaning "good news," has been part of the Black church experience since its inception. Specifically, Black Christians have proclaimed the good news of Jesus with an emphasis on Conversion, Walking in the Spirit, and a high view

---

[5] See vol. 2 for an excerpt from Bailey's sermon "Does Jesus Care?"
[6] Besheer Mohamed, Kiana Cox, Jeff Diamant, and Claire Gecewicz, "10. A Brief Overview of Black Religious History in the U.S.," Pew Research Center, February 16, 2021, www.pewresearch.org/religion/2021/02/16/a-brief-overview-of-Black-religious-history-in-the-u-s/#fnref-34217-47.

of Scripture. These evangelical affirmations have been upheld and cherished outside the churches and institutions of White evangelicalism. However, doctrinally evangelical Black Christians have not always been affiliated with institutions directly associated with the broader evangelical movement.[7]

BLACK IN THE EVANGELICAL ACADEMY

Black evangelicals, on the whole, have had a bittersweet relationship with evangelical Bible colleges and seminaries. On the one hand, there is deep resonance because we are part of the same family, share the same heavenly Father, and affirm core doctrinal convictions. On the other hand, Black evangelicals commonly sense that they are accepted as long as they take on White evangelical cultural forms of worship and theological heroes, and explore the faith's implications for issues more prominent among White believers. Assessing Black cultural issues in the evangelical academy is often relegated to the "secular" realm, while matters important to their White counterparts are deemed "gospel issues." It follows that budding Black evangelical pastors and ministers feel the illegitimate tension in attending a school that either shares their doctrinal convictions or legitimizes the context in which they hope to minister.[8]

> **Black evangelical scholars and the Evangelical Theological Society** have had a frustrated relationship, crippled by the same challenges found with the evangelical academy—being welcomed to attend but with sporadic attention to Black evangelical needs. Since faculty have limited time and resources to allocate toward participating in academic societies, countless Black evangelicals have chosen to participate in the American Academy of Religion or the Society of Biblical Literature, despite doctrinal incongruence, to actively engage the theological and exegetical challenges commensurate with their communities of origin.

Many evangelical institutions of higher education have desired to diversify their faculty and administration. This desire has been met with several challenges. One seeming insurmountable challenge for evangelical institutions is that they are not aware of Black evangelicals with PhDs. This lack of awareness leads to the false assumption that there are very few Blacks qualified to teach. Since the time when William Pannell served as a Black forerunner in the evangelical academy,

---

[7]See vol. 2 for an excerpt from Claude Alexander Jr.'s sermon "Washbasin Religion."
[8]See vol. 2 for an excerpt from Jarvis Williams's *One New Man*.

the number of Black evangelicals who hold PhDs has risen and quickly climbed in the second and third decades of the twenty-first century. The real challenge these institutions face is whether their own graduates, and Black evangelicals from nonevangelical institutions, are willing to hold teaching posts in contexts where they will embody the illegitimate tension described above throughout their teaching career.[9]

Due to the central role Black ministers have played in African American communities, Black doctoral graduates, whose credentials often grant them opportunities for more prestigious pastorates, continually choose the pulpit over embodying ongoing tensions in White evangelical institutions. Moreover, many Black PhDs have a deep desire to be useful to their kinsmen in the flesh because of the unique needs within the community. This point is especially poignant because the flow of ministers is almost exclusively Black ministers moving *to* White evangelical churches and institutions—the inverse occurs on the rarest occasions.

BLACK EVANGELICALS AND DOCTORAL DEGREES

Historically, bright Black evangelicals were encouraged to pursue the Doctor of Ministry (DMin), a degree for ministry practitioners, rather than the Doctor of Philosophy (PhD), the highest terminal research degree. Blacks were often advised toward the DMin because of the false assumption that evangelical questions in Greek, Hebrew, biblical interpretation, and theology had been satisfied, and all Blacks had to do was take White evangelical theological and exegetical paradigms and apply them to their ministries. In addition to missed opportunities to convey orthodox doctrine in new ways and to apply right doctrine to additional issues, this paradigm stunted the Black faculty pool because the PhD is the standard credential for teaching most disciplines in a Bible college or seminary.

Bruce L. Fields (1951–2020) was a professor at Trinity Evangelical Divinity School from 1988 until he stepped down for medical reasons in 2019. He followed the trajectory of many early Black evangelicals by serving on the staff of an evangelical ministry, in his case Campus Crusade for Christ. His six years of parachurch ministry preceded his matriculation to Trinity Evangelical Divinity School, where he earned both a Master of Divinity and a Master of Theology. After completing his Doctor of Philosophy from the prestigious Marquette University, he

---

[9]See vol. 2 for an excerpt from Anthony B. Bradley's book *Aliens in the Promised Land*.

returned to his alma mater to serve as a faculty member. Fields's position at Trinity was groundbreaking. Despite not having authored a long list of books, he broke out of practical or applied theology disciplines, where most African American evangelical scholars resided at the time, into biblical and systematic theology, and he inspired a generation of Black evangelicals to follow in his footsteps.

Fields's theological convictions are apparent in his assessment of Black liberation theology in his short book *Introducing Black Theology: Three Critical Questions for the Evangelical Church*. In his assessment, he critiques Black liberation theologians in ways that correspond to multiple doctrinal Anchors of African American faith. In supporting the authority of the Good Book, Fields critiques James Cone for his method of biblical interpretation:

> My concerns, however, stem from two possible scenarios that arise from allowing experience to have the foundational interpretative role for theological formulation. Experience, apart from the transcendent perspective of revelation as embodied in Scripture and practiced in the community yielded to Scripture, cannot itself be elevated. . . . One possible resultant scenario is for black theological reflection to degenerate to something more in line with sociology that is merely baptized with Christian terminology.[10]

Fields's apprehension about experience manipulating doctrine does not end with biblical interpretation; it extends to Black liberationist and womanist assessments of Christ. Fields's primary concern is that for Cone the utility of the cross lacks substitution:

> Cone's definition of the cross robs the cross of both its endurance of suffering force and its substitutionary nature. As I intimated above, I do not wish to suggest that there is not a multiplicity of meanings properly proposed for the single event of Christ's death on the cross. I am arguing that some understandings lie outside of biblical parameters, and are therefore non-Christian. Not all interpretations of the atonement offered in the name of constructing a relevant understanding of the event and driven by a unique set of experiences may be called Christian.[11]

Of preeminent womanist scholar Delores Williams, Fields writes, "According to Williams, the suffering and death of Jesus on the cross cannot have redemptive

---

[10] Bruce L. Fields, *Introducing Black Theology: Three Critical Questions for the Evangelical Church* (Grand Rapids, MI: Baker Academic, 2001), 73.
[11] Fields, *Introducing Black Theology*, 91.

force for black women because that would be a type of baptism of their own suffering through the evil of surrogacy. Williams argues that 'there is nothing divine in the blood of the cross.'"[12] Fields is troubled by the primacy of the Black female experience overriding what he deems as a historic Christian understanding of Christ's person and work.

The final theological Anchor Fields assesses is the first dimension of Anchor 3, Conversion. His concern is that the way of salvation among Black theologians is more immediately associated with social activism on behalf of the oppressed, which Fields is certainly not unconcerned about, and not a dependence on Christ's finished work on the cross. Fields queries, "Does a person become a member of the community of the redeemed simply because he or she is a member of the community of the oppressed? . . . According to some, at least, the answer would be yes. However, right standing before God, contrary to the idea above, is accomplished through faith in Jesus Christ alone." Consistent with the Reformation tradition, Fields insists, "I am deeply burdened by any appearance of works-righteousness, whereby a person may gain the understanding that it is through good works that he or she gains forgiveness from God and obtains new life with him."[13]

In a personal encounter turned interview in the summer of 2015, when I was serving as a theology instructor at an evangelical seminary, I thanked Fields for his enduring example of faithfulness. His existence at Trinity Evangelical Divinity School demonstrated that serving in a predominantly White institution in the classical theological disciplines was possible. Fields proceeded to weep in a conference ballroom because he wondered whether he had squandered his teaching career at an institution where he embodied the illegitimate tension detailed above for so long. In that ballroom, I reassured him that his labors were not in vain. Five years later, he crossed the river into glory as a groundbreaking figure among Black evangelicals. Fields's legacy initiated a surge of African American biblical and theological scholars serving in evangelical institutions who will continually weaken the illegitimate tension he embodied throughout his career.

BLACK SCHOLARS WHO HAVE SERVED IN EVANGELICAL INSTITUTIONS FOLLOWING BRUCE FIELDS

Biblical studies: Quonekuia Day, Dennis Edwards, Esau McCaulley, Cleotha Roberts, Jarvis J. Williams

---

[12]Fields, *Introducing Black Theology*, 91-92.
[13]Fields, *Introducing Black Theology*, 101-2.

Theology: Uche Anizor, Vince E. Bacote, Anthony B. Bradley, Sherelle Ducksworth, Daniel Lee Hill, Kenneth Reid, Walter R. Strickland II

History: Vince Bantu, Eric M. Washington[a]

[a]See vol. 2 for an excerpt from Vince Bacote's *Reckoning with Race and Performing the Good News*.

BLACK AND REFORMED

Reformed theology has appealed to some African Americans because of its explicit focus on biblical exegesis and theology. The interpretative and theological structure within Reformed theology gives shape to the Bible-centric focus embodied throughout the African American Christian tradition. Many are like Doug Logan Jr., who serves as the inaugural president of Grimké Seminary in Richmond, Virginia, who, after sitting under the preaching of Philip Ryken, "discovered he was Reformed" based on his preexisting theological beliefs.[14]

Ken Jones, senior pastor of Greater Union Baptist Church in Compton, California, and former longtime cohost of the internationally syndicated radio program *White Horse Inn*, points to the five points of Calvinism or the doctrines of grace as a summation of Reformed theology, often referred to with the acronym TULIP.[15] Jones insists that the Reformed doctrine, summarized in TULIP, highlights the sovereignty and glory of God in salvation. Reformed theology begins with humanity's depravity, due to the fall, which renders humanity incapable of responding to the gospel. Through his long-suffering love, God's saving act warrants never-ending glory from his people.

The TULIP acrostic, which was developed at the Synod of Dort (1618–1619) by John Calvin's followers after his death and summarizes his teaching, stands for

- Total depravity
- Unconditional election
- Limited atonement
- Irresistible grace
- Perseverance of the saints

---

[14]See vol. 2 for an excerpt from Eric C. Redmond's essay in *Glory Road* called "Sovereign in a Sweet Home, School, and Solace."

[15]Ken Jones, "Introduction," in *Glory Road: The Journey of Ten African-Americans into Reformed Christianity*, ed. Anthony J. Carter (Wheaton, IL: Crossway, 2009), 16.

Jones also describes how Reformed theology provides a means of interpreting Scripture. He insists that the substructure of the Bible is covenantal in nature. "Reformed theology unwraps the covenant language of scripture, bringing to light important concepts and terms such as covenant of works, covenant of grace, covenant mediator, federal head, and signs and seals." Jones concludes that in Reformed theology, "Christ is the theme of all of scripture," and in him all of the covenants are fulfilled. Moreover, all prophets who came before Christ prefigured and pointed to his unique prophetic office. Every faithful preacher since his coming declares the word and stands in his authority.[16]

Pastor Michael Leach of All Saints Reformed Church in Stone Mountain, Georgia, is an example of how a desire to be biblically formed led to a thoroughgoing advocacy for Blacks becoming explicitly Reformed in their theology. Leach discovered Reformed theology in 1991 after ministering to inmates at Rankin County Correctional Facility in Peal, Mississippi. A fierce storm caused a lockdown at the prison, and during the downpour he noticed several donated resources from a pastor's library. He picked up a periodical titled *Tabletalk*, the monthly publication of Ligonier Ministries, led by R. C. Sproul.[17] Leach testifies that Sproul's ongoing impact has been foundational in his life. He purchased, read, and listened to various resources from Sproul. Sproul's impact on Leach's theology led him to transfer from Liberty University to Reformed Theological Seminary in Jackson, Mississippi.

Leach's account of entering Reformed circles contains a critical assessment of traditional Black churches that is not uncommon among Reformed Blacks. Reflecting on Black churches in Atlanta, he says,

> Most of the African-American churches in this sweltering reserve of fluid eclecticism have their own brand of theology. It is a waning residual of historic orthodoxy; an unquestioned default system of Arminianism, with heavy influences by the Prosperity Gospel and Word of Faith teachings; deep inroads by local and national politics, especially that of the National Democratic Party; and deep encrustations of the Civil Rights Movement. It maintains many troubling aspects of liberation theology evidenced by the growing popular appeal of Afrocentrism and the Feminist Gospel. There is also a continuing retreat from the transcendent supernaturalism of biblical

---

[16]Jones, "Introduction," 16-17.
[17]See Michael Leach, "I Remember It Well," in Carter, *Glory Road*, 97-110.

theology into an entrenched liberalism known for its commitment to pragmatism, the Social Gospel, and the confusing of the church with (and even its submergence under) the broader stratum of the community.[18]

Leach's critical disposition toward stereotypical Black Christianity is a holdover from the negative gaze commonly noted among early National Negro Evangelical Association leadership and members. Leach's disposition toward Black churches notwithstanding, he maintains a vibrant ministry at a predominantly Black church that reaches into its community with its ministries.

While Reformed theology has provided a helpful doctrinal framework for Blacks who have adopted it, its history remains an active stumbling block for many African Americans. The same doctrinal system that gave shape to some Bible-centric African American Christians was used to perpetuate the evil of slavery in America. The most prominent slaveholding Reformed thinkers include Jonathan Edwards (1703–1758) and Archibald Alexander (1772–1851). In a stark turn of events, Edwards's followers, New Light Calvinists, promoted slavery's undoing energized by their Reformed convictions, but proslavey Reformed theologians are more notable than their abolitionist-minded counterparts. It follows that Black Christians who are aware of Reformed thought yet do not subscribe to it commonly contemplate whether the theological system is inherently racist.

As a subset of Black evangelicals, the Black Reformed community has had a disproportionately difficult time finding a place to call home. This homelessness spawned several networks, including the Reformed Blacks of America, The Witness: A Black Christian Collective, and the Front Porch, to name a few. Despite the close attention to Reformed doctrine, there remains a significant amount of diversity among Reformed Blacks, especially at the intersection of politics and culture. Reformed Blacks span from the ultraconservative Darrell B. Harrison and Virgil Walker to the more socially progressive yet theologically orthodox Thabit M. Anyabwile, Darryl Williamson, and Vermon Pierre. Shared theological convictions notwithstanding, bitter theological skirmishes have resulted in significant division among Black Reformed leaders.

The division among contemporary Reformed Blacks is reminiscent of the tensions within the National Black Evangelical Association during the late 1960s and early 1970s.

---

[18]Leach, "I Remember It Well," 109.

Throughout the Black Reformed community, there are varying levels of desire to interact with the broader African American Christian community. The organization originally called the Reformed African American Network was discontent to allow the "Reformed" label to keep non-Reformed Black Christians at a distance. In a release announcing Reformed African American Network's transition to The Witness: A Black Christian Collective, cofounder Jemar Tisby affirmed that the name change was to intentionally pursue affinity with Black Christians who bear witness to the truth of Jesus Christ:

> By including "Reformed" in our name, we indicated that a significant part of our identity was a theological system. An emphasis on clear doctrine is important, but it comes with inherent drawbacks. Identifying primarily with a set of theological standards tends to make faith overly intellectual and theoretical. It becomes less about people and more about ideological precision.... While there is always a place for theological clarity, we did not want our work to end there. Changing our name to The Witness identifies both who we are and what we do.... We are witnesses to what God has done for humanity in and through Jesus Christ. A move away from a theological label is not a move away from historic Christianity. We still boldly preach Christ crucified (1 Corinthians 1:23). At the same time witnessing is what we do.[19]

The state of the Black Reformed movement has in some ways taken a page from The Witness and has de-emphasized "Reformed" in comparison to the days of Anthony J. Carter's *On Being Black and Reformed: A New Perspective on the African-American Christian Experience*, originally published in 2003, and the 2009 *Glory Road: The Journeys of Ten African-Americans into Reformed Christianity*, edited by Carter. Both politically conservative and socially progressive Reformed Blacks have remained in an array of ministry contexts, with the numbers of their followings steadily increasing.[20]

THE MULTICULTURAL MOVEMENT

The roots of the American multicultural church movement stretch back to 1943 with the establishment of the Church for the Fellowship of All Peoples in San

---

[19]Jemar Tisby, "The Journey from RAAN to 'The Witness: A Black Christian Collective,'" The Witness, October 31, 2017, https://thewitnessbcc.com/raan-witness-black-christian-collective/.
[20]See vol. 2 for an excerpt from Anthony J. Carter's "Sample Orders of Worship."

Francisco under the leadership of Howard Thurman, who vacated his position as dean of the chapel at the prestigious Howard University, and Alfred G. Fisk, a Presbyterian clergyman and professor of philosophy. This was the first intentionally interracial pastoral leadership duo documented in American history. Although this interracial and interfaith congregation would begrudgingly accept the label "evangelical," it broke new ground in the racially hardened American landscape.

John M. Perkins (1930–) is a forerunner for evangelical reconciliation who has labored for decades for unity and to eliminate the legacy of racism in communities. He was born in New Hebron, Mississippi, into the grip of Jim Crow segregation. After being raised by his sharecropping grandmother and extended family, he was urged to leave Mississippi because they feared for his life after his brother was fatally shot and killed by law enforcement. With a disdain for his native Mississippi, Perkins moved to California and married Verna Mae Buckley in 1951 after being drafted into the US Army. After serving in Okinawa during the Korean War, Perkins came to faith in Jesus Christ by the influence of his son, Spencer.

Despite vowing never to return to the South, his faith compelled him to go back to his childhood home in 1960 and proclaim the gospel of Jesus Christ where he had experienced a great deal of racially motivated pain. He was an outspoken advocate of civil rights for Blacks and endured harassment, incarceration, and violence at the hands of White resistors for his convictions. His impact is ongoing through the John and Verna Mae Perkins Foundation and as cofounder of the Christian Community Development Association, which has afforded him the opportunity to travel and speak internationally as one of the leading evangelical voices for reconciliation and unity emerging from the American civil rights movement.[21]

Perkins's efforts are legendary around the globe, but a widespread racial reconciliation movement that built on Perkins's work began throughout the broader evangelical movement in the 1990s through the ministry of Promise Keepers. Promise Keepers was a parachurch organization founded by former University of Colorado football coach Bill McCartney in 1990. Promise Keepers heralds itself as a "Christ-centered organization dedicated to introducing men to Jesus Christ as their Savior and Lord; and then helping them to grow as Christians." After successfully urging men to be better husbands and fathers for the first six years of their revival-style gatherings, in 1996 the organization's attention turned to racial reconciliation with the motto "Breaking Down the Walls." It is estimated that 1.1

---

[21] See vol. 2 for an excerpt from Perkins's book *One Blood*.

million men in twenty-two stadiums throughout the United States attended the gatherings aimed at racial reconciliation.[22]

Nationwide, the late 1990s featured fewer overt catalysts for racial tension, and there was a growing hope of leaving America's racist past behind. This resulted in Promise Keepers adopting a largely colorblind model of racial reconciliation. Colorblindness insists that the best way to cure racial strife is to ignore the racism of the past and its negative consequences, forgive one another, and move forward together. This method of pursuing reconciliation ignores how race and racism have ongoing implications in daily life beyond the words and attitudes of individuals.

> **Colorblind unity** does not always mean that unity is forged on biblical grounds. Too often, Christ is added to as the unifier, and the additional characteristic fuses a group together. The addition to the gospel that unifies people is a stumbling block for those who do not meet the criterion (be it political, cultural, or economic). Counterfeit unity diminishes the Savior's ability to bring his children together.

The colorblind model resulted in predominantly White ministries inviting people of every ethnic background to participate in their gatherings. This resulted in many upwardly mobile Blacks (and other minorities) attending churches where they worshiped with their colleagues, fellow college alumni, and families from their neighborhoods. Despite becoming more multiethnic, many of these ministries remained monocultural. Despite the imperfections of the evangelical racial-reconciliation movement, God began revealing the deep racial wounds that remained in the American psyche through the turn of the century, and some Christian groups began taking genuine steps toward having "all things in common" (Acts 2:44).

The Promise Keepers movement changed the evangelical racial climate enough for predominantly White organizations to expand the scope of their ministries and intentionally pursue non-White participation. The "Breaking Down the Walls" effect also created an opportunity for Black leaders to vie for unity within some White-led organizations. A vivid example of a ministry that expanded its scope was Cru (formerly Campus Crusade for Christ). In 1991, Campus Crusade established a subsidiary ministry named Impact Movement to reach Black students on university campuses. However, in the 2000s, the ministry embraced an enhanced

---

[22]"Promise Keepers on Quest for Revival," *Tampa Bay Times*, April 16, 2005, www.tampabay.com/archive/2005/04/16/promise-keepers-on-quest-for-revival/.

vision of students from different backgrounds worshiping together, so the ministry actively pursues both models.

The new millennium brought about new possibilities to pursue Christian unity within evangelicalism. In addition to faithful Black exegetes, theologians, and ministers serving throughout evangelicalism, there was a new ability to pursue biblical unity amid diversity. Reformed Theological Seminary began its African American Leadership Initiative under the leadership of Jemar Tisby in 2011, which was expanded to include the Center for the Study of the Bible and Ethnicity under the direction of Karen Ellis. This movement of ethnic unity continued with the emergence of the Kainos Movement, led by Bryan Loritts, whose purpose was "to gather leaders who either seek to start multi-ethnic ministries or churches, or who aspire to transition their current homogenous ministries into a multi-ethnic trajectory," with the goal of 50 percent of American churches becoming multiethnic before 2050. The year 2050 was pointed to as significant during the 2014 advent of Kainos because that is when sociologists projected the United States would become majority minority.[23]

A multiethnic church is one where no ethnicity makes up more than 80 percent of the local church body.

Black leaders have contributed to the multicultural church movement in a variety of ways. African American pastors Chris Williamson of Strong Tower Bible Church (Nashville) and Derwin Gray of Transformation Church (Indian Land, South Carolina) founded intentionally multicultural churches. Versatile African American leaders such as Chris Brooks are shepherding churches such as Woodside Bible Church (a multisite church in the Detroit area), which was historically Anglo but is intentionally pursuing a multicultural witness. This trajectory is becoming more common. H. B. Charles pastors the thriving Shiloh Metropolitan Baptist Church in urban Jacksonville, Florida, which subsumed the predominantly White Ridgewood Baptist Church in 2015—the first widely known merger of its kind in American history. Likewise, Black authors such as Priscilla Shirer and Trillia Newbell have expansive multiethnic followings.[24]

In addition to church and thought leadership, artistic expression and worship are the two most common vehicles that take Black faith beyond African American

---

[23]See vol. 2 for an excerpt from Karen Ellis's address "My People, My People: A Letter to the Church in America."
[24]See vol. 2 for an excerpt from H. B. Charles Jr.'s sermon "The Glory of God in Diversity."

communities. Black cultural art forms express joys and sorrows through a medium that transcends their original audience. The joy of Black faith was spread throughout evangelicalism through Kirk Franklin's "Stomp" and through the artistic genius of Richard Smallwood. In addition to the more traditional sounds of Yolanda Adams and Tasha Cobbs, the contemporary gospel fusion sounds of Israel Houghton, Tamala Mann, and Tye Tribbett continue to carry gospel sounds to new cultural contexts. In addition to gospel music, Christian hip-hop was legitimized by the cross-genre movement and paved the way for Reach Records, and together they reached a generation.[25]

> **William "Duce" Branch, a.k.a. the Ambassador** (1971–), is arguably the father of Christian hip-hop. Branch's father was a faithful Christian evangelist who raised Branch to abide by evangelical principles, filtered through the Black experience. The mainstream release of hip-hop artists such as Rapper's Delight awakened an affection for hip-hop culture in Branch that caused a cultural clash with his father and a stint of rebellion against his faith. After being theologically trained at Philadelphia College of the Bible and Dallas Theological Seminary, Branch concluded that hip-hop was a valuable tool for spreading the Christian message. The Ambassador's accomplishments and influence have affected a generation of Christians expressing their faith within the context of urban America.[a]
>
> [a]See vol. 2 for an excerpt from the Ambassador's song "One Two, Sela, Hold Your Ground, Hand in the Air."

During the second decade of the twentieth century, the multicultural church movement was frustrated because of several racialized acts of violence, many involving the use of police force on Black civilians. Fellow church members within multicultural congregations had clashing perspectives on several nationally reported stories. The initial blow was the tension that emerged during the murder trial of Trayvon Martin in 2013. In addition, the rise of mobile devices and social media, including Facebook, Instagram, and Twitter (now X), as well as cellphone cameras, provided the means to nationally broadcast a series of highly racialized homicides. This culminated in 2020 with the murders of Ahmaud Arbery, Breonna Taylor, and George Floyd. The pressure of these events slowed overt efforts toward multicultural unity in many churches and evangelical institutions, but in others it offered an opportunity to bear each other's burdens like never before.

---

[25]See vol. 2 for an excerpt from Shai Linne's song "Greatest Story Ever Told."

CONCLUSION

The conflation of evangelical doctrine with White evangelical culture and politics has caused most surveys of African American Christianity to avoid the label "evangelical." However, the roots of African American Christianity are unmistakably evangelical, and orthodox doctrine has flourished outside White evangelical denominations and institutions. Nevertheless, the African American Christian tradition is incomplete without incorporating the testimonies and contributions of faithful ministers and laypeople who have been theologically trained in or serve in predominantly White evangelical circles.

The tension between ministering to the priestly (gospel proclamation) and prophetic (temporal) needs of God's people is pronounced among Black evangelicals. This balancing act is an ongoing cause for spirited debate among Black Christians and tension among the broader evangelical family. This tension, driven by the brokenness of sin, will give way to evangelicalism's hope of a kingdom where Jesus will redeem the relational and social brokenness that Black evangelicals labor to mend in the present.

13

THE ARRIVAL OF BLACK LIBERATION

THE LEADERSHIP VACUUM FOLLOWING the assassination of Martin Luther King Jr. was filled with hopelessness and rage, and a new religious expression emerged from that cocktail called Black liberation theology. Some notable Black clergy and scholars alike expressed concern that popular Christian theology was incapable of addressing the struggles of being Black in America. They concluded that a society that is racialized in every sphere calls for a theological response that is self-consciously Black. As a result, these leaders intentionally departed from White doctrine to develop a theological formulation that addressed the concerns of the Black community.

The formalization of this self-consciously Black theology featured a bold reordering of the doctrinal Anchors of African American theology. While the method of the Anchors' rearrangement is unique to each scholar, there is a shared insistence on social, political, and economic Deliverance that shapes each proponent's doctrinal formation in distinct ways. Despite investing little effort in defining the White theology from which it departed, characteristics of that corpus are apparent in the writings of Black liberation theology. White theology, especially in the academy, is often shaped by the topics covered by the ecumenical councils at Nicaea in 325, Constantinople in 381, Chalcedon in 451, and others that shaped nascent Western theological thought. The church counsels convened to debate almost strictly doctrinal issues, such as the nature of the incarnate Son and the deity of the Holy Spirit, without consideration of their impact on Christian practice. Black theologians lamented theology that was devoid of engagement with the Christian life. The church councils and influential theologians of the Protestant Reformation codified the loci, or topics, of theology that emerged as the major branches of theological study (Christology, soteriology, eschatology, etc.).

Branches of doctrine serve as both a starting point and an organizing structure for many seminaries, divinity schools, and systematic theology texts. Inherent to this theological framework is an acute lack of contextual awareness. Consequently, renowned theological masterpieces produced in the West (Europe and North America) have significantly contributed to the development of doctrine to the exclusion of engaging the pressing issues of the contexts from which they emerged. The lack of contextual awareness resulted in theological frameworks that emphasize knowledge and piety that are disassociated from daily life.

In addition, the detachment of White fundamentalism from daily life was lamented not only by Black liberationists but by noteworthy White fundamentalists as well. In 1947 Carl F. H. Henry's *The Uneasy Conscience of Modern Fundamentalism* evaluated the state of his beloved fundamentalism in its inability to engage the needs of Black life in America:

> Modern fundamentalism does not explicitly sketch the social implications of its message for the non-Christian world; it does not challenge the injustices of the totalitarianisms, the secularisms of modern education, the evils of racial hatred, the wrongs of current labor-management relations, the inadequate bases of international dealings. It ceases to challenge Caesar and Rome, as though in futile resignation and submission to the triumphant Renaissance mood. The Christian social imperative is today in the hands of those who understand it in sub-Christian terms.[1]

Henry's appraisal criticized fundamentalist theology for its inability to influence public life to the exclusion of petitioning alcohol consumption, condemning smoking, and boycotting movies.

The lack of contextual awareness among White theologians did not generate an a-cultural theology; rather, their culture was standardized and assumed to be transcultural. As a result, the White experience became normalized in the theological task. Consequently, questions and concerns generated outside the "normal" context of theology were deemed invalid, including the social, political, and racial challenges faced by Blacks.

On the whole, the social concerns and bodily needs of White Americans were met by government and civil authorities that were favorably disposed toward them; thus, social needs became a secular concern, not a theological matter. By

---

[1] Carl F. H. Henry, *The Uneasy Conscience of Modern Fundamentalism* (repr., Grand Rapids, MI: Eerdmans, 2003), 39.

contrast, the Black experience was characterized by individual and systemic racism, which transformed what Whites considered to be social or political problems into theological issues. These dynamics explain the inability of White theology, which is largely focused on piety and knowledge, to engage the most pressing social and political needs of the Black community.

Among Black liberationists, the overwhelming silence of White Christians during the social crisis of Jim Crow segregation and the civil rights movement was a theological problem. Those who emerged as the initial generation of Black theologians were the first to collectively identify this oversight and condemn White theological paradigms as incapable of guiding Blacks out of oppression. Black theology emerged with an expressed concern for doing what "standard" theology was unable to do, that is, holistically engage the Black experience.

> **The Black experience** is a challenge to define—especially as it becomes increasingly diverse. Regrettably, racialization produces a comparatively shared set of experiences that cause Blacks to have a united history, sorrows, joys, and a need for perseverance. These realities produce genuine solidarity that Blacks avail themselves of to varying degrees, but ignoring these facts causes self-harm because it disallows reckoning with certain experiences and emotions. The Black experience also produces cultural artifacts including movies, songs, literature, and food. Identification with Black cultural expression is elective. Those who desire to assimilate into the dominant culture will diminish their participation in it, and those who cherish Black cultural expression will amplify its significance and beauty.

In addition to the critique of White theology, James Cone and others sought to provide a theology that would disallow the Black church to slip back into what Gayraud Wilmore called a state of deradicalization. Following the 1915 death of Presbyterian minister Henry McNeal Turner, Wilmore insisted that a state of deradicalization characterized the loss of the Black church's prophetic voice until the emergence of King during the Montgomery bus boycott in 1955. As such, Cone insists that Black theology is an internal critique of the Black church because its existence insists that the Black church's theological vision was unable to identify the shortcomings of White theology and maintain the institutional Black church's prophetic voice.[2]

---

[2] See vol. 2 for an excerpt from Gayraud Wilmore's "Blackness and Sign and Assignment."

THE EMERGENCE OF LIBERATION THEOLOGIES

The 1960s was a time of pioneering new intellectual terrain that coalesced with a revolutionary social moment that forged a path for liberation theology to emerge. The most notable liberation theologies that appeared were Latin American, feminist, and Black. A confluence of ideas converged in the academy to foster this eruption of theological imagination. Two significant methodological developments that fostered Black theology were perspectival awareness and studies "from below."

Perspectivalism is a theory of knowledge that considerers human limitation. Not privileging a single perspective of the human story over another invites previously silenced voices to contribute to the historical and theological dialogue. The perspectival nature of knowledge does not necessarily challenge the authority of Scripture and other sources of knowledge; rather, it considers human situatedness in the process of interpreting these resources.

"From below" can also be phrased as "from the margins." The story of history is largely generated by those with wealth and power, and first-person accounts of subdominant actors are limited or nonexistent. When depicted, common people are often characterized as being foolish or driven by unsavory appetites. Most often, the masses appear as large, unruly mobs and rarely as well-developed protagonists.

The status quo of Western historiography was challenged when British historians George Rude and E. P. Thompson, respectively, published *The Crowd in the French Revolution* (1959) and *The Making of the English Working Class* (1963). Rude and Thompson offered personhood and agency to the often-anonymous impoverished faces in the crowd during seminal moments in European history. These pioneers developed accounts from the margins that described the agency of ordinary people, acknowledged their contributions to the historical narrative, and examined the ideological commitments that informed their actions. These shifts in historical studies set a precedent for theological scholarship and were an academic forerunner for theology from the Black experience.

In addition to the intellectual context of liberation theologies, the mid-twentieth-century social and political climate—featuring the civil rights and Black power movements—are commonly understood as catalysts of Black theology. These two movements drove Black theologians to reject White racism and passivity more strongly in order to affirm that the struggle for liberation is consistent with the gospel of Jesus Christ.

JOSEPH WASHINGTON'S *BLACK RELIGION*

The civil rights movement signaled an invigorated social consciousness among Black scholars and ministers, who attempted to offer historical and theological accounts of Black Christianity. The first widely recognized attempt to account for the African American religious experience was Joseph R. Washington's *Black Religion*, published in 1964. The crux of Washington's argument is that Black religion exists only because of its exclusion from White faith and is therefore illegitimate. As a result, Black Christianity is a deviation from genuine faith, and the Black church ceases to be a true church and lacks any formidable theological contributions. Washington says,

> Those who join a religious community in search of meaning and relevance are thwarted in this quest, not because there is no ultimate belief in God but because there are not middle guide-lines for the faithful in this world. In this perspective, Negro congregations are not churches but religious societies—religion can choose to worship whatever gods are pleasing. But a church without theology, the interpretation of and response to the will of God for the faithful, is a contradiction in terms.[3]

A consequence of the Black church being illegitimate is its inability to produce genuine theology; Washington claims,

> The absence of theology in Negro religious communities [churches] and the opposition to all forms of intellectual endeavor within the sphere of religion have not provided a place for creative, independent thinkers. Unlike White communions which continue to attract brilliant laymen and clergy as spokesmen for the faith, Negro communions can only boast of leaders in the field of race relations. There are no first-rate Negro theologians, and a limited number of Negro scholars and teachers of repute are to be found in non-Negro institutions.[4]

Washington concluded that Black exclusion from White European Christianity was a break from genuine Christianity. Much like today, many White Christians welcome a Black man who disparages his own, and Washington was given significant opportunities to justify indifference to the Black plight and position White Christianity at the center of the American Christian story. However, Black scholars and clergy vehemently rejected his conclusions.

---

[3] Joseph R. Washington, *Black Religion: The Negro and Christianity in the United States* (Boston: Beacon, 1966), 143.
[4] Washington, *Black Religion*, 143.

THE NATIONAL COMMITTEE OF NEGRO CHURCHMEN AND "BLACK POWER STATEMENT"

African American clergy rallied to counter Washington's claims that Black faith was less than Christian because it was not Eurocentric. As a result of the stir caused by Washington's book, the rising enthusiasm for the Black power movement, and the waning influence of King's nonviolence, Black Christian leaders stood at a crossroads. In the midst of titanic cultural and political shifts, an ad hoc committee named the National Committee of Negro Churchmen organized to offer a theological account for social developments in America. The committee elected to address the nation by publishing a full-page statement in the July 31, 1966, edition of the *New York Times*. The piece, titled "Black Power Statement," offered a theological interpretation of Black power.

The release of "Black Power Statement" is commonly regarded as the beginning of a self-consciously Black theology because of its theological contemplation of disenfranchised African Americans. For the first time, Blacks sought an independent theological perspective that departed from White theology. By contrast, the "Black Power Statement" identified the nature of power and explored it theologically in a racialized society.

The introduction to the 1966 statement describes power and its usage. It is best heard in its own words:

> The fundamental distortion facing us in the controversy about "Black power" is rooted in a gross imbalance of power and conscience between Negroes and White Americans. It is this distortion, mainly, which is responsible for the widespread, though often inarticulate, assumption that White people are justified in getting what they want through the use of power, but that Negro Americans must, either by nature or by circumstances, make their appeal only through conscience. As a result, the power of White men and the conscience of Black men have been corrupted. The power of White men is corrupted because it meets little meaningful resistance from Negroes to temper it and keep White men from aping God. The conscience of Black men is corrupted because, having no power to implement the demands of conscience, the concern for justice is transmuted into a distorted form of love, which in the absence of justice, becomes chaotic self-surrender. Powerlessness breeds a race of beggars. We are faced now with a situation where conscienceless power meets powerless conscience, threatening the very foundations of our nation.[5]

---

[5] National Committee of Negro Churchmen, "Black Power Statement," *New York Times*, July 31, 1966.

This theologically informed prelude is followed by three sections that call on specific groups within the American populace to move away from conscienceless power and powerless conscience. The first appeal is to the leaders of America (i.e., civil authorities) to wield their power for freedom. The second appeal is to White churchmen to employ their power in love for their fellow citizen. The third appeal is to "Negro" citizens to use power for justice, and last there is a call to mass media to exert the power of the press for truth.

The loving yet stern tone of "Black Power Statement" calls the authors' Black counterparts back to the ideas of love and nonviolence expressed in the speeches and writings of Martin Luther King Jr. The publication signaled the arrival of a new era for many Black clergy who believed that theology that emerged from suburban Whiteness was incapable of engaging riots, urban religions, and the Black power movement that was sweeping America.

The ad hoc group of ministers who united to publish the statement discerned the importance of their contribution and met three times between 1966 and 1969, drafting multiple statements decrying the political and racial state of America. During that three-year span the declining influence of King's nonviolence and the emphasis on the beloved community within the National Committee of Negro Churchmen began giving way to Malcolm X's nationalist ideology. This shift was signaled in a name change from the National Committee of Negro Churchmen to the National Conference of Black Churchmen. Along with acknowledging an ideological shift from *Negro* to *Black*, the change from *committee* to *conference* also indicated the intent for this body to be permanent.

Black theology emerged from the ministries of pastors who were familiar with fire hoses, cattle prods, and dog bites. These practitioners preached the funerals of nonviolent civil rights workers and had their churches destroyed by White supremacists. The earliest stages of development for Black theology are most accurately identified as emerging from the church and influenced by the lived experience of Blacks in America.

THE TERM "BLACK THEOLOGY"

The term "Black theology" was not coined until the waning years of the 1960s, but its origins are the topic of conversation. One of the earliest uses of the term "Black theology" was in Gayraud Wilmore's theological commission project report in fall 1968. Its first known published usage was in a *Time* magazine in an article from November 15, 1968, that is a summary of the National Conference of Black

Churchmen gathering in St. Louis, titled "Is God Black?" Months later, the term appeared in Grant S. Shockley's February 12, 1969, article "Ultimatum and Hope" in *The Christian Century*. James Cone, Leon Watts, and Wilmore agree that the spirit of Black theology (defined as "an interpretation of the faith in light of Black history and culture and completely separate from White religion") was present at the outset of the National Conference of Black Churchmen, although it was not employed until years later.

The formalization of the term "Black theology" was with Cone's usage in his 1969 monograph *Black Theology and Black Power*, which formally established Black theology as an academic theological movement. Despite the term "Black theology" emerging in the late 1960s, twentieth-century pastors and theologians do not consider themselves the first to formulate theology that emerged from the Black experience. However, the adoption of the term "Black theology" was a declaration of intent to cease theologizing from the Black experience in the shadows.

BLACK THEOLOGY AS A THEOLOGICAL DISCIPLINE

In 1969, the establishment of the Society for the Study of Black Religion continued to establish Black theology as a formidable theological discipline. This society provided the primary context for the ongoing development of Black theology. In contrast to its predecessor—the clergy-dominated National Conference of Black Churchmen—the professors and graduate students of the Society for the Study of Black Religion took a far less radical posture when challenging racism in their seminaries and in society. This is in part attributed to the nature of scholarly debate in the academy, which tends to become disconnected from the needs of common people. In hindsight, Cone lamented:

> I myself was too much focused on the internal debates of Black theologians. Those debates were useful in sharpening our critical tools for the intellectual development of Black theology. But we conducted those debates too much outside the life of the Black community, thereby making Black theology an abstract, academic discipline in the worst sense.[6]

The concerns of Black academics provided a stark contrast to the struggles of ministers in the urban centers. This distinction developed into an ongoing tiff with respect to Black theology being the property of the church or the academy.

---

[6]James H. Cone, *For My People: Black Theology and the Black Church* (Maryknoll, NY: Orbis Books, 1984), 27.

The tension between the church and the academy is inherent to Black theology's establishment and development as a grassroots movement whose content was initially produced by pastors but shifted to the ivory towers of academia. Among the ranks of Black theologians, the relationship between the scholar and the church takes on various forms, but two common dispositions are embodied by two of Black theology's most established and respected scholars, namely, Cone and J. Deotis Roberts. On the one hand, Cone was an ardent proponent of Black theology's nonacademic roots but insisted that his body of work, produced in the academy, functioned as a critique of the Black church from within. On the other hand, Roberts produced a corpus that bears an overarching constructive engagement with the issues most pressing to the Black church. These internal dialogues continually surfaced among Black theologians over time.

FIRST-GENERATION BLACK THEOLOGIANS

In his *Introducing Black Theology of Liberation* (1999), Dwight N. Hopkins presented an indispensable framework that is the standard for quantifying the macro developments of Black theology. Hopkins identified the rise of Black theology's first generation with the publication of the 1966 "Black Power Statement" by the National Committee of Negro Churchmen in the *New York Times* and the 1969 publication of Cone's *Black Theology and Black Power*.

A common misconception among those unfamiliar with Black theology is that each proponent undertakes the theological task in a similar fashion, with Cone serving as the lone paradigm for all Black theologians. While Black scholars agree that liberation is an essential theme of Black theology, each theologian attributes unique nuances to the term and employs different methods of pursuing liberation. However, it is common for ill-intended onlookers to construct a caricature of Black theology with Cone's more radical positions in an effort to marginalize the Black theological enterprise as a whole. While a more nuanced view of Cone is needed throughout the theological academy, it is also apparent that there are a variety of ways to undertake Black theology. Roberts wrote in 1984, "While White scholars have accepted Cone as the spokesperson for Black theology (when they considered the movement worthy of attention), Black theologians have persistently made the point that James Cone speaks mainly for himself."[7]

---

[7] J. Deotis Roberts, *Black Theology Today: Liberation and Contextualization* (Lewiston, NY: Edwin Mellen, 1984), 41.

The Arrival of Black Liberation

In an effort to nuance the discipline, Hopkins identified two significant methodological trends within the first generation of Black theologians. He classifies the first group as "political theologians." The political interpreters of Black Christianity are more prominent because of preeminent theologians such as Cone and Roberts. Their goal is to oppose racism in society, in the church, and in theology with a call to end inhumane abuses of White power. By contrast, "cultural theologians," exemplified by Wilmore and Charles H. Long, call for a fundamental shift in the construction of Black religion (Christianity included). These thinkers issue a call for a departure from the categories established by White theologians because of the conviction that liberation will not be achieved using the theological tools previously used to maintain White supremacy.

Frederick L. Ware provides further classification and analysis of perspectives in Black theology in *Methodologies of Black Theology* (2002). Ware offers three schools to conceptualize the field of Black theology. His first, and admittedly the most common, contingent is the Black hermeneutical school, embodied by Jacquelyn Grant and James Evans, who employ biblical hermeneutics to construct a theology that engenders moral and ethical action leading to liberation. The Black philosophical school, seen in the work of William R. Jones and Cornel West, achieves liberation by utilizing social and political philosophies that Ware notes may or may not be compatible with all points of the biblical story. Last, the human-sciences school seeks to overcome and transform the conditions of Black life through the interpretative tools of the social sciences and the exploration of Black religion, most clearly demonstrated in the work of C. Eric Lincoln and Cheryl Townsend. The theological diversity among first-generation Black theologians warrants consideration of their unique contributions to the field.

JAMES H. CONE

James H. Cone served as the Bill and Judith Moyers Distinguished Professor of Systematic Theology at Union Theological Seminary (of Columbia University) in New York City and is widely noted as the "father of Black theology." Born on August 5, 1936, and raised in Bearden, Arkansas, Cone recalls being introduced to the patterns and feelings of Black life in the South through the Black church. Yet during his formal theological training, he was educated in the depths of European and (Anglo) American theological approaches. In his words,

> Like most college and seminary students of my generation, I faithfully studied philosophy and theology—from the pre-Socratics to modern

existentialism and linguistic analysis, from Justin Martyr, Irenaeus, and Origen to Karl Barth, Bultmann, and Tillich. I was an expert on Karl Barth and knew well the theological issues that shaped his theology. I wrote papers in seminary on the Barth and Brunner debates, the knowledge of God in contemporary theology, Bultmann's program of demythologization, the Tillichian doctrine of God as being-itself, and concluded my formal education with a Ph.D. dissertation on Barth's anthropology.[8]

But the theological paradigms of Cone's education did not answer the questions raised amid the Black experience. In his search for answers, he fought the historical Jesus of White liberals at Garrett Theological Seminary, which received his tuition but maintained an overwhelming indifference to his lived situation.

Cone began teaching at Philander Smith College in Little Rock, Arkansas, after completing his PhD at Northwestern University. During his time at the college, he realized the disjunction between his theological education and his class of Black students. This experience forced Cone to raise the question, "What could Karl Barth possibly mean for Black students who had come from the cotton fields of Arkansas, Louisiana, and Mississippi?" The disconnect from Nicaea and Chalcedon to the social, political, and economic realities of the Jim Crow South forced Cone to reimagine the theological task away from what he deemed the "irrelevancies of American theology."

Following Martin Luther King Jr.'s assassination, civil rights activists grew weary of nonviolent tactics, and the rhetoric and logic of Malcolm X grew in its appeal. Despite Malcom X's allure, the theology of the Black church remained a central catalyst in the struggle for racial equality. Cone sought to integrate the methods of Black power (embodied my Malcolm X) with the faith of the civil rights movement (embodied by King) in order to renew the pre–Civil War spirit of Richard Allen, Nat Turner, and others in Black faith. Cone's efforts to catalyze the Black church to revolutionary action are clearly seen in *Black Theology and Black Power*. Cone argues, "It is my thesis, however, that Black Power, even in its most radical expression, is not the antithesis of Christianity, nor is it a heretical idea to be tolerated with painful forbearance. It is, rather, Christ's central message to twentieth-century America."[9] Cone later defines Black power as

---

[8]James H. Cone, *God of the Oppressed* (Maryknoll, NY: Orbis Books, 1975), 5.
[9]James H. Cone, *Black Theology and Black Power* (Maryknoll, NY: Orbis Books, 1997), 1.

[the] complete emancipation of Black people from White oppression by whatever means necessary. The methods may include buying, boycotting, marching, or even rebellion. Black Power means Black freedom, Black self-determination, wherein Black people no longer view themselves as without human dignity but as men, human beings with the ability to carve out their own destiny.[10]

In short, Cone attempts to encourage the Black church not to disregard Black power, and Black power proponents not to disregard the Black church.

> **Revolutionary violence** is not Cone's immediate recourse; but he affirms it as a means of pursuing liberation. He rejects simplistic ethical conclusions that arise by asking the question, "What would Jesus do?" because the premise that Jesus did not use violence cannot function as a guiding principle for twentieth-century Blacks responding to racial oppression. Cone also argues that the Black man "must make a choice. If he decides to take the 'nonviolent' way, then he is saying that revolutionary violence is more detrimental to man in the long run than systemic violence. But if the system is evil, then revolutionary violence is both justified and necessary."[a]
>
> [a] James H. Cone, *Black Theology and Black Power* (Maryknoll, NY: Orbis Books, 1997), 143.

Cone rounds out what he called his intellectual trinity (which begins with King and Malcolm X) with poet James Baldwin. Cone insists, "Baldwin shared Martin King's incredible *love* of humanity. And he shared his *rage*, defined by love of *Blackness*, with Malcolm X."[11] The most profound lesson Cone learned from Baldwin was to identify beauty from destruction:

What was beautiful about slavery? Nothing, rationally! But the spirituals, folklore, slave religion, and slave narratives *are* beautiful, and they came out of slavery. How do we explain that miracle? What's beautiful about lynching and Jim Crow segregation? Nothing! Yet the blues, jazz, and great preaching, and gospel music *are* beautiful, and they came out of the post-slavery brutalities of White supremacy.[12]

Baldwin provided Cone a means of viewing Black people not as a people in need of protection or as victims but as agents—sources of beauty—amid horrific circumstances.

---

[10] Cone, *Black Theology and Black Power*, 6.
[11] James H. Cone, *Said I Wasn't Gonna Tell Nobody* (Maryknoll, NY: Orbis Books, 2018), 159.
[12] Cone, *Said I Wasn't Gonna Tell*, 164.

> **James Baldwin** (1924–1987) was a writer and activist during the height of the American civil rights movement. Of his poems, novels, and essays, *Go Tell it on the Mountain* (1953), *Notes of a Native Son* (1953), and *Fire Next Time* (1963) are the most acclaimed. As the oldest of nine children, this Harlem native featured themes of race, sexual identity, and masculinity in his writings. With the faith of his childhood in the background, Baldwin applied himself to racial and social commentary that pushed society's established norms during his lifetime.

Despite Cone's revolutionary pairing of Christian theology and Black power, his ideas were not all well received by other emerging Black theologians. Initial critiques following the publication of his second monograph, *A Black Theology of Liberation* (1970), regarded Cone's overuse of White sources, including Karl Barth, Paul Tillich, H. Richard Niebuhr, and others, as antithetical to the goal of liberation. After seeking to legitimize Black theology among his peers in the academy—seen in the traditional systematic theological structure of *A Black Theology of Liberation*—Cone broke away from traditional Western form and sources with the publication of *The Spirituals and the Blues: An Interpretation* (1972). Cone's prolific contributions continued with his most thorough theological text, *God of the Oppressed* (1975), and his corpus includes over a dozen books and over 150 scholarly and popular articles. Cone's writing career climaxed with a treatment of Christology and the Black experience in *The Cross and the Lynching Tree* (2011).[13]

Cone's theological commitments are laid bare in his Christology. He describes his understanding of Christ by employing a question that proponents of the Black power movement often pose to Black Christians, "What has the gospel of Jesus to do with the oppressed Black people's struggle for justice in American society?" Cone insists that demonstrating Christ's existence is not merely to provide spiritual salvation but to break into social existence and establish the truth of freedom among the oppressed of his day. Likewise, Christ liberates the oppressed today and places them into a new sociopolitical reality.

Cone continued his christological reflection by affirming 1 John 3:8, saying, "Christ came into the world to destroy the works of Satan." This verse is applied directly to social and political oppression and made into a purpose statement for Christ because he came to destroy oppression and White oppressors. For Cone, the resurrection is the key to unlocking the mystery of how Jesus becomes the universal Christ to all who "labor and are heavy laden" (Matthew 11:28). The good

---

[13]See vol. 2 for excerpts from Cone's *A Black Theology of Liberation* and *The Spirituals and the Blues*.

The Arrival of Black Liberation

news of the resurrection is its tangible victory over oppression for contemporary African Americans. For Cone, this means that Black power characterizes the resurrection as Jesus becomes embodied in the conscience of Black Americans. Consequently, the resurrection is evidence that the oppressed can triumph over oppression, which invigorates Cone's imperative for political engagement to enhance the Black experience.

> **White salvation** is a theme veiled in Cone's writings, but it is not intentionally obscured. Blackness (and Whiteness) is not a direct reference to skin pigmentation. Blackness is associated with the reality of social, political, and economic oppression. Salvation is liberation from oppression, so White people are saved by becoming "Black" (i.e., taking on Black oppression as their own) and joining in the fight for freedom.

The imperative of the incarnation is central in Cone's Christology. Cone highlights that, when Christ walked the earth, he identified with the oppressed by locating himself with the social, political, and racially disenfranchised. Cone stressed the importance of the incarnation by drawing attention to the significance of Christ's Jewishness. Not only does Christ's ethnicity further establish his personhood, but it identifies him with a specific people who are at the center of God's salvation drama, rooted in the exodus from Egypt. The connection between Christ and the exodus is intended to encourage the disheartened and oppressed with the significance of the Christ event on their behalf because he is an exemplar of how to endure suffering in the contemporary struggle for freedom.

The result of Christ's kingly rule is the imperative for the oppressed Christian community to join Christ in the fight for liberation. Cone's emphasis on the incarnation intersects with contemporary racism because Christ saves the oppressed to afford them the ability to rebel against forces that make them less than human. For Cone, human action in response to Christ is not optional—it is a necessity, because surrendering to Christ in salvation is submitting to the call to rebel against oppression in pursuit of liberation. Cone offers painstaking detail about contemporary participation with Christ because "liberation is not a human possession, but a divine gift . . . to those who struggle in faith against violence and oppression."[14] For Cone, the task of Black theology in the struggle for freedom is

---

[14]Cone, *God of the Oppressed*, 128.

to offer a new understanding of Black dignity and provide a new soul among Blacks to destroy racism.[15]

> **Cone's view of salvation** is exclusively social and political in scope. It excludes notions of Conversion, sanctification, and being filled with the Holy Spirit, which were passed down through the African American Christian tradition.

Cone's ongoing influence among African American theologians is undeniable. As he is the "father of Black theology," it is difficult to understand the contemporary theological landscape among African American scholars without grasping his influence. In his scholarship, Cone granted permission for Blacks from across the theological spectrum educated in White seminaries and divinity schools to bring the totality of themselves into the theological task. Cone's insistence that theology is an inherently contextual reality allowed Blacks to unashamedly bring their struggles, their joys, and the uniqueness of being Black in America to the theological table. In addition to the immediate influence of his written corpus, over the years Cone committed himself to mentoring a cadre of doctoral students, who carried his influence into their scholastic contributions and into strategic leadership as deans, provosts, and presidents of institutions around the world.

Unlike many of his first-generation counterparts who conducted their scholarship from historically Black colleges and universities, Cone served as a precedent for Black scholars holding a teaching post in a predominantly White institution without setting aside Black consciousness. In a real sense, Cone served as a forerunner to every contemporary African American theologian who theologizes on the Black experience in their scholarship. As the pioneer of a new theological movement, Cone was prone to asserting his ideas to the point of overstatement to generate energy in a new direction, but it is undeniable that Black Christians, no matter their theological persuasion, owe Cone a debt of gratitude because he did the initial groundbreaking work of not having to leave Blackness at the door of the theological academy so that others could follow with more nuance and precision from various theological traditions.

A scholar labeled the father of a theological movement receives a mixture of admiration, skepticism, and at times goodhearted critique. In the sea of ill-willed grievances of Cone's corpus, there are erudite criticisms that are noteworthy. The

---

[15]See vol. 2 for an excerpt from Cecil Cone's critique of first-generation Black theologians, called "The Identity Crisis in Black Theology."

first is related to Cone's understanding of Black theology's historical context. In *A Black Theology of Liberation*, Cone argues that Black history is a source of Black theology. His explanation of Black history raises two concerns about the nature of this fundamental element of his theology. Cone's explanation of Black history reduces the Black historical narrative to its engagement with White supremacy. He insists, "Black history refers to the way Blacks were brought to this land and the way they have been treated in this land.... Black history in North America [means] that Whites used every conceivable method to destroy Black humanity." Later Cone describes Blacks as proactive agents in the historical narrative, yet still in response to White hatred, he says, "Black history is more than what Whites did to Blacks. More importantly Black history is Black persons saying no to every act of White brutality."[16]

Cone's understanding of Black history disallows theological reflection that extends beyond the catalyst of White supremacy. In this sense, African American history, as a source for Black theology, is always dependent on the oppression to which it responds.[17] As a result, Cone's theology is limited to being a response to racial oppression and has little ability to bring biblical imperatives to bear outside the liberation-oppression binary.

Cone's historical perspective caused him to fixate on a specific period as the default context for doing Black theology. Eddie Glaude rightly notes that a particular historic moment, the late 1960s and early '70s, disproportionately shaped the theology of early Black theologians, specifically Cone.[18] Several of Cone's mid-career and later books are masterful accounts of the civil rights and Black power movements, or accounts of Black theology itself. This is in contrast to Cone's prophetic (i.e., constructive) voice, which was formative for Black thought in the 1960s and '70s and forever enlarged the scope of African American theology.[19] The historical starting point of Cone's theological approach makes it impossible for young African Americans to employ Cone's version of Black theology despite being Black.

Due to Cone's truncated historical and therefore theological gaze, he dramatically reorders and redefines the theological Anchors that marked the African

---

[16]James H. Cone, *A Black Theology of Liberation* (Maryknoll, NY: Orbis Books, 1970), 25-26.

[17]Victor Anderson, *Beyond Ontological Blackness: An Essay on African American Religious and Cultural Criticism* (New York: Continuum, 1999), 51.

[18]Eddie S. Glaude, *In a Shade of Blue: Pragmatism and the Politics of Black America* (Chicago: University of Chicago Press, 2007), 73.

[19]See Cone's *Black Theology and Black Power* (1969), *A Black Theology of Liberation* (1970), *The Spirituals and the Blues: An Interpretation* (1972), and *God of the Oppressed* (1975).

American Christian tradition for generations. His good and laudable desire to affirm Black humanity causes a nearly exclusive fixation on the oppressive dire straits that threaten Black personhood. As a result, Cone's theological corpus focuses on addressing the social, political, and economic plight of Black people, which elevates the Deliverance Anchor and makes it his prevailing aim. Consequently, the other doctrinal Anchors that previously maintained independent integrity as part of an integrated whole are stratified or redefined in service of Deliverance.

A Big God serves Cone's liberation imperative because God is able to deliver modern Blacks from oppression the same way he delivered Israel out of Egypt. Jesus is also leveraged in service of liberation because his oppressors did not have final victory over him, so now contemporary Blacks are emboldened to seize liberation as Jesus did. Cone also insists that the Good Book is useful insofar as it promotes liberation.[20]

Finally, Cone reimagines the Conversion and Walking in the Spirit Anchor by departing from the historic African American assertion that held Conversion as the individual's freedom from sin's penalty (which is death) because of the resurrection of Jesus. Cone collapses Conversion and Deliverance by insisting that salvation is from temporal social, political, and economic oppression. It follows that Walking in the Spirit does not have a place in Cone's theology because salvation is an external reality that does not include internal transformation. These theological moves erode Cone's ethical foundations, which allows for his acceptance of the Black power movement's "by any means necessary" approach to social engagement.

J. Deotis Roberts was among Black scholars who appreciated Cone's efforts but thought it necessary to contribute another approach, beginning with his book *Liberation and Reconciliation* (1971).[21]

J. DEOTIS ROBERTS

Roberts was born in Spindale, North Carolina, on July 12, 1927. After graduating from high school, he embarked on an academic journey that offered him a unique perspective as a Black theologian. During his time at Johnson C. Smith University, Dr. A. O. Steele impressed on Roberts the importance of both *thinking* and

---

[20] In an exploration of Scripture's infallibility and verbal inspiration, Cone insists, "It matters little to the oppressed who authored scripture; what is important is whether it can serve as a weapon against the oppressors" (*Black Theology of Liberation*, 31).

[21] See vol. 2 for an excerpt from a work by J. Deotis Roberts's protégé Olyn Moyd, "Membership or Movement: Luke 9:57-62."

believing. His quest to think more carefully about the Christian faith drove him to study at Shaw University in Raleigh, North Carolina, where he received a Bachelor of Divinity, and then at Hartford Seminary for a Master of Sacred Theology in philosophy of religion. Last, in 1957, Roberts earned a Doctor of Philosophy from the University of Edinburgh in Scotland.

In the 1950s, it was rare for an African American to study in Europe. Roberts's distance from the Black experience in America allowed his scholastic interest to extend beyond conducting a formal study of race and injustice. Roberts hoped to tether faith and reason, and his interests were arrested by the study of epistemology among Cambridge Platonists. His formal studies resulted in the publication of his first two books, *Faith and Reason* (1962) and *From Puritanism to Platonism in Seventeenth Century England* (1968).[22]

In addition to his first two volumes on Platonism, **Roberts's broad theological interests** are evident in his publication list, which includes books titled *A Black Political Theology* (1974), *Roots of a Black Future: Family and Church* (1980), *Christian Beliefs* (1981), *The Prophethood of Black Believers* (1994), and *Bonhoeffer and King: Speaking Truth to Power* (2005).

Roberts's formative years—which included growing up in the American South, attending multiple historically Black universities, and living abroad for his doctoral studies—made him an unusual voice among Black theologians:

[I'm] avowedly Black. The reader will note that the theological positions of neo-orthodoxy and the British post-liberal theologians have shaped my thought. I have been aided in my thinking by existentialism and theology of hope. To be honest, it would be well for me to mention how much classical Western philosophy and theology that impinged upon my mind and spirit. My study of Christian Platonism will always be in focus. The study of Eastern and African religions will be reflected from time to time, but I want to speak from the Christian faith claim in its healing and social dimensions. My purpose is to speak to the whole man, body and spirit, in solitude and in the encounter with the man, body, and spirit, in solitude and in the encounter with other persons-in-community.[23]

---

[22] See vol. 2 for an excerpt from J. Deotis Roberts's autobiography *The Seasons of Life*.
[23] J. Deotis Roberts, *A Black Political Theology* (Philadelphia: Westminster, 1974), 13. Roberts's theological themes were self-identified in an interview with the author on May 23, 2014.

Roberts's unique formation fortified unique values, witnessed in his fourteen monographs, three multiauthored volumes, ten book chapters, and numerous academic journal articles. The first major theme of his teaching and writing is the relationship between faith and reason, an interest that drove him to the classroom, where he began teaching classical (European American) philosophical theology in 1957. Roberts's teaching career was Anchored by a tenure at Howard University (1958–1980), the hub of Black consciousness in higher education; a presidency at the Interdenominational Theological Center in Atlanta (1980–1983); and professorates at the prestigious Yale and Duke Universities. His commitment to coupling faith and reason also emerged in his reflections on theological method in Black theology. Unique among first-generation Black theologians, Roberts's commitment to theological foundations is most clearly seen in a collection of essays, titled *Black Theology Today* (1984).

A second theme of Roberts's theological program is the formation of the Black community and its two fundamental units, namely, the family and the local church. In these areas, Roberts's pastoral tone is consistent with the various ministry posts he occupied during his years of formal theological study. Roberts was deeply concerned with the disintegration of the nuclear family and its consequences for the Black community's ability to pursue liberation and reconciliation. In the absence of family, the church is God's familial provision for those without the support of a nuclear family. The plight of Black America drove Roberts to a two-pronged approach to combating racial injustice. First, he focused on the common top-down approach that directly challenged unjust social and political structures. Second, Roberts did not neglect a bottom-up approach that strengthened the two most fundamental units in society to support people in the struggle of daily living. Roberts's twin concerns for family and church in liberation led to the publication of *Roots of a Black Future: Family and Church* (2002).

The third major theme of Roberts's written work is a passion for reconciliation among God's people that transcends racial division. Roberts's crosscultural experiences during his doctoral studies and throughout his career drove him toward a missiological posture and a desire for reconciliation among the whole people of God. This characteristic transitions to his final and most distinctive themes, liberation and reconciliation, which are considered at the same time and in relation to each other. In his estimation, "the all-or-nothing, victory-or-death, approach to race relations appears to be more rhetoric than reality."[24] In order for there to be

---

[24] J. Deotis Roberts, *Liberation and Reconciliation*, 2nd ed. (Louisville, KY: Westminster John Knox, 2005), 1.

genuine peace, Roberts insists that liberation and reconciliation must coexist. Dwight N. Hopkins describes Roberts's views: "Liberation implies black people's freedom from the bondage of white racism. And reconciliation suggests that black freedom does not deny white humanity but meets whites on equal ground."[25]

Roberts acknowledged that many Blacks accused him of moving toward reconciliation too quickly, but he reassured his detractors that true liberation was logically prior to reconciliation. If one reads Roberts's writings and seizes on reconciliation without the prerequisite of liberation, Roberts says, one has misinterpreted his writings. Reconciliation includes cross bearing for Whites as well as for Blacks. It can take place only between two equals and cannot coexist within the historic American situation of Whites over Blacks.[26]

Throughout his writings, Roberts confesses that his commitment to a distinctively Christian approach to race relations is unpopular among frustrated youth who are enamored with the Black power movement. However, since Roberts insists that Christians be motivated by liberation as well as reconciliation, liberation by "any means necessary" is not a Christian ethic because it might cause irreconcilable damage to the prospect of reconciliation.[27]

At the outset of Roberts's career, he remained distant from formal discussions about race and racism because his views were being well represented by Martin Luther King Jr. Upon King's assassination, Roberts was compelled to respond to the mounting racial tension in the Black political arena as the Black power ideology sprang up in the urban centers in America. In the wake of Cone's *Black Theology and Black Power*, Roberts determined that he was not represented in that theological vision, and despite crediting Cone for doing the demolition work to develop Black theology. Roberts burst onto the scene in 1971 with what Patrick Bascio calls the first major critique of Cone's theological program.[28] The distinguishing themes of Roberts's theology appear most poignantly in his christological centerpiece, with Christ being both liberator and reconciler of all humanity.

Jesus is a holistic Savior, which is the foundation for spiritual and physical ministry, embodied by the Christian faith. Roberts fuses Christ's restorative work with spiritual realities by identifying Christ's universal work of salvation, coupled with

---

[25] Dwight N. Hopkins, *Black Theology USA and South Africa: Politics, Culture, and Liberation* (Eugene, OR: Wipf & Stock, 2005), 48.
[26] Roberts, *Liberation and Reconciliation*, 22.
[27] See vol. 2 for an excerpt from J. Deotis Roberts's *Liberation and Reconciliation*.
[28] Patrick Bascio, *The Failure of White Theology: A Black Theological Perspective* (New York: Peter Lang, 1995), 114.

the contemporary redemptive implications of Jesus' mission in particular contexts. He explains, "We seek a Christ *above* culture who is at the same time at work *in* culture and history for redemptive ends—setting free the whole person, mind, soul, and body."[29] To that end, Roberts summarizes the good news of Christ as God, by his grace, forgiving sin and reconciling humanity to God:

> The good news is that where there is repentance and faith, there is forgiveness and reconciliation. The gospel is also good news to man in his social relations. Because of a broken relationship between man and God, there is hostility between man and man. Through God's redemptive action in Christ, the wall of participation between men has been removed. This means that the gospel which reconciles us to God also brings us together. Because of man's fall, man being the crown of creation, all creation groans to be redeemed. The good news is that in and through Christ there is a new order of reconciliation between nature, man, and God.[30]

Roberts's definition of the gospel presents a holistic scope that binds people to God and one person to another. He explains that the brokenness of the individual becomes the brokenness of a society; conversely, that which heals the individual heals the society, which individuals comprise. The implication is that personal brokenness blossoms into social problems, which cause fractured relationships from one person to the next. Central to Roberts's message is humanity's objective change before God—Conversion. Salvation is the change elicited in the hearts of all who are redeemed, and the cumulative effect is that people who are restored by Christ's work undertake the missiological task of demonstrating Christ's salvific message in public life.

The significance of Roberts's Christology for the world and for the individual hinges on his universal-and-particular framework. Roberts argues that Christ is the desire of all nations (universal), but he is the Savior of each person (particular).[31] The import of the incarnation for Roberts is that the universal Son became particular in the person of Christ, and the demonstration of his redemptive power came to bear on a specific context. In Roberts's schema, Jesus redemptively entered into the particulars of the struggle for Black equality in America yet remains universally able to meet others at their point of need. Roberts insists, "In moving to

---

[29]Roberts, *Black Political Theology*, 119, emphasis added.
[30]Roberts, *Black Political Theology*, 139.
[31]Roberts, *Black Theology Today*, 328.

the universal, it must not abandon the concrete particular, for that is where we meet the human situation. There is no abstract universal that makes any difference in the relief of human misery. There is no universal revelation that separates salvation history from world history. Systematic theology must become theological ethics."[32] Moving from the particular to the universal is not the abandonment of concrete specifics because the particulars are the realities of the human situation. Thus, the details of world history (the particulars) should never be divorced from salvation history (the universal).

The actualization of Blackness is not Roberts's central tenet in salvation, as with Cone; rather, it is an implication of a mended relationship between God and humanity through Christ's saving work on the cross. Roberts's holistic paradigm tethers the personal, social, and interracial realities together by insisting that the restorative work of Christ is applicable to each context respectively, thus binding them together. As a result of persons being liberated from nonbeing, genuine reconciliation occurs between equals (i.e., fully human Blacks and Whites), which is made possible by Christ's death and resurrection.

Roberts's christological convictions influenced his pursuit of racial justice. For Blacks and Whites to interact on equal footing, a nuanced articulation of Black power was necessary. Roberts defines Black power as the freedom to pursue a state of Black liberation.[33] Roberts has a distanced relationship with classic Black power, not because of its emphasis on Black consciousness but due to the "by any means necessary" ethic it employs to reach its goals.

Roberts insists that the "by any means necessary" ethic needs careful examination by Black theologians in the face of militant biblical interpreters who seek to justify violence with biblical narratives such as that of Jesus and the moneychangers. Roberts stipulates that these texts must be understood through the words of the apostle Paul, who taught Christ-followers to overcome evil with good because love is the most excellent way. Roberts is convinced that using Scripture to sanction violence is not biblical interpretation but using the text to promote an ideology. His commitment to a nonviolent ethic is tethered to a kingdom vision that upholds both liberation and reconciliation. The ethical paradigm that emerges from Roberts's liberation/reconciliation binary limits ethical action to that which encourages reconciliation between Blacks and Whites.

---

[32]Roberts, *Black Theology Today*, 108.
[33]Roberts, *Black Political Theology*, 72.

> **ROBERTS'S ETHICS AS TIED TO ESCHATOLOGY**
>
> Roberts insists that ethics and eschatology are interdependent and indispensable and lead Christians toward either withdrawal or action regarding contemporary issues. Convinced that deep engagement with the Christian faith leads to contemporary social engagement, Roberts explores the kingdom by plumbing the essence of the faith, namely, Christ, who is the agent of God's kingdom and provides the interpretative trajectory for the church's mission.[a]
>
> [a] J. Deotis Roberts, *A Black Political Theology* (Philadelphia: Westminster, 1974), 184.

A contribution Roberts made to the field of Black theology is the undercurrent of the mutual dependence between pastor and theologian. He insists that theologians need to be thoroughly attuned to the worship and life of the local church. Roberts understands that theologians are caught in the crossfire between an academic discipline and practical responsibilities in the church. Time demands notwithstanding, theologians should temper their desire for academic respectability, which causes the sole driver of Black theology to be academic prestige and leads them to lose the purpose for which they begin.

> **"The theologian of balance"** is a widely recognized title given to Roberts by Dwight Hopkins because of Roberts's thoughtful engagement with the Black experience and his deep commitment to the Black church.

Like Cone, Roberts made a fundamental contribution to the Black theological enterprise, but unlike Cone, Roberts is regularly overlooked because of his more moderate disposition on controversial issues. Despite his more amiable tone, Roberts's corpus is thoroughly prophetic and is a helpful entry point to understand a fuller register of Black theologians. While Roberts insisted on the Deliverance imperative of theology, it did not drive his engagement with the other Anchors of the African American theological tradition; rather, a robust understanding of the other Anchors informed how he conceived of Deliverance and the ethical commitments that guided his pursuit of liberation.

Roberts's engagement with each theological Anchor further warrants his title, "the theologian of balance," during a time when the discipline of Black theology was undergoing drastic shifts in the academy. Interestingly, Roberts was commonly numbered among liberationists because they are his primary interlocutors, but his theological register is consistent with scholars such as George Kelsey and Benjamin Elijah Mays, who came before him. Roberts's incorporation with Cone and other liberationists was not because of a shared theological methodology but because Roberts endeavored to propose a distinct vision for Black theology, which ironically bound his legacy closely with Cone's.

WILLIAM R. JONES

William R. Jones (1933–2012) was an anomaly among first-generation Black theologians as a Unitarian Universalist pastor and humanist philosopher. Jones's contribution to the movement was distinctive because it was not an addition to the theological discussion—it was a critique. Jones argued that Black theologians assumed that God was a proponent of Black liberation without sufficiently proving that fact. As a result, Jones endeavored to return theodicy (the problem of evil) to the center of the Black theological conversation.

Jones converted to Protestant fundamentalism but concluded his religious journey with a form of humanism. Billy Graham was his theological hero, and following in Graham's footsteps, he became a licensed Baptist minister. As time progressed, Jones identified what appeared to be inconsistencies between spiritual and physical readings of Scripture, and he began doubting the validity of the Christian faith. Jones employed Carter G. Woodson's iconic phrase "mis-education" to coin his own term, "mis-religion." In his effort to reeducate himself, he jettisoned White religious influences for African American theologians, historians, and activists, including Benjamin Elijah Mayes, E. Franklin Frazer, and Harriet Tubman. Jones later turned to the humanist tradition, including Ralph Ellison, John Paul Sartre, and David Hume, to round out his influences. Jones spent the most productive years of his career teaching philosophy of religion and directing the Afro studies program at Florida State University until his death in 2012.

Jones's lone monograph, *Is God a White Racist?* (1973), marked the entry of Black philosophers into the discussion of Black theology and simultaneously introduced insights from humanism and philosophical analysis into the conversation. Jones argues for the centrality of theodicy based on a two-pronged argument: First, Black theology defines itself as a theology of liberation in the face of the magnitude of Black suffering. Second, the unique character of Black suffering forces the question of divine racism, and to pose that question is to initiate the theodicy debate. Beyond the centrality of theodicy, Jones locates the source of racial injustice in God himself, arguing for "divine racism."[34]

Jones follows the logic of Rabbi Richard Rubenstine in *After Auschwitz*, which analyzes Jewish suffering and poses the troublesome question, "Is God an anti-Semite?" Jones's logic to determine whether "God is a White racist" begins with the assertion that God, like humanity, is the sum of his acts. The logic continues by developing a "two-category system" that divides humanity into an in-group and an out-group. In the equation of divine racism, the out-group refers to those whose suffering is imbalanced in regard to the rest of the population. Jones asserts that God is directly responsible "for the imbalance of suffering that differentiates the 'in' and the 'out' groups." God's disfavor, therefore, "is correlated with the racial or ethnic identity of the group in question." Thus, "God must be a member of the 'in' group."[35]

Jones develops a critical distance from God that results in the conclusion that God is a divine racist. His continued exploration of God drives him to examine theodicy with the admittedly nontheological resources of secular humanism. Jones's humanistic leanings necessitate questions about divine assumptions among first-generation Black theologians, including that God is the liberator of the oppressed. For example, rather than Blacks identifying with Christ's suffering on the cross, Jones explains,

> In this new setting it becomes a public relations gimmick concocted by God to improve His image by reducing His accountability for human suffering. By arguing that human suffering should be endured and accepted because God Himself has suffered even more, the strategy is laid to keep man, particularly the oppressed, docile and reconciled to his suffering.[36]

Fundamentally, Jones's concern is that the residue of the "oppressor's" Christian worldview is bound up in the assumption of God's goodness (i.e., God as liberator). Convinced that he was not the founder of Black theistic skepticism, as an ongoing side project Jones identified a thoroughgoing stream of religious humanism within the African American spiritual heritage extant since slavery.

In place of Black theology's theistic assumption, Jones proposes "humancentric theism," which includes empirical and philosophical analysis, biblical and

---

[34]William R. Jones, *Is God a White Racist? A Preamble to a Black Theology* (Boston: Beacon, 1997), xxv-xxvi.
[35]Jones, *Is God a White Racist?*, 3-4.
[36]Jones, *Is God a White Racist?*, 8.

philosophical hermeneutics, and deductive argumentation.[37] Two significant affirmations lie at the center of humanism, according to Jones: (1) freedom is the essence of human being, and (2) human choice is logically prior to the authority of faith, reason, science, method, and so forth. In an effort to distinguish the source of liberation from God, Jones locates humancentric theism as the last point on the theistic spectrum before humanism. The human-centered nature of Jones's proposal disallows a single source of truth (including Scripture); instead, social and political philosophies emerge from specific contexts to function as the source of liberation. As a result, the methods of pursuing freedom from oppression vary depending on the details of the oppressive context.

The culmination of Jones's philosophical program is that Black theologians cannot survive racial oppression in the political, economic, and social spheres and rely on a racist supernatural being to liberate them. Jones suggests that ultimately, humanity must conclude either that God is for liberation, and then act with him, or that God is a White racist, in which case humanity becomes the arbiter of truth and ethical action for the sake of its own well-being. In either case, Jones insists, the buck stops at Black people acting for their own liberation. For Jones, championing liberation outside a theological imperative is the most viable pathway to escaping oppression. Since Jones's critique of Black theology is admittedly from a non-Christian perspective, it is self-evident that his contribution does not accord with the theological Anchors of historic African American faith but the starting point determined by his discussion partners.

Cone, Roberts, and Jones are examples of the groundbreaking scholarship that characterized first-generation Black theologians. In addition to the voices above, their noteworthy contemporaries include Allan Boesak (1945–), Cecil Cone (1937–2016), Vincent Harding (1931–2014), C. Eric Lincoln (1924–2000), and Charles Long (1926–2020). Despite the advent of the second generation of Black theologians, the first generation continued to produce seminal works that progressed the field of Black theology.

BLACK JESUS

A significant development during Black theology's first generation was the consideration of Black Jesus, with echoes of Henry McNeil Turner's "God Is a Negro" in the background. The question of Jesus' Blackness was emerging from the

---

[37]Jones, *Is God a White Racist?*, 171-72.

insistence that "Black is beautiful" but more importantly to identify Jesus with a people who had in many ways been despised and rejected. Black theologians highlighted elements of Christ's human life that demonstrated that the Black experience was not beyond the purview of the God-man.

Black theologians identify Christ with one of the most unappealing facets of the Black experience, namely, suffering. Black liberationists insist that Christ took sides with the oppressed as he entered into economic suffering in his humble birth by not dwelling in the mansions of kings but in a stable and lying in a manger. Cone equated Jesus' lowly birth with being born in a city alley and laid into a beer case in the ghetto.[38] Roberts embraced Christ's suffering, especially on the cross, because it was the chief symbol and example of passing through suffering into a larger and fuller life. For Roberts, this robust life was one in which Black men and women were reconciled to God through the cross of Christ, were purified through suffering, and were given a heightened compassion to be healers as agents of reconciliation. For Roberts, this transformation became the rod in the hands of Black people to pursue the redemptive purposes of God.

Black Jesus was also used to describe Christ as a source of dignity and significance in a society where Blackness was given negative meaning. Roberts explained that Black-White color symbolism influenced Christianity's core because the color Black (or Blackness) had come to represent the antithesis of Christ, namely, evil, immorality, and nonbeing. On the other hand, the Whiteness commonly attributed to Christ took on religious significance that indicated love and purity. The contrast was clear: Blackness was associated with reprobation, and Whiteness was affiliated with moral conversion and redemption.[39] Historically, these deeply engrained ideals about Whiteness and Blackness offered White Christians a theological justification for slavery and intensified the contemporary struggle for Black equality.

The power of iconography in the church cannot be overstated. Christians and non-Christians alike are subconsciously taught countless lessons without opening a book because images train the mind in powerful ways. Interestingly, an extrabiblical "White Jesus" was so engrained in American folklore that some Blacks reflexively adopted that imagery, and it appeared in the aesthetics of historic Black churches.

---

[38]Cone, *Black Theology of Liberation*, 114.
[39]Roberts, *Black Theology Today*, 11-12.

While the majority of Black liberationists would encourage a discussion of Black Jesus, there is a spectrum that contains significant differences about how Jesus' Blackness manifests. On one end of the continuum, Detroit minister Albert Cleage argues that Jesus was a Black man when he walked the earth.[40] Few identified with Cleage's attempt to make the Jesus of the Bible Black, but he was not without followers. The well-founded fear of Cleage's explanation was that it started down a slippery slope that stripped Christ of his Jewishness. Throughout history, exchanging Jesus' race for another is often linked with abuse by the powerful to help achieve their goals.[41]

In the middle of the spectrum, Cone took a mediating position that described Christ's Blackness as both literal and symbolic. Cone explains Christ's literal Blackness as being united with contemporary Blacks in their suffering. On the other hand, Christ's Blackness is symbolic because the Jesus of Scripture remains ethnically Jewish. Jesus' Jewish heritage is also important to Cone because it connects him to the oppressed nation of Israel, and most importantly situates Jesus within God's grand drama, which includes exodus and Jubilee.[42]

On the other end of the spectrum, Roberts argued that Jesus was symbolically Black because he met Blacks amid the Black experience. Roberts insists that Jesus is simultaneously the "desire of all nations" and the Savior of each person and every people. Roberts explains:

> The universal Christ is particularized for the Black Christian in the Black experience of the Black Messiah, but the Black Messiah is at the same time universalized in the Christ of the gospel who meets all persons in their situation. The Black Messiah liberates the Black person. The universal Christ reconciles the Black person with the rest of humankind.[43]

For Roberts, the significance of Black Jesus is symbolic because it allows Blacks to find dignity and self-awareness rooted in affirmation from Christ. Despite being understood through the lens of Blackness, for Roberts, Jesus remains the universal Savior and is applicable to every human context—yet purposefully not captive to the Black experience. The intentional use of racial categories to describe Christ is a foreign concept for most Westerners, but it is regrettably common to meddle

---

[40] Albert Cleage Jr.'s argument in his monograph *The Black Messiah* (London: Guilford, Sheed and Ward, 1968).
[41] See vol. 2 for an excerpt from Cleage's sermon "We Are God's Chosen People."
[42] Cone, *God of the Oppressed*, 125.
[43] Roberts, *Liberation and Reconciliation*, 73.

with Christ's ethnicity. In most Western depictions of Jesus, he is of European descent despite the obvious biblical data that testifies to Christ's Jewish background. Symbolic identification with Christ is a natural inclination, but disregarding his Jewish heritage is to wrongly manipulate the biblical witness.

14

HEIRS OF BLACK LIBERATION

DWIGHT HOPKINS IDENTIFIED the rise of Black theology's second generation with the appearance of two articles in 1979 that both affirmed and critiqued the first generation. The first article, by Jacquelyn Grant, is titled "Black Theology and Black Women," and the second, authored by Cornel West, is "Black Theology and Marxist Thought," which West expanded on in his famed 1982 book *Prophesy Deliverance! An African-American Revolutionary Christianity*. Grant's article addresses the marginalization of African American women in Black theology's first generation, and the latter insists that Black theology must take more proactive steps toward addressing economic issues if Blacks are to be liberated from oppression.

SECOND-GENERATION BLACK THEOLOGIANS

Grant and West's new avenues of engagement continued the liberative energies of the first generation and firmly established them in the second. Hopkins identifies seven notable themes among second-generation Black theologians. The first is an engagement with popular culture, which accentuates widely accepted works from artists and intellectuals who explored Black life in America. Examples of Black theology's interface with popular culture include Jon Spencer's *Protest and Praise: Sacred Music of Black Religion* (1990) and the emergence of "theomusicology" and its journal, *Black Sacred Music: A Journal of Theolomusicology*, published by Duke University Press. The second theme is reliance on the religious experience of Black poor folk as a norm for theological development. This is evident in George C. L. Cummings and Dwight N. Hopkins's edited volume *Cut Loose Your Stammering Tongue: Black Theology in the Slave Narratives* and in Riggins R. Earl Jr.'s *Dark Symbols, Obscure Signs: God, Self, and Community in the Slave Mind*. The third theme among second-generation Black theologians is an Afrocentricity that attempts to remove Eurocentric language and practices from the faith of Black people and replace them with elements from African spirituality. Examples of

Afrocentricity are Robert Earl Hood's *Must God Remain Greek? Afro Cultures and God Talk* (1990) and Theodore Walker's *Empower the People: Social Ethics for the African-American Church* (1991).

The fourth theme of the second generation is remaking traditional disciplines. This struggle is most acutely identified with African American professors who employ the intellectual tools of their disciplines in creative ways to be more relevant to Black communities and churches. *Experience and Tradition: A Primer in Black Biblical Hermeneutics* (1991), written by Baylor University's Stephen B. Reid, and Thomas L. Hoyt Jr.'s *A Study of the Book of Romans: The Church in Your House* (1991) are prototypical examples of remaking traditional disciplines.

The fifth second-generation theme is engagement with global connections that link allies of Black liberation from the African diaspora across the globe. Noel L. Erskin's *Decolonizing Theology: A Caribbean Perspective* (1981) is a notable contribution exploring the African diaspora by identifying how the problem of identity plagues oppressed peoples in the Caribbean. The sixth second-generation characteristic is a challenge to Black theology's liberation theme in the line of William R. Jones. Most notably, Anthony Pinn questions God's desire to liberate Black people in *Why Lord? Suffering and Evil in Black Theology* (1995), and David Emmanuel Goatley does similarly in *Were You There? God-Forsakenness in Slave Religion* (1996).

The final theme among Hopkin's second generation is interdisciplinary studies, which describes efforts to put African American religious thought and Black theology into dialogue with other bodies of scholarship. This theme is evident in Shelia Greeve Davaney and Dwight N. Hopkins's edited volume, *Challenging Conversations: Religious Reflection and Cultural Analysis* (1996), where contributors interact with postmodern theory, pragmatic historicism, Christian social criticism, and radical philosophy. The complexity of Black theology's second generation abounds because the liberation motif was applied to an ever-increasing number of concerns. Of these innovations, however, gender inclusion was the most widely acknowledged and is emphasized with the nomenclature "womanist theology."

Womanist theology. Theologian Jacquelyn Grant defines a womanist as "a strong Black woman who has sometimes been mislabeled as domineering and castrating."[1] The term *womanist* had a historically negative connotation as used in Black folk culture, but Alice Walker redefined the term and in so doing turned

---

[1] Jacquelyn Grant, "Womanist Theology: Black Women's Experience as a Source for Doing Theology, with Special Reference to Christology," in *Black Theology: A Documentary History*, vol. 2, *1980–1992*, ed. James H. Cone and Gayraud S. Wilmore (Maryknoll, NY: Orbis Books, 1993), 278.

a negative term into a positive description.[2] The origin of the term *womanist* offers insight into the disposition of Grant's womanist theology. Grant argues that Black and White women's experiences are so drastically different that their liberation enterprises must bear distinct names.

Grant affirms Walker's use of the term *womanist* because it is indigenous to the Black community. Walker describes *womanist* in the following way:

> Womanist from womanish. (Opposite of "girlish," i.e., frivolous, irresponsible, not serious.) A Black feminist or feminist of color. From the Black folk expression of mothers to female children, "You acting womanish," i.e. like a woman. Usually referring to outrageous, audacious, courageous or willful behavior. Wanting to know more and in greater depth than is considered "good" for one. Being grown-up. Interchangeable with another Black folk expression: "You trying to be grown." Responsible. In charge. Serious.[3]

Grant is convinced that Black female theologians should adopt Walker's term *womanist* because it rightly captures Black femininity as "being responsible, in charge, outrageous, courageous, and audacious enough to demand the right to think theologically and do it independently of White and Black men and White women."[4] In short, the term represents an experience that is familiar to most, if not all, Black women.

Grant consistently roots the womanist ethos in historical figures to establish a precedent for womanism; the womanist tradition serves as a baseline for its incorporation into Grant's theological program. She identifies historical figures such as Sojourner Truth, Jarena Lee, Amanda Berry Smith, Ida B. Wells, Mary Church, Mary McLeod Bethune, Fannie Lou Hamer, and countless others, who were often forgotten in historical accounts, as carrying the womanist disposition through the ages.[5]

The development of womanist theology benefited from decades of contemplating the Black self in society and within the Black community. In scholarly circles, this evolution is referred to as exploring Black subjectivity. In the early to mid-twentieth century, W. E. B. DuBois and E. Franklin Frazier challenged the

---

[2]Jacquelyn Grant, "Womanist Theology in North America," *Journal of the Interdenominational Theological Center* 16 (Fall 1988–Spring 1989): 287-88.
[3]Quoted by Jacquelyn Grant in *White Women's Christ and Black Women's Jesus: Feminist Christology and Womanist Response* (Atlanta: Scholars Press, 1989), 204-5.
[4]Grant, *White Women's Christ*, 209.
[5]Grant, *White Women's Christ*, 205; also see Grant, "Womanist Theology: Black Women's Experience," 278.

assumption that Blacks were monolithic. The concept of double consciousness offered a more expansive Black subjectivity that allowed Blackness to be a hyphenated reality composed of various factors. In addition, in the foreword to his groundbreaking study *The Negro Family in the United States* (1939), Frazier concludes that differences in Black familial behavior can only be understood in light of social forces that shaped them—most chiefly, growing economic disparities within the Black community. The diversity of the Black experience caused Black people to exist within shared experiences in unique ways.

> **Subjectivity** relates to understanding the self is the quality or condition of viewing things exclusively through the medium of one's own mind or individuality.[a]
>
> [a]*Oxford English Dictionary*, 2nd ed. (Oxford: Clarendon, 1989), s.v. "subjectivity."

Womanists insist that a single Black masculine narrative remained the central catalyst for the civil rights and Black power movements. As a result, the needs of Black women, who were estranged from the front lines, were often unrepresented and disregarded.[6] This lack of consideration in the 1950s and '60s urged Black women to rethink the complexity of their own composition as it related to Black men on issues of public policy, social issues, gender, and affiliation to religion. As Black people thought about their relationship to society at large (and Christians within the church), Black women sought to discover their place among Black theologians.

Acknowledging the Black experience as a multifaceted reality was the precursor to womanist theologians' highlighting the substantive distinction between the experience of Black women and that of Black men. Among Black women, there was ample enthusiasm about Black theology's emergence, but their excitement turned to frustration as they sensed their exclusion from the movement's first generation. Accordingly, Black women indicted the first generation of Black theologians for upholding an ideology of (gender) superiority that mirrored the (racial) superiority Black theologians fought to escape.

Black women sought a more suitable theological home where their concerns would be addressed. The feminist movement emerged, and Black women hoped that the sorrows of a shared female experience would form a productive theological partnership. Unfortunately, the dynamics within the feminist movement mirrored other attempts to include dominant and subdominant cultural groups

---

[6]Grant, "Womanist Theology: Black Women's Experience," 279.

in the same movement—the dominant group defined the shape and priorities of their association while inviting others to join the cause. While the invitation was to give voice to the concerns of "all women," in reality, it promoted the cause of White women. Black women concluded that because the feminist movement championed the needs of White women alone, the feminist theological movement was no place for Black women.[7]

Because Black theology normalized the Black masculine experience, and feminist theologians standardized the White woman's experience, both theological paradigms were deemed incapable of liberating African American women. Grant explains, "Where racism is rejected, sexism is embraced. Where classism is called into question, racism and sexism have been tolerated. And where sexism is repudiated racism and classism are often ignored."[8] Consequently, Black women creatively spawned a new theological paradigm that accounted for their unique otherness.

In an effort to fully account for the Black women's experience, womanist theologians considered the two historically disenfranchised characteristics they embodied (femininity and Blackness). The significance of these traits is not the sum of their parts but results in a unique interplay of characteristics that creates a new situation requiring distinct attention. The conclusion was that they were three times removed from normative White masculine culture. Black women endured race, class, and gender discrimination that comprised the context of womanist theology.

Womanist theologians have termed the result of race, class, and gender discrimination the *tridimensional* of the Black women's experience, or being in "triple jeopardy."[9] Grant insists that addressing racism and sexism in isolation is inadequate because each "ism" has a life of its own and they must be thwarted together for Black women to be liberated.[10] Other influential womanist voices include Emilie M. Townes, Marcia Riggs, Linda E. Thomas, and Cheryl Townsend Gilkes, who not only forged a new theological paradigm but successfully challenged first-generation Black theologians to consider the plight of Black women in the Black theological paradigm. The influence of womanist theologians on first-generation Black theologians is most evident in the later editions of widely read texts, such as Cone's *Black*

---

[7] Grant, *White Women's Christ*, 200.
[8] Jacquelyn Grant, "Black Theology and the Black Women," in *Black Theology: A Documentary History*, vol. 1, *1966-1979*, ed. James H. Cone and Gayraud S. Wilmore (Maryknoll, NY: Orbis Books, 1993), 323.
[9] Jacquelyn Grant, "Subjectification as a Requirement for Christological Construction," in *Lift Every Voice: Constructing Christian Theologies from the Underside* (San Francisco: HarperCollins, 1990), 203.
[10] Grant, "Womanist Theology: Black Women's Experience," 279.

Theology and Black Power: A Black Theology of Liberation and Roberts's *Liberation and Reconciliation*, which were amended to address gender dynamics and to employ gender-inclusive language when describing the Black theological task.[11]

> **PIONEERING WOMANIST BOOKS**
>
> Katie G. Cannon, *Black Womanist Ethics* (1988); Renita J. Weems, *Just a Sister Away* (1988); Jacquelyn Grant, *White Woman's Christ and Black Woman's Jesus* (1989); Delores S. Williams, *Sisters in the Wilderness* (1993); Emile M. Townes, *Womanist Justice, Womanist Hope* (1993).[a]
>
> [a]See vol. 2 for an interview with leading womanist Katie G. Cannon.

The scope of oppression. The occasion of Black theology's second generation expanded the scope of oppression addressed by Black liberationists. Grant and West insisted on gender and class engagement, but the expanded scope of any movement runs the risk of perpetually widening after an initial evolution. By the height of the second generation, the gospel had become "liberation from oppression," and oppression was anywhere people identified it.

Grant's criterion for liberation was twofold: first universal salvation, and second image-bearing capacity. Regarding universal salvation, Grant's concern, like Cone's, was not spiritual or eternal salvation but social relations. Since God does not privilege one race or demographic over another, she insists: "The crucifixion was for universal salvation, not just for male salvation or, as we may extend the argument to include, not just for White salvation. Because of this, Christ came and died, no less for the woman as for the man, no less for Black as for Whites."[12] Grant employs the concept of universal salvation to challenge traditional gender roles in the church and in society because the reality of salvation resists any type of functional gender distinction, since humanity shares common salvific ground.[13] As a result, any type of subordination or differentiation, even the potential of divinely appointed gender roles, is interpreted as oppression.

Grant also utilizes the concept of image-bearing capacity to legitimize claims of oppression.[14] In tandem with universal salvation, image-bearing capacity is

---

[11]See vol. 2 for an excerpt from Jacquelyn Grant's "Black Theology and the Black Women."
[12]Grant, "Womanist Theology: Black Women's Experience," 286.
[13]Jacquelyn Grant, "Come to My Help, Lord, For I'm in Trouble: Womanist Jesus and the Mutual Struggle for Liberation," in *Reconstructing the Christ Symbol: Essays in Feminist Christology* (New York: Paulist Press, 1993), 68.
[14]Grant, "Come to My Help," 65.

fundamental to all of humanity and places all people on an equal plane of existence. For Grant, one person of equal standing has no ability to exert force of any type over another. Consequently, anyone who impedes the process of self-liberation with any source of authority—including Scripture—commits an oppressive act.

Beyond gender and class, the most profound circumstance to which liberation from oppression was applied among certain second-generation liberationists was deliverance from traditional sexual norms. While virtually every liberationist would decry poor treatment for anyone, not every liberationist affirmed this development in the early days of the second generation. In contrast to the historic Black Christian tradition, a growing number of liberationists affirm that individuals determine their sexual orientation however they choose and must be liberated from oppression based on that choice.

> **RESOURCES ON BLACK LIBERATION AND SEXUALITY**
> Kelly Brown Douglas, *Sexuality and the Black Church: A Womanist Perspective* (Maryknoll, NY: Orbis Books, 1999); Dwight N. Hopkins and Linda E. Thomas, eds., *Walk Together Children: Black and Womanist Theologies, Church, and Theological Education* (Eugene, OR: Wipf & Stock), 183-250; Sallie M. Cuffee, "On Sex and Sexuality in the Black Churchwomen's Lives: A Womanist Call for a Moral and Just Conversation in the Black Church," *The Journal of Religious Thought* 59-60, no.1 (2006–2007): 45-65; Roger A. Sneed, *Representations of Homosexuality: Black Liberation Theology and Cultural Criticism* (New York: Palgrave Macmillian, 2010); Renee Leslie Hill, "Who Are We for Each Other? Sexism, Sexuality and Womanist Theology," in *Black Theology: A Documentary History*, ed. James H. Cone and Gayraud S. Wilmore (Maryknoll, NY: Orbis Books, 1993), 345-51.

Liberation versus prosperity. The introduction of economic critique among second-generation Black theologians raises the common question, Has Black liberation theology transformed into the prosperity gospel? While the prosperity gospel is difficult to summarize, its proponents affirm that benefits of being born again include material wealth and physical health. Another common name for the movement is the "health-and-wealth gospel" because of its emphasis on these two earthly realities. Its ideas find their roots in the "Word of Faith" movement, which was popularized by Kenneth Hagin Sr. and Oral Roberts in the 1980s.

This question is reasonable because the two movements have similar themes. They start with freedom from economic bondage. Second, the movements mirror each other ecclesiastically in that both liberation theology and the prosperity gospel are a composite of theological convictions that are not the possession of a specific church or denomination. Despite having shared themes, Black theologians almost unanimously agree that the prosperity gospel did not develop from Black theology. This renunciation is primarily because the prosperity gospel abandons a central feature of Black theology with its all-encompassing interest in personal prosperity over the well-being of the community. Said differently, there can be personal prosperity without social justice. Furthermore, the economic philosophy of the prosperity gospel opposes the core of Black theology because it attributes economic success to individual spiritual flourishing, rather than considering both the individual and systemic realities that contribute to a person's economic state. In short, the prosperity gospel short-circuits the social activism and community mobilization that has characterized the mood of Black theology.

James H. Evans Jr. claims that the prosperity gospel's deviation from Black theology is located in its revisionist Christology. Evans raises the question, How can one claim a Christ whom the church has historically described as a poor and oppressed member of a poor and oppressed community and still hold on to the notion of material prosperity as an ultimate value? In response to the question, Evans indicts prosperity preachers by insisting that they eliminate Christ from their preaching by resorting to motivational and self-help sermons that rarely mention Christ or his social, political, and economic setting.[15]

Many second-generation womanists and Black theologians followed in the footsteps of Cone by radically prioritizing Deliverance among the doctrinal Anchors of the African American theological tradition. They similarly departed from the tradition's affirmation of Conversion as a matter of internal transformation based on Christ's redemption and framed it as a universal phenomenon focused on salvation from social, political, and economic oppression. There was also a move away from placing liberation in the hands of a Big God, instead asserting divine authority in Blacks' pursuit of liberation. Similarly, it was common for second-generation liberationists to leverage the Good Book in service of deliverance without close exegesis pertaining to other topics. The most pronounced departure within the second generation, especially among some womanist scholars, was a departure from viewing Jesus' death as a welcomed, exemplary act and instead outright rejecting redemptive suffering—including Christ's crucifixion.

---

[15]James H. Evans Jr., "The Future of Black Theology," in *The Cambridge Companion to Black Theology*, ed. Dwight N. Hopkins and Edward P. Antonio (New York: Cambridge University Press, 2012), 314-21.

THIRD-GENERATION BLACK THEOLOGIANS

Hopkins's *Introducing Black Theology of Liberation* marked the first two generations of Black theology as beginning in 1966 and 1979, respectively. He justified establishing a second generation by identifying a new set of challenges worthy of innovative theological activity. Despite the wide use of this model and four decades of elapsed time since the establishment of the second generation, there has been no broadly recognized attempt to identify a third generation. It is long overdue.

The chief difficulties of identifying a third generation are their decentralization in the academy and their participation in a variety of scholarly societies and institutions. The first generation were few in number and marginalized in mainstream academics; as a result, they were compelled to find solidarity in their theological endeavors among one another. By contrast, young Black scholars have found relatively broad acceptance in the academy and are less motivated to participate in racially delineated groups than their predecessors.

This diaspora throughout the academy is amplified by the increasing number of Black and womanist theologians and the increasing acceptance of contextual theologies. Prior to Cone's tenure at Union Theological Seminary, Blacks had to assimilate to the dominant culture by undertaking the theological task from a White cultural framework or risk career sabotage for theologizing from a marginalized social location. Cone set a precedent for persisting as a Black scholar in a White-dominant space without assimilation. He stood in contrast with influential voices in Black theology's early years whose vocational homes were historically Black colleges, divinity schools, and churches. The current number of scholars situated outside historically Black institutions reflecting on Black life is inconceivable without Cone.

While neither geography nor institutional affiliation characterizes the third-generation Black theologian, three characteristics are relatively consistent. The first is engagement with literature produced by first- and second-generation Black theologians. Interaction with Cone is especially common, and the nature of the engagement is generally respectful, yet with a critical eye. This kind of interaction is typified in J. Cameron Carter's *Race: A Theological Account* (2008) and Brian Bantum's *Redeeming Mulatto: A Theology of Race and Christian Hybridity* (2010).

The second characteristic of third-generation Black theologians is an increasing interaction with traditional Western theological sources. First-generation scholars such as Cone were determined to unearth a distinctively Black set of theological resources, but the newest generation has reengaged traditional theological sources, often looking to identify the ways that European colonialist racial logic became pervasive in Western theology. This is typified by womanist Eboni Marshall Turman's assessment of conciliar orthodoxy in *Toward a Womanist Ethic of Incarnation* (2013). In addition, these scholars are identifying undiscovered theological intersections between the dominant Western and the Black theological narrative, which is evident in Reggie L. Williams's *Bonhoeffer's Black Jesus* (2014). The expanded engagement with sources produced in the patristic period through to the Reformation in the sixteenth century is a shift that further establishes third-generation Black theologians in the broader academic theological community.

Third, Black theology's third generation is characterized by an increasing disposition toward assessing and decolonizing ideas due to a growing consensus that discrimination inhabits human thought forms as well as institutional systems and structures. This is over against the first generation, for whom social and political concerns dominated, and the second generation, which insisted on the expansion of the Black liberationist enterprise and the integration of Black voices into traditional divinity-related disciplines. The highly academic orientation of the third generation presupposes the deployment of various expressions of critical theory in the theological process. While engagement with critical theories varies in usage and dependence, Black theology's now virtually uncontested home in the academy assumes that liberationists have facility with these critical resources. Examples of Black theology intermingling with race theory include Willie James Jennings's award-winning *The Christian Imagination: Theology and the Origins of Race* (2010), featuring his emphasis on place in the theological task, and Kelly Brown Douglas's *Stand Your Ground* (2015).[16]

One of the most profound contributions of third-generation Black theologians interfaces with the second Anchor of the African American Christian tradition: Jesus. Former Duke Divinity School colleagues J. Kameron Carter and Willie James Jennings endeavored to dismantle Enlightenment racial analysis that encouraged humanity to transcend its human particularity and strive to achieve a universal conception of the world. The pursuit of universal knowledge was followed by the quest for the universal man, and that man was embodied as White. As a result, non-White bodies were deemed peculiar and thus inferior. Carter and Jennings take down this racial assessment by asserting Jesus' Jewish identity over

---

[16]See vol. 2 for an excerpt from Willie James Jennings's *The Christian Imagination*.

against the notion of Enlightenment transcendence.[17] Furthermore, they say, Gentiles were grafted into Jesus' Jewish body and fulfill God's covenant with Israel. This kind of welcoming and joining upends discriminatory racial logic that has marked Christian theology and the Christian church.[18]

In addition to the analytical approach to theology that describes much of this generation, the influence of pastor-scholars such as Raphael G. Warnock, a doctoral student of Cone, cannot be ignored. His quest to examine and define the mission of the Black church in his *The Divided Mind of the Black Church: Theology, Piety, and Public Witness* is a near playbook for Warnock's life and ministry. Warnock's answer to the missional witness of the church is embodied in his own social protest, which includes applying his unapologetically liberationist disposition to his role as the senior pastor of the historic Ebenezer Baptist Church in Atlanta and to his political endeavors as a US senator (Georgia).

The unapologetically scholastic nature of Black theology's third generation is prone to narrow their scope of theological concern from the breadth of the doctrinal Anchors that epitomize the African American Christian tradition. The often-theoretical modes of inquiry are driven by an underlying desire for Deliverance and are inclined toward an analytic (not constructive) disposition. To that end, this generation's study has not featured systematic explorations of the nature and attributes of a Big God who is able to deliver but instead has assessed what has been done in God's name throughout the history of the church. Similarly, the explorations of Jesus have not been dedicated to the skirmishes of the conciliar tradition but focus on Jesus' humanity and constitution as a means of undoing racialization and otherness. Third-generation biblical scholars have been relatively quiet but have remained steady contributors to the Black interpretative tradition as they research at the nexus of Scripture and the Black experience.[19] In addition to biblical interpretation, there is an emerging focus on hermeneutics, reexamining Black religion from a Black radical disposition that has been reenergized.[20]

---

[17]J. Kameron Carter, *Race: A Theological Account* (New York: Oxford University Press, 2008), 7-8.

[18]Willie James Jennings, *The Christian Imagination: Theology and the Origins of Race* (New Haven, CT: Yale University Press, 2010), 252-65.

[19]Examples include Allen Dwight Callahan's *The Talking Book* (New Haven: Yale University Press, 2006) and Mitzi J. Smith, Angela Parker, and Ericka S. Dunbar Hill's *Bitter the Chastening Rod: Africana Biblical Interpretation After Stony the Road We Trod in the Age of BLM, SayHerName, and MeToo* (Lanham, MD: Rowman & Littlefield, 2023).

[20]Sylvester A. Johnson, *African American Religions, 1500–2000: Colonialism, Democracy, and Freedom* (New York: Cambridge University Press 2015), and J. Kameron Carter, *The Anarchy of Black Religion* (Durham, NC: Duke University Press 2023), embody this trend.

THE SCHOLAR AND THE CHURCH

The ongoing skirmish for the home of Black theology is of ongoing interest in the third decade of the twenty-first century, but the answer to the question is obvious. Black theology has become an academic enterprise despite the insistence of seminal figures such as Cone and the determination of statesmen such as Hopkins. At the apex of the second generation's influence, Hopkins guarded against the allure of the academy over against the church, saying:

> Most educational systems in the United States, particularly for full-time professors, pull [professors] away from meaningful organized faith communities. . . . Still, African American theologians must maintain creative and critical relationships to the Black church—whether in the forms of teaching and preaching in the church, being associate pastors, leading workshops and seminars, consulting, or regularly sharing ongoing academic work with laypeople.[21]

In addition to the all-consuming culture of the academy, the increasing demand for African American theologians and biblical scholars adds to the appeal of the academy, which previous generations did not have to contend with.

Coupled with the allure of the academy, Black theology's initial intent to function as an internal critique of the Black church's waning prophetic zeal set Black theologians on an overly critical trajectory regarding rank-and-file Black Christianity. Prominent Black liberationist Jeremiah Wright recalls that he was constantly put down and "beat up" during his academic studies because he would not give up his constructive relationship with the local church. Wright recalls:

> Many of the theologians in Cone's age group—Dwight Hopkins calls them the "first generation of Black theologians"—did not "do church." They did not and do not belong to church. They did not and do not attend church regularly. They were upset with the "other worldly" focus of far too many Black churches. . . . As a result they cut themselves off from the very congregations for whom and to whom they should have been writing.[22]

The increasing integration of theoretical resources and concerns that originate from the academy enhances an ideological rift between scholar and pastor. This

---

[21]Dwight N. Hopkins, *Heart and Head: Black Theology Past, Present and Future* (New York: Palgrave, 2002), 165.
[22]Jeremiah A. Wright Jr., "Protestant Ecclesiology," in Hopkins and Antonio, *Cambridge Companion to Black Theology*, 191-92.

rift promotes an elitism among liberation scholars and ministers with graduate-level training. While the third generation's contributions are needed in their own right, they have not forged a meaningful meeting ground for scholar and clergy to interact.

Black theology's strength is its insistence on theologizing about the challenges of daily life. Its rejection of the mid-twentieth-century ethereal theological paradigms that dominated seminaries and divinity schools gave rise to a mode of theology that not only was contextual but also took aim at the challenges of Black life and served as an inherent critique of the Black church.

As time passed, however, the critiques of several Black and womanist theologians became the scope of their theological inquiry. In doing so, they ceased to theologically explore the breadth of historic Black Christianity and fostered a nearly exclusive focus on its problems, namely, the truncated pursuit of its priestly and prophetic mission and latent theological malformation. As a result, the Black church is heavily critiqued but remains underengaged by Black liberationists in ways the Black churchgoing masses recognize.

Despite Black theologians having composed the bulk of Black Christianity's written theological witness in the academy, their influence in the church is limited. In a now dated 1990 study of urban Black pastors in historic Black denominations, they reported little influence from Black theology:

> Both in survey data and the qualitative responses show that thus far that the movement of Black liberation theology had relatively limited influence upon the urban clergy and their congregations. A little more than one-third of Black pastors interviewed claimed any influence from this movement. Further analysis of urban church data indicates that age, education, and denomination were the most significant variables in determining the responses.[23]

The study continues by noting that recently theologically trained ministers under forty, along with those among them who had been formally educated, were more likely to be influenced by Black theology. The date of the study's publication indicates that it was reporting on a relatively young movement (twenty-one years after *Black Theology and Black Power* was published), but the data offers a keen insight—that the movement took hold in the academy, but those who had no formal theological training, or who were trained before the movement was formalized, were

---

[23] C. Eric Lincoln and Lawrence H. Mamiya, *The Black Church in the African American Experience* (Durham, NC: Duke University Press, 1990), 179.

unlikely to be able to identify the names of those associated with the movement. Although Cone's name recognition increased as his career developed, active ministers consulted other resources to assist with the pastoral task.

In a sample from a 2003 study of Black church leadership, 25 percent of ministers in historically Black denominations had a master's degree from a seminary.[24] As the trajectories indicate, Black theology has been on the periphery of the churchgoing masses, and it will remain that way until it bridges the gap between the academy and the church by taking its chief concerns from the church, not primarily from the ivory towers of the academy. Ironically, the popularization of Black theology occurred not by the pen of a scholar but by the thundering pulpit of Rev. Jeremiah Wright during Barack Obama's 2008 presidential campaign.

---

[24]Michael I. N. Dash and Christine D. Chapman, *The Shape of Zion: Leadership and Life in Black Churches* (Eugene, OR: Wipf & Stock, 2007), 153.

15

INTO THE TWENTY-FIRST CENTURY

As THE TWENTY-FIRST CENTURY COMES OF AGE, Black Christianity in the United States continues to thrive in its diasporic expression, spanning various denominations, institutions, and ministries. While it is too soon to make definitive judgments about recent developments, it is evident that there is a surge of Black consciousness forged on the heels of an era marked by growing racial unity and hope for a renewed America.

At the dawn of 2012, there was a budding notion that the United States was becoming a postracial society. Beacons of hope included a growing Black middle class and the election of America's first Black president, Barack Obama (2008). For Black Millennials and Generation Z, Malia and Sasha's arrival at the White House was yet another milestone of progress for America. Among Christians, there was a growing number of historically White churches and parachurch organizations taking on racial reconciliation as an essential part of their mission since the 1990s. This state of affairs forged a renewed hope for race relations in America and fanned the flame of racial reconciliation in the church.

For older Millennials, the American story of racial violence and tension was the stuff of history books, and the 1992 Rodney King riots were a faint memory. During their childhood, there were only a few racialized events that were elevated to national news. Relatively minor bumps in the road included the 2006 Jena Six case, where nooses were hung in a tree at a school in Louisiana, and President Obama's famous July 2009 "Beer Summit." This meeting was convened after renowned Harvard professor Henry Louis Gates had been detained while attempting to enter his home, which had a jammed front door. The gathering involved Gates, the officer who arrested him, and President Obama. This situation ended peaceably and illuminated hope for a new way of addressing racial tension.

The progress toward a postracial society was seemingly shattered on February 26, 2012, when seventeen-year-old African American Trayvon Martin was fatally shot and killed while walking home from a convenience store wearing a hoodie and carrying Skittles and iced tea. Martin's death, at the hands of neighborhood watchman George Zimmerman—a murder that shattered the innocence of younger generations—polarized the nation. Throughout Zimmerman's trial and "Stand Your Ground" hearings, lines hardened across America.

The nation grew more polarized as incidents reminiscent of Martin's murder swept the country. Americans were bewildered by a string of widely publicized Black murders, including those of Eric Garner (2014), Laquan McDonald (2014), Tamir Rice (2014), Walter Scott (2015), Freddie Gray (2015), Sandra Bland (2015), the Charleston nine (2015), Philando Castile (2016), Terence Crutcher (2016), and Alton Sterling (2016). These traumatic events drove Millennials and Generation Z back into the horrors of their grandparents' America—especially those by the hand of law enforcement.

A time that many hoped would be a new chapter of the American story characterized by racial unity and empathy witnessed the formation of the largest protest organization since the civil rights and Black power movements—namely, #BlackLivesMatter. This series of events sparked a Black consciousness movement, both inside and outside the church, among Millennials and Gen Z, with leaders who extend into the younger ranks of Generation X. This relatively new movement is in its infancy, but among the movement's participants there is a collection of Christians characterized by being doctrinally Anchored, socially conscious, and culturally liberated.[1]

> **#BlackLivesMatter** began in 2013 as a slogan to oppose racial injustice aimed at Blacks. Due to its intentionally ambiguous nature, people from various backgrounds employed the term and asserted that Black lives mattered in a variety of ways (spanning from nonviolence to looting). Among Christians, there were those who insisted that #BlackLivesMatter because African Americans were made in God's image. Over time, #BlackLivesMatter evolved into an organization that upholds ideological commitments that are inconsistent, at several points, with the Christian social ethic historically associated with the doctrinal Anchors of African American Christianity. These various uses of #BlackLivesMatter are simultaneously deployed by groups that hold a wide array of ideological commitments.

---

[1] See vol. 2 for an excerpt from Christina Edmonson's essay "Freedom of Speech for You, of Him."

> Unlike the civil rights movement, with its recognized leader and well-known nonviolent methodology, the ideological commitments of those who utter the slogan #BlackLivesMatter are nearly impossible to pigeonhole.

Anchored, conscious, and liberated Black Millennial and Generation Z Christians are marked by a passionate ethos that is grounded by the doctrinal Anchors of Black faith. On the whole, there is a continued affirmation of the Good Book, which remains the theological bedrock for the largest Black denominations. In addition to doctrinal clarity, there is enthusiasm about the ancient creeds because of the often-forgotten contributions from North African church fathers. There is also a resistance to socially indifferent pietism and an insistence on upholding a robust Christian ethic that the creeds stopped short of.[2]

Among Generation X and Millennial leaders of this movement, there is a growing desire to decolonize their faith. The decolonization effort is driven by a desire to embody doctrinal and ethical clarity within the Black experience. This process has been especially marked among those with extended exposure to the cultural and political assumptions of White evangelicalism and mainline Christianity. Christian hip-hop artist Lecrae Moore recounted the beginning of his decolonization process in the wake of Mike Brown's murder:

> I was interviewed by the *Washington Post*. I remember the questions I was getting.[3] You know, it was kinda like they were making me to be like the poster child for evangelicalism and I was like, "Wait, wait, wait . . . I didn't sign up for this." Like, time out. And then, when the article came out, Christena Cleveland, you know? [She] had written that . . . she believed I could be more (I don't know the words she used specifically) but more potent, more effective. And she said right now, I was an evangelical mascot. . . . God bless her for that. I value people who can be direct and upfront. That for me was just so riveting and challenging that I had to take a look at myself and process who I was. And so yeah, it was a long journey. A lot of depression. A lot of identity, you know, struggles, but I'm better on the other side. I mean, I'm much better.[4]

---

[2]See vol. 2 for an excerpt Thabiti Anyabwile's address "Speak Up for the Vulnerable."
[3]See Michelle Boorstein, "This Rapper Is Trying to Get Fellow Evangelicals to Talk About Race. Not Everyone Is on Board," *Washington Post*, July 1, 2016, www.washingtonpost.com/news/acts-of-faith/wp/2016/06/14/this-black-rapper-might-be-americas-next-evangelical-leader/.
[4]Lecrae Moore, "Facts About Lecrae," *Truth's Table*, podcast audio, September 30, 2017. See vol. 2 for a larger excerpt of this interview with Lecrae Moore.

While the beginning of every decolonization process is not this public, Lecrae's testimony accounts for the moment when he deemed decolonization was necessary. The initiation of Lecrae's decolonization process is characteristic of many, but unlike Lecrae's, however, some decolonization processes result in apostasy because appalling acts done by Christians are mistaken as the essence of the faith itself.[5]

> **The decolonization process** often includes (1) assessing doctrinal commitments for affirmations that intentionally or unintentionally oppress others, (2) evaluating whether there are ethically significant issues that have not been appraised theologically, (3) intentionally diversifying theological influences by adding African American voices, and (4) pursuing healthy spiritual formation practices that emerge from the African American Christian tradition.

The Jude 3 Project, led by Lisa Fields, is an asset to Christians conducting introspection similar to Lecrae's. Jude 3 facilitates seminars, trainings, podcasts, and blogs with a mission to "help the Christian community know what they believe and why they believe it. Distinctive in its strong emphasis in equipping those of African descent in the United States and abroad."[6] Organizations such as Jude 3 facilitate a public discourse equipping believers to apologetically engage issues that emerge from the African American context. Educational initiatives such as the Meachum School of Haymanot, led by Vince Bantu, provide formal, degree-seeking training to redemptively engage the Black experience.

The Meachum School of Haymanot exists to

> bring biblical, graduate-level theological education to African American, ethnic minority and low-income communities in a contextualized and affordable manner. MSH is committed to theological education that is biblical, contextual and accessible: biblical as rooted in the Gospel, the sole lordship of the risen Jesus Christ and the authority of Scripture; contextual as having indigenous leadership and deploying contextualized pedagogical methods and content arising from the African American and other diverse traditions; and accessible as offering theological education at an affordable cost located in under-resourced communities.[7]

---

[5]See vol. 2 for an excerpt from Jasmine L. Holmes's book *Mother to Son: Letters to a Black Boy on Identity and Hope.*

[6]"About Us," Jude 3 Project, https://jude3project.org/aboutus (accessed October 1, 2022).

[7]"About Us," Meachum School of Haymanot, https://meachum.org/about (accessed October 1, 2022). See vol. 2 for an excerpt from Vince Bantu's *A Multitude of All Peoples.*

Black-conscious and Afrocentric initiatives such as the Jude 3 Project and the Meachum School of Haymanot benefit from a growing number of scholars and ministers establishing a written tradition. Volumes including Esau McCaulley's *Reading While Black* and Vince Bantu's *A Multitude of All Peoples* proactively connect the dots between orthodox faith and the Black experience with a view toward the broader people of God. In addition, psychologists, including Sheila Wise Rowe and Christina Edmondson, are addressing topics from a Christian perspective that have been the source of significant existential angst for Blacks, including racial trauma.[8]

These Anchored, conscious, and liberated believers express their social consciousness by "doing justice, loving mercy, and walking humbly with God" (Micah 6:8). The desire is driven by the theological affirmation captured in the words of Pastor Charlie Dates in his address at the fifty-year commemoration of Martin Luther King Jr.'s assassination:

> Righteousness is the root of justice and justice is the offspring of righteousness. . . . The implication is that the notion of righteousness is related to justice. This is what makes the claim of the gospel so scandalous. It is that we who are sinners are, now, through the shed blood of Jesus Christ made righteous before God and have peace with God. We have been justified. That is, righteousness has been credited to our sin's depleted accounts. At the cross God got justice and we got righteousness. So now, in the church, we who are righteous ought to be found fighting for justice. Through the Scripture, the notions of righteousness and justice are not to be separated.[9]

The affirmation of a God who provides salvation and upholds justice through his atoning death and resurrection drives social engagement. Bryan Stevenson's bestselling book-turned-film *Just Mercy: A Story of Justice and Redemption* is a model often noted by these young people. Stevenson is a forerunner for Black Millennial and Generation Z Christians in engaging public life in their vocations in a way that is driven by faith in Jesus and has an eye toward Black struggles. Politically, movements such as the & Campaign, led by Justin Giboney, typify the political ethos of this group, who reject down-the-line partisan politics because neither major party consistently represents Christian virtues.[10]

---

[8]See vol. 2 for an excerpt from Esau McCaulley's *Reading While Black*.
[9]Charlie Dates, "The Most Segregated Hour in America: Overcoming Divisions to Pursue MLK's Vision of Racial Harmony" (speech), April 4, 2018, Memphis, https://vimeo.com/263070525.
[10]See vol. 2 for an excerpt from Amisho (Sho) Baraka's "Maybe Both, 1865."

Black cultural affirmation is also a vital component to this movement. Throughout American history, the beauty of Black culture has been contested and subjected to the standards of the dominant culture. Without deifying Black culture, Afrocentric cultural expression including worship forms, literature, and fashion are enthusiastically affirmed if they accord with Christian virtue. The denial of White cultural normativity is especially poignant for those who were "discipled" out of their culture because another was made to seem inherently more godly.

The explosion of Poets in Autumn, which features Christian spoken-word artists who seamlessly converge the African American Christian tradition with contemporary issues, typifies Black cultural liberation. Relatedly, working with classic Black literature, Claude Atcho's *Reading Black Books* highlights Black Christian cultural expression as he offers a theological reading of popular Black novels and poetry to unearth the joys, sorrows, and longing that often mark Black life.[11]

> **Poets in Autumn** is the largest poetry tour in the world. The poets aim to deliver a culturally relevant and distinctively Christian message to those who are drifting from the faith or those who do not claim Christ. The tour features the top Christian spoken word artists in the nation. Each artist featured has created their own demand and has reached millions online utilizing the vehicle of spoken word to convey hard-hitting, transparent messages that challenge and encourage audiences.[a]
>
> [a]See volume 2 for an excerpt from Preston Perry's poem "New Woke Christian."

Anchored, conscious, and culturally liberated Black Christians serve and worship in a variety of denominational and ecclesial contexts. In search of a worship environment that is doctrinally Anchored, socially conscious, and celebrates Black cultural expression, there is a reinvigorated affection for historic Black churches. This fervor is evident in ministers such as C. J. Rhodes, who continuously embodies the virtue of Black church life as pastor of the charismatic Baptist hotbed Mount Helm Baptist Church. In addition to relatively young fellowships such as the Bridge Church in Brooklyn, New York, church-planting movements are growing in number, sparked by the Crete Collective, which endeavors to grow churches in communities of color, and MyBVLD, led by Dhati Lewis, which coaches urban church leaders to overcome a scarcity mindset. Others have reentered historically Black churches from White

---

[11]See vol. 2 for an excerpt from Quina Aragon's poem "What's a Woman Worth?"

evangelical churches for a more holistic worship experience that includes soul care needed as a result of the trials of living in a racialized world.[12]

One facet of this ecclesiastical shift was captured by a March 9, 2018, *New York Times* article titled "A Quiet Exodus: Why Black Worshipers Are Leaving White Evangelical Churches." This exposé captures the sentiment of numerous Black worshipers who found a home in White evangelical churches in record numbers by 2012. As White ministers failed to address police shootings and overwhelmingly supported presidential candidate Donald Trump—despite his well-documented racial bigotry—Black worshipers were troubled that their spiritual family declined to hear their cries. Journalist Campbell Robertson reports, "[White evangelicals] cheered the [election's] outcome, reassuring uneasy fellow worshipers with talk of abortion and religious liberty, about how politics is the art of compromise rather than the ideal." Many Black worshipers were convinced their burdens were not being borne (Galatians 6:2) by fellow church members. These pressures, among others, have generated a diversity of sentiments toward partnering with and worshiping in predominantly White churches within this movement.[13]

The tale of Anchored, conscious, and culturally liberated Christians will continue to develop in contrast to Black liberationists and adjacent to Black evangelicals in the days ahead. The major question for the future is not regarding doctrinal commitments, which accord with the historic doctrinal Anchors of Black faith. Rather, the question is where these believers will find their homes in terms of local churches, established Christian ministries and institutions, and church-planting movements.

The story of African American Christianity is one of a determined people driven by faith to pursue spiritual and social uplift for themselves and others to God's glory. May this story be interwoven into the tapestry of the "cloud of witnesses" (Hebrews 12:1) from "all nations, tribes peoples, and tongues" (Revelation 7:9) who bear witness to Christ. The ongoing story of Black evangelicalism, Black liberation, and Anchored, conscious, and liberated believers is a story that continues to unfold. Where will all of this take us in the coming decades? We will soon find out, but one thing is certain, there is a balm in Gilead.[14]

---

[12]See vol. 2 for an excerpt from Rasool Barry's sermon "Esther: God Remembers You."
[13]See vol. 2 for an excerpt from Jackie Hill Perry's *Gay Girl, Good God.*
[14]"There Is a Balm in Gilead" is a popular gospel song covered by numerous artists. The phrase emerged from Jeremiah 8, when Israel is in exile and the Babylonians are poised to violate their homeland. As the Jews are far from home, the question was uttered, "Is there no balm in Gilead? Is there no physician there? Why then has the health of the daughter of my people not been restored?" (Jeremiah 8:22). Resonating with Israel's diasporic plight, African American Christians confidently answer Jeremiah's question, saying, "Jesus is the balm in Gilead."

GENERAL INDEX

African American Pentecostalism, 165
African Methodist Episcopal Church, 35-36, 70-71
Allen, Richard, 31, 35-36, 52, 54, 67-68
antilynching, 104, 118-19
Bailey, E. K., 191-92
Baldwin, James, 217-18
Bantu, Vince, 252
Baysmore, Joseph, 25
Bentley, William H., 165-66, 168-69, 172, 174-75, 182-86
Bethel African Methodist Episcopal Church, 35
Bishop College, 191-92
Black evangelical Black theology, 182-87
Black evangelicalism, 153, 161, 167, 175, 181, 187, 189
Black, Leonard, 58-59
Black Panther Party, 156, 159
Black power, 216-19, 227
Black power movement, 154-59, 176, 181, 211-12, 222, 225
"Black Power Statement," 211-12, 214
Boothe, Charles Octavius, 74-75, 86, 90
Boulden, Jesse Freeman, 76
Boyd, Richard Henry, 85, 90, 191
Brooks, Walter H., 91
Buckaloo, Solomon, 75
Cain, Richard Harvey, 77
Carey, Lott, 30
Carmichael, Stokley, 154-56, 159
Carter, Anthony J., 200
Charles, H. B., 203
Coppin, Fanny Jackson, 80-81
Church of God in Christ, 125-29, 165
Cleage, Albert, 233
Coker, Daniel, 35-36, 67
colorblind model, 202
Cone, James H., 3, 187, 195, 208, 213-22, 225, 232-33, 243
Congress of Racial Equality, 104, 145, 154, 157-59
Colley, William W., 94
Crummell, Alexander, 94
decolonization, 251-52
Dennis, David, 158

Dorsey, Thomas, 107
Douglass, Frederick, 41, 43, 56-58
Drumgoold, Kate, 81-83
Dubois, W. E. B., 64, 88, 105, 116-18, 131, 144, 237-38
Dunbar, Paul Laurence, 97-99
Elaw, Zilpha, 32
Ellis, Carl F., Jr., 186
Ellis, Karen, 203
Evans, Tony, 183-84, 192
Fields, Bruce L., 194-96
Fisk, Alfred G., 201
First Great Awakening, 21-23, 50
Fleming, Louise Celestia, 95
Freedman's Bureau, 87-88
"from below," 209
Garnet, Henry Highland, 53, 57-58
Garvey, Marcus, 109
Grace, Charles Manual, 109
Grant, Jacquelyn, 235-37, 240
Great Migration, 104-10, 114
Grimke, Francis James, 111-12
Hamer, Fannie Lou, 144-45
Haynes, Lemuel, 23-24
Heard, Josephine Delphine Henderson, 99
Henry, Carl F. H., 163, 207
Hill, Edward Victor, 172
Hood, James Walker, 74
Hopkins, Dwight N., 214-15, 235-36, 246
Jackson, Joseph H., 112-13
Jackson, Mahalia, 145
Jennings, Willie James, 244
Jim Crow, 102, 105, 112
Johnson, Mordecai Wyatt, 135-36
Jones, Absalom, 35, 52
Jones, Charles P., 125-26
Jones, Howard, 166, 168, 170, 174
Jones, Ken, 197-98
Jones, William R., 229-31
Jude 3 Project, 252-53
Kelsey, George, 137-40
King, Martin Luther, Jr., 143-52, 159
Liele, George, 33-34
Lee, Jarena, 31-32
Leach, Michael, 198-99

Lynch, James, 70
lynching, 100-101, 106
Malcom X, 154, 212, 216-17
Marrant, John, 29-30
Martin, Trayvon, 250
Mason, Charles, 125-27
Mays, Benjamin Elijah, 85, 136-38, 140-41
McCaulley, Esau, 253
Meeks, James T., 192
Moore, Lecrae, 251-52
Morris, Elias Camp, 68-69
multicultural church movement, 200, 203-4
National Association for the Advancement of Colored People (NAACP), 104, 105, 108, 116, 118-19, 141-45, 157
National Association of Evangelicals, 163-64, 179
National Baptist Convention, 37, 68, 69, 71-72, 80, 112-13, 127
National Baptist Convention of America, 191
National Baptist Convention U.S.A., 37, 69
  See also National Baptist Convention
National Black Evangelical Association, 182-84, 187-89
  See also National Negro Evangelical Association
National Committee of Negro Churchmen, 174, 211-12
National Conference of Black Churchmen, 174, 212
National Negro Evangelical Association, 161-72, 174-75, 181-82
new negro, 105, 115-16
Nottage, Berlin Martin, 165
Nottage, Whitefield Talbot, 165
Obama, Barack, 77-78, 249
Pannell, William, 173, 180-81
Paul, Nathaniel, 28
Payne, Daniel Alexander, 62, 70-71, 80, 96
Pearce, Charles H., 75
Perkins, John M., 201-2
Perry, George, 171, 182
Perry, Rufus L., 90-91
perspectivalism, 209
Poets in Autumn, 254

Potter, Ronald, 168-69, 171, 173, 175-76
Powell, Adam Clayton, Sr., 110-11
Prentis, Marvin, 164, 166, 168
Progressive National Baptist Convention, 114
Promise Keepers, 201-2
Prosser, Gabriel, 53, 59
Reconstruction, 4, 6, 64-68, 72-90, 97
Rhodes, Joseph J., 191
Roberts, J. Deotis, 222-29
Salley, Columbus, 173, 176
Second Great Awakening, 43-45, 49, 121
Seymour, William Joseph, 121-25
Skinner, John, 183
Skinner, Tom, 173, 177-81
slave codes, 20-21, 39, 48-49, 66
Smith, Lucy Turner, 125
Society for Propagation of the Gospel in Foreign Parts, 18, 21, 26
Southern Christian Leadership Conference, 143-47
Stockton, Betsy, 1-2, 11
Student Nonviolent Coordinating Committee, 145-47, 154, 157-59
Tanner, Benjamin Tucker, 67
Tate, Mary Magdalena, 125
Taylor, Gardner C., 113-14
Thurman, Howard, 136-38, 140-41
Truth, Sojourner, 54-55
Turner, Henry McNeal, 76-77, 92-93
Turner, Nat, 37, 47, 57, 61
United Pentecostal Council of the Assemblies of God, 166
Vesey, Denmark, 47, 50-51, 53, 60-61
Walker, David, 57
Ware, Frederick L., 215
Washington, Joseph R., 210
West, Cornel, 235
Wheatley, Phillis, 24
Whitefield, George, 21, 22-23, 30
Wilmore, Gayraud, 105, 208, 212-13
womanist theology, 236-39
Wright, Jeremiah, 246, 248
Ya'qob, Zar'a, 15
Young Turks, 172-73, 176-77, 181, 183

SCRIPTURE INDEX

OLD TESTAMENT

Genesis
1:26-28, 17
1:31, 19
9, 38
9:18-27, 38
9:25, 38
45:4, 68

Exodus
3:7-8, 52

Joshua
6, 60

Judges
16:17, 59

Jeremiah
8, 255
8:22, 255

Micah
6:8, 6, 253

Habakkuk
3:17-19, 58

Zechariah
14, 60

NEW TESTAMENT

Matthew
6:33, 61
11:28, 218
22:37, 73
22:39, 73
25:14-30, 67
25:25, 67
27:46, 101

Mark
1:24, 75

Luke
9:57-62, 222
19:11-27, 67

John
3:3, 24

Acts
2, 123
2:44, 202
8, 12
26:18, 151

1 Corinthians
1:12, 68
1:23, 200
12, 126

2 Corinthians
5:17, 178

Galatians
3:28, 23
5:22-23, 5
6:2, 255

Ephesians
3:20, 4, 23
6:1, 18

Philippians
2:12-13, 24

Hebrews
4:12, 190
12:1, 2, 255

James
2:19, 75

1 John
3:8, 218

Jude
3, 12, 252, 253

Revelation
5:9, 17
7:9, 2